AF606047

Louis Ginzberg's *Legends of the Jews*

Louis Ginzberg's *Legends of the Jews*

Ancient Jewish Folk Literature Reconsidered

EDITED BY GALIT HASAN-ROKEM
AND ITHAMAR GRUENWALD

WAYNE STATE UNIVERSITY PRESS
DETROIT

Manufactured in the United States of America.
18 17 16 15 14 5 4 3 2 1
ISBN 978-0-8143-4047-9 (paperback) / ISBN 978-0-8143-4048-6 (e-book)
Library of Congress Control Number: 2014936571
∞

Designed and typeset by Adam Bohannon
Composed in Gentium and Cronos Pro

Published in cooperation with
the World Union of Jewish Studies

In memory of Dov Noy ז"ל
Great teacher of Jewish folk literature

Contents

Preface: Legends and Folklore

Louis Ginzberg's *Legends of the Jews* in Historical and Critical Perspective

Galit Hasan-Rokem

The century that has passed since Louis Ginzberg initiated the publication of his monumental *Legends of the Jews* has been an especially productive one for the critical, scholarly, and cultural study of the aggadic texts of the Rabbis of late antiquity. Like Ḥaim Naḥman Bialik, some have viewed those texts as part and parcel of Hebrew belletristic creativity, others as important historical sources. These texts certainly constitute an important point of reference and fountainhead for contemporary Hebrew literature—in no small measure due to both Bialik and Ravnitzki's *Sefer ha-aggadah*[1] and Ginzberg's *Legends of the Jews.*

The two plenary sessions devoted to the centennial of *Legends* at the Fifteenth Congress of the World Association of Jewish Studies at the Hebrew University of Jerusalem in August 2009 were included in the Folklore Section of the Congress.[2] The first of the two sessions was chaired by Avigdor Shinan, one of the initiators of the celebratory sessions; in the course of his introductory remarks, he aptly recited his beautiful Hebrew translation of the entire Friedrich Schiller poem whose final lines are the motto of the first volume of Ginzberg's *Legends of the Jews:*

> Was sich nie und nirgends hat begeben,
> Das allein veraltet nie![3]

David Golinkin, Daniel Boyarin, and Hillel Newman delivered papers in this session. Menachem Hirshman, another of the event's initiators, chaired the second session, where the papers were delivered by Jacob Elbaum and Galit Hasan-Rokem. The sessions concluded with the comments of Yaakov Kaduri (James Kugel).

In order to provide the broadest possible view of both the extent of Ginzberg's colossal project and its repercussions in contemporary scholarship, the present volume brings together five essays based on the papers delivered at the two sessions, along with a new introduction and two additional essays that address Ginzberg's project. All the authors have taken as their point of departure the academic expertise and professional identity of the author of the *Legends* as a folklore scholar. They have included discussions on the folkloristic underpinnings of *Legends of the Jews* and have pointed out, each according to her or his disciplinary framework, the uniqueness, strengths, and weakness of the project. The disciplinary variety among the authors of the present volume vouches for the diversity of the perspectives—historical, philological, philosophical, and methodological—represented here.

Rebecca Schorsch, who did not participate in the sessions mentioned above, was invited to write an introduction especially for the English edition, based on her comprehensive study on Ginzberg's folkloristic approach in her 2003 dissertation at the University of Chicago, "The Making of a Legend: Louis Ginzberg's *Legends of the Jews.*"

David Golinkin, who was active in the preparation of the 2009 Hebrew edition of *The Legends of the Jews* for the Schechter Institute in Jerusalem, set the stage for the Congress sessions—as well as this volume—with a presentation of Ginzberg's life story and academic career as the background and matrix for the project. In his essay, Golinkin further elaborates on the biographical details and complexities that surrounded the work and that partly resulted from it. In addition, he reviews the impressive reception of the *Legends,* which was heralded with much praise as well as some criticism, and he introduces some of Ginzberg's own reflections on the project, culled from written and oral sources.

Hillel Newman's chapter "Louis Ginzberg, *The Legends of the Jews,* and the Church Fathers," begins by introducing Ginzberg's doctoral dissertation on the aggadic literature in the writings of the Church

Fathers, both as complementary to the larger and later project and as a source for better understanding it. Newman shows how Christian authors adapted Jewish legends to their religious system, pointing out that Ginzberg's identification of common motifs does not necessarily determine the direction in which the motifs have traveled. He also emphasizes Ginzberg's definition of the corpus as Jewish rather than Rabbinic; such a categorization could denote a wider corpus than the talmudic-midrashic texts alone and specifically encompass the Hellenistic Jewish literature and the Apocrypha. According to Newman, Ginzberg was convinced that some Rabbinic aggadah had been transmitted orally to the Church Fathers. Ginzberg's view concerning the dominance of oral transmission converged with his ambition to reconstruct the popular nucleus of aggadah; the example that Newman gives for revealing the interreligious dynamics in the development of aggadic materials concerns the traditions about King Hezekiah.

With all his appreciation for the author of *Legends,* Newman does not remain uncritical; he sees no contradiction in both acknowledging the grandeur of the project and pointing out its limitations. For Newman, however, it is not the shortcomings and failures that should surprise us but the immensity of the achievements of the author.

In his chapter "An Unimagined Community: Against *The Legends of the Jews*," Daniel Boyarin draws the broad contours of the ideological, theological, and philosophical context of Ginzberg's project and situates it within his own vision of Judaism as embedded in multiple intercultural contexts. Like some other essays in this volume, Boyarin identifies Ginzberg's ideological roots in Romanticism; he interprets *The Legends of the Jews* as an attempt to prove that Jews are a "people among peoples," since they have folk literature as other peoples do. Boyarin's criticism of the project is based on this premise. He emphasizes Ginzberg's omission of the biblical text as the basis for his compilation of the parabiblical materials. Boyarin adopts theoretical models from folklore research, primarily the concept of oikotype or ecotype, to address questions of the transmission of traditions from one place to another or from one group to another. Boyarin oscillates between the idea (Richard Kalmin)[4] that Babylonian Jews shared an elite culture with their neighbors and his own critique that Ginzberg imputed a dichotomy between elite culture and popular or folk culture. Boyarin tentatively resolves the tension by suggesting that talmudic culture has adapted folk culture in refined forms.

Jacob Elbaum navigates the discussion into a more distinctively literary discourse in his essay "The Quiet Revolution: Louis Ginzberg's *The Legends of the Jews* and Jewish Anthological Literature." He outlines the vast chronological span of the sources that served Ginzberg in his project, from the Second Temple period until the late Middle Ages. He then sketches the tradition of Jewish and Hebrew anthologies, from *Pitron Torah* (not earlier than the eighth century CE, according to Ephraim E. Urbach's dating) through the heyday of tenth- to fourteenth-century *yalqutim*, and continuing to those of the sixteenth century. Elbaum considers the eighteenth-century Judeo-Spanish *Me'am lo'ez* to be the exception that proves the rule that the genre "disappeared" between the seventeenth and nineteenth centuries. After reviewing the "moderns"—Bialik and Ravnitzki, and Berdyczewski (Bin-Gorion)—he arrives at Ginzberg, whose scholarly methodology surpassed theirs.

For Elbaum, the peculiar characteristic of the anthological genre is its reflexive "consciousness" of its status as secondary, and its inherent use of texts that are fixed in form and have acquired "canonical" authority. He adds that it is of course not possible to assign identical goals to all anthologists across the generations, but one can postulate some common motivations. Elbaum's historical analysis encompasses the radical change in the genre that occurred when the incorporation of kabbalistic writings and especially passages of the Zohar became a cultural necessity. Following his historical description, Elbaum highlights the aspect of authority involved in Ginzberg's selections and editorial decisions, especially his decision to include long passages from texts that are not particularly authoritative in Jewish tradition: the Apocrypha, Hellenistic Jewish texts, and even passages from the Church Fathers when he thought that they involved borrowings from Jewish sources. Elbaum considers Ginzberg more daring in these cases than even Berdyczewski. On the one hand, Ginzberg rejected the absolute hierarchy of Jewish post-biblical texts in which Mishnah and Talmud outrank everything else, and on the other, he unabashedly based his decisions on folkloristic considerations. Another, no less important, set of considerations belongs to the literary realm. The preference for longish narrative selections follows almost automatically from the principle of the continuous, linear narrative—such selections are found, however, not in Tannaitic and Amoraic sources, but elsewhere. The elements of Rabbinic thought were integrated into the narrative continuum rather than isolated in specific sections, in contrast to Bialik and Ravniztki's *Sefer ha-aggadah.* Elbaum considers the comparison to Berdyczewski's German-language collection, *Der Born Judas* (1924)—which may already have made use of the early sections of Ginzberg's *Legends*—to be of utmost importance. This comparison emphasizes the status of Ginzberg's project as a post-Enlightenment (or, in emic terms, post-maskilic) endeavor, which allowed him to write in a "non-Jewish" language, as did Berdyczewski.

My essay, "Ancient Jewish Folk Literature: *The Legends of the Jews* and Comparative Folklore Studies at the Beginning of the Twentieth Century," is based on the indications amply reflected in Ginzberg's own writings, as well as in those of his contemporaries and the students of his works—namely, that he had a thorough education in folklore like many of the philologists who attended German universities in his generation. Moreover, he identified himself as a scholar of folklore, particularly at one of the most prestigious events in which he participated, Harvard University's tri-centenary, at which he was invited as the sole representative of Jewish studies and delivered the paper that later became the article "Jewish Folklore—East and West." Ginzberg's association with folklore studies takes form in two aspects of *The Legends of the Jews.* First, he uses the narrative genre as the vehicle for telling the *Legends;* he highlights the centrality of this genre to the study of folklore in his explanations of the choice of the term "legend" as the unifying label of his project. Second, his use of the comparative method, the dominant method of folklore studies from the mid-nineteenth century until the mid-twentieth century, as the conceptual basis for the notes of the *Legends* is the main scholarly contribution of the project. This strategy aligns Ginzberg in a discernable association with Johannes

Bolte and George (Jiři) Polívka, whose comparative notes to the folktales of the Brothers Grimm were published more or less in parallel to *The Legends of the Jews.*[5] After delineating the theoretical folkloristic basis of Ginzberg's project, the essay points at two additional aspects of Ginzberg's association with folklore and folkloristics: his view of *The Legends of the Jews* as an inclusive reconstruction of the universe of the imagination of ancient Jews, on the one hand, and his self-conception—with which others concurred—as an excellent storyteller, on the other.

Here I want to evoke some points of the concluding comments at the Fifteenth World Congress from Yaakov Kaduri (James Kugel), whose introduction to the 1998 Johns Hopkins University Press edition of *Legends* stands as one of the strongest contributions to the study of the project. Kaduri summed up both plenary sessions of the folklore section. Reinforcing Boyarin's critical observation about the detachment of the aggadah from its exegetical basis in the verses of the Hebrew Bible, Kaduri maintained that Ginzberg's choice of the Hebrew word *aggadah* reveals a double approach to the texts, highlighting the genre aspect of the Sage/legend on one hand and the rabbinical aspect of the *beit midrash* on the other. Moreover, Kaduri stressed the concrete affinity of Ginzberg's project with the anthological tradition of Jewish literature, which, he argued, began even before the yalqutim, with the classical midrashic compilations by the Rabbis of late antiquity themselves. He also noted Ginzberg's referencing of Slavic, especially Ukrainian, folklore. Kaduri ended with a slightly tongue-in-cheek tone, musing on what Judaism might have looked like had *Yalqut shimoni* rather than Rashi become the most prominent commentary on the Pentateuch.

In addition to the introduction by Schorsch mentioned above, the lectures collected here from the Fifteenth World Congress have been amplified by the inclusion of two essays that widen the scope of the volume in other directions. Ithamar Gruenwald's chapter "The Legend about *The Legends:* Methodological Reflections on Ginzberg's *The Legends of the Jews,*" approaches the project critically. The author's point of departure is his own grounding in the history of religions. This leads him to question the lack of references to such categories of analysis, which are almost totally absent from *Legends,* according to Gruenwald; instead, Ginzberg mobilizes analytical categories that are relevant to his own disciplinary roots, such as "culture." Gruenwald focuses on the genre category of "legend" as a central problem in Ginzberg's conceptualization of the corpus, since it according to him isolates the materials in a literary, textual world and disconnects them from their contexts in the belief system and ritual practices of ancient Jews.

Moreover, Gruenwald accuses Ginzberg of blurring the boundaries between the canonical text of the Hebrew Bible and later texts. According to Gruenwald, this introduces a real change in the basic definition of Scripture, resulting in a "conceptual umbrella" of *Legends* that may create an impression that aggadah is Scripture and Scripture is aggadah. On the other hand, Gruenwald also demonstrates, by means of a few examples, that the Hebrew Bible itself is a polyphonic text and thus subverts the idea of a fundamental unity.

Another issue considered problematic by Gruenwald is what he calls Ginzberg's "lack of consistency" with regard to his declared focus on individuals and personalities. Gruenwald then proposes his own methodological innovation in this respect by introducing midrashic narratives originally excluded by Ginzberg, since they do not actually refer to biblical figures. His main example here is the story of Ḥoni the Circlemaker, whose acts fall within the ritual "protocol" of rainmaking. Basing himself on premises intimately related to the myth and ritual theory of James Frazer, Gruenwald expands on the study of biblical and midrashic rainmaking rituals, quoting in detail Dov Noy's study based on Raphael Patai, which in turn is indeed based on Frazer.[6]

The volume is rounded off by Johannes Sabel's "Aggadah in 'Higher Unity': The German Manuscript of *The Legends of the Jews.*" The German manuscript of *Legends,* the existence of which was merely an informed guess, was recently discovered in the library of the Jewish Theological Seminary of America in New York. Sabel, along with his mentor Andreas Kilcher, has commenced a project to publish the manuscript, and his essay is a result of his research for it. First, the author demonstrates the process of Ginzberg's selection of the materials and their unification into a linear narrative. Analyzing selected passages in the German manuscript, he demonstrates how Ginzberg sometimes blurred the boundaries between the separate sources from which his final text was culled. The second topic Sabel addresses is Ginzberg's characteristic code-switching. This phenomenon is most clearly expressed in his mixed use of German and English; particularly at the early stages of the writing, English phrases and even longer passages are interspersed with German (in later volumes German predominates, but his ability to write it well shows deterioration). Sabel attributes this phenomenon to Ginzberg's diasporic situation, according to accepted theory in translation studies. Naturally, the author is aware of Ginzberg's earlier diasporic removal from his Lithuanian Jewish–Yiddish linguistic and Hebrew educational roots, at the time when he began his academic career in German universities.

Another text-critical aspect that Sabel clarifies relates to the differences between the German and English versions, with special reference to omissions, additions, and changes. He thus reaches an unambiguous definition of the German version as the "source" for the final English version. The last part of Sabel's discussion addresses the issue of genre, which is also addressed by a number of other chapters in this volume. Sabel sets out the complex evolution in Ginzberg's thinking that finally leads him to define as *legend* the genre that he presented to the American audience. The triple system in which he operated (unlike the tripartite genre system of the Grimm brothers: myth, legend, folktale) included the following genres: folktale (*Märchen*), legend (*Sage*), and sacred legend (*Legende*). According to Sabel, Ginzberg chose for the basic genre of *The Legends of the Jews* the last of these three, the sacred legend. For Sabel it was the similarity of the Jewish midrashim to the German *Legende* that led Ginzberg to name his collection of Jewish sacred legends *The Legends of the Jews;* the Hebrew term *aggadah* thereby retains a multiple signification, participating in both the literary and rabbinic realms of discourse.[7]

This multidimensional discussion of Ginzberg's monumental *Legends of the Jews* grants us an opportunity to investigate not only Ginzberg's work, but also contemporary scholarly discourse that addresses aggadah in a folkloristic perspective. Both are illuminated here by multiple points of view, some among them critical, which produce, if not a synthesis, at least a shared platform. The essays highlight the power of Ginzberg's great work to lead scholars to think productively about the continuous entanglement of oral and written creativity in Jewish sacred texts as a particularly characteristic source for their development.

Notes

1. Ḥ. N. Bialik and Y. Ḥ. Ravnitzki, *Sefer ha-aggadah: Mivḥar ha-aggadot sheba-Talmud uva-midrashim,* 1st ed., vols. 1–4 (Krakow, 5668 [1907/08]); vols. 5–6 (Odessa, 5670–5671 [1910/11–1911/12]).
2. Most of the essays were published in Hebrew as volume 47 of the publication of the World Union of Jewish Studies, *Mada'ey ha-yahadut* (2010).
3. Friedrich Schiller, "An die Freunde" (1803), quoted in Louis Ginzberg, *Legends of the Jews,* 7 vols., trans. Henrietta Szold and Paul Radin (Philadelphia: Jewish Publication Society, 1909–1938), 1:vii. Anonymous English translation: "What has happened nowhere,—happened never,—That has never older grown." Project Gutenberg, "The Poems of Schiller—Third Period by Frederich [*sic*] Schiller," http://www.gutenberg.org/files/6796/6796-h/6796-h.htm, accessed March 8, 2011. The poem's meaning in the context of Ginzberg's work is further discussed below in Hasan-Rokem's essay.
4. Richard Kalmin, *Jewish Babylonia Between Persia and Roman Palestine* (Oxford: Oxford University Press, 2006).
5. Jacob Grimm, *Anmerkungen zu den Kinder- u. Hausmärchen der Brüder Grimm,* newly rev. Johannes Bolte und George Polívka (Leipzig: Dieterichische Verlagsbuchhandlung, 1913–1932).
6. See James G. Frazer, *Folk-Lore in the Old Testament: Studies in Comparative Religion, Legend, and Law* (London: Macmillan, 1918); Dov Noy, "Tefilat ha-tamim moridah geshamim" (The prayer of the righteous brings down rain), *Maḥanayim* 51 (1961), 34–45; Robert Graves and Raphael Patai, *Hebrew Myths: The Book of Genesis* (Garden City, N.Y.: Doubleday, 1964); Rapahel Patai, "The Control of Rain in Ancient Palestine: A Study in Comparative Religion," *HUCA* 14 (1939), 251–86.
7. See Kaduri's remarks, quoted above.

Introduction: The Past in the Service of the Present

Rabbinicizing Folklore or Folklorizing the Rabbis?

Rebecca Schorsch

At the beginning of the last century, many perceived American Jewry to be in a state of crisis: would American Judaism "continue God's work or cease to be"?[1] A loosely bound American Jewish awakening emerged in response. Louis Ginzberg's *Legends of the Jews* took part in this cultural and religious battle for the future of American Jewry.[2] Published in multiple volumes beginning in 1909, *Legends* marked Ginzberg's answer to the contemporary crisis. While emerging out of a worldview born and nurtured in the traditional institutions of talmudic learning of eastern Europe and the academies of western Europe, Ginzberg's vision shared the broadly defined goals of this American Jewish renaissance, "to revitalize and deepen the religious and spiritual lives of American Jews . . . to strengthen Jewish education . . . and . . . to promote the restoration of Jews as a people."[3]

Individuals differed about how to create a vibrant Jewish future. Some critiqued others for abnegating concern for the needs of the present, as did Mordecai Kaplan, who in 1914 wrote in his journal that while "I hold science in proper respect . . . I would not permit any but those who are crippled and maimed to pursue it." Objecting to scholarship with its concern only for the past, Kaplan wished to "compel men like Ginzberg . . . men of brains, to build up a living Judaism with content to it."[4] Ginzberg, however, viewed the scientific or academic study of Judaism as integral to creating a living Judaism. He thus decided to extend *The Legends of the Jews* far beyond the original commission for a one-volume compilation of Jewish lore.

Rather than a popular volume, Ginzberg produced a comprehensive popular and scholarly hybrid. Instead of a solely popular project, Ginzberg annotated the narrative by two copious academic volumes of notes filled with sources and extensive comments.[5] Instead of a single volume, Ginzberg produced an encyclopedic collection, a vast array of biblical legends, tales, myths, and Rabbinic interpretations transformed into a grand legendary narrative of ancient Israelite history. Though ostensibly the narrative served to entertain the folk while the notes addressed the concerns of scholars, the two components of this multi-volume set reflected Ginzberg's broad conception of the importance of a dual and intertwined approach to enliven and define contemporary Jewry by speaking to scholars as well as lay people, using the tools of history as well as of storytelling. *Legends,* designed to instruct scholars and crafted to interest the masses, set out to reclaim Jewish originals borrowed and buried in the traditions of others. It aimed to ground the Jewish awakening on American soil in past traditions. Above all, to shape the understanding of Jewish history while actively participating in it, it exemplified Ginzberg's inseparable academic and affective commitments and marked his greatest effort to combine them in a single work.

Legends took its inspiration from and shared in the vision of several key scholars and teachers from Ginzberg's life. Many Jewish leaders and figures of the nineteenth century embodied the commitments Ginzberg prized above all else. Ginzberg wrote about them in many biographical essays, a particularly accessible genre enabling him to characterize Judaism before a wide, non-expert audience. Most seemed to share what Ginzberg aspired for himself: a perfect balance of intellectual and spiritual work. Repeatedly Ginzberg characterized the Jewish teacher, rabbi, and scholar—his intellectual and religious heroes—as devoted to the formation of a "living Judaism," a part of, or addition to, their educational and academic pursuits. Through these many character portraits Ginzberg offered his ideal of religious and intellectual leadership.[6] Ginzberg's sketch of Isaac Hirsch Weiss praises his understanding of Judaism as an "active religion," a religion of deeds "whose prime function . . . is to give form to religious consciousness, to express or present the religious feeling or thought of man."[7] In describing the greatness of Israel Salanter, Ginzberg wrote of his dedication "toward the achievement of two objects, the attraction of the masses of the people by emphasizing the emotional element of religion, and the training of men who would in the true sense of the word be spiritual leaders of the people."[8] Active and intellectual commitments characterized all his religious scholarly heroes.

One of his most powerful portraits depicted the *melammed*, the Jewish teacher of Ginzberg's early schooling. Ginzberg's depiction of the melammed underscored the importance of emotions in the attachment to the past, as illustrated in the melammed's recounting of Jewish history through traditional Jewish legends. In the melammed's tearful recitation of the legends describing the destruction of the Temple, Ginzberg viewed this Jewish teacher as doing "more for the preservation of Jewish nationalism than all the well-tuned phrases of modern orators."[9] Neither historical studies nor the study of the past would link Jews to the significance of these monumental moments in Jewish history. Rather, legends more than history could sustain the people. Indeed, the melammed's lasting impact on Ginzberg undoubtedly contributed to his use of Jewish lore as a source of contemporary sustenance. In the introduction to *Legends,* Ginzberg wrote that "the sadder the life of the Jewish people, the more it felt the need of taking refuge in its past." Jewish legends, he contended, have "the magic means of making a sordid reality recede before a glorious memory."[10] Choosing, it would seem, to imitate traditional educational role models, such as the melammed and the traditional rabbinical student, Ginzberg continued the tradition of turning to "national literature for draughts of spiritual refreshment."[11]

Thus the duality of the popular and scientific components of *Legends* reflected Ginzberg's dual educational inheritance. As one who was raised in the eastern European world of traditional academies of talmudic learning, a descendant of the Vilna Gaon, a childhood prodigy singled out for rabbinic greatness at a young age, and undoubtedly a child impressed by the tears of the Jewish melammed, Ginzberg opted nonetheless to pursue western scholarship, the academic path. The eastern European religious sensibilities always remained close to the surface for Ginzberg, however. Hardly coincidental, Louis Finkelstein, the successor of Solomon Schechter at the Jewish Theological Seminary, singled out Ginzberg's recitation of the traditional dirges on Tisha b'Av to indicate his deep emotional attachment to the Jewish past. While reading these lamentations of the destruction of the ancient Temples in Jerusalem, tears apparently streamed down Ginzberg's face. Finkelstein depicted Ginzberg as Ginzberg had characterized the melammed: tearfully transported into the past. Similarly, when Ginzberg led the congregation in the closing service of Yom Kippur, Finkelstein noted that "the ancient melodies rendered with beauty and skill, combined with the stirring words and his obvious absorption in the prayers, communicated to all a profound sense of the ineffable holiness of the place and the time." Finkelstein characterized those present as bearing witness to the disappearance of "the modern scholar, trained in German universities . . . [into] the intimacy of the ancient service; and before the Ark of the Torah there would stand the successor to the authors of the *Sha'agat Aryeh* and the *Lebush.*"[12] Ritual, prayer, and the imaginative recounting of the ancient past bridged the distance between past and present.

Ginzberg explicitly rejected those who wished to present the "past as separate and apart,"[13] embracing the vision of those whose work brought the two together. For Ginzberg, as for many practitioners of *Wissenschaft des Judentums,* scholarship served this purpose. Prayer and biography joined scholarship in Ginzberg's work to efface the costly distance between the present and the past. Scholarship for Ginzberg informed the present, served the present, and necessarily must be connected to the present. The scientific study of Jewish history could close the gap between the past and the present. Solomon Schechter, one of the greatest scholars and popularizers of Judaism at the turn of the twentieth century, exemplified Ginzberg's activist and scholarly commitments. Schechter led JTS in its efforts toward Jewish renewal, spearheading its reorganization and revitalization in 1902. Ginzberg was his first faculty appointment. Schechter knew of Ginzberg's dissertation in which he had culled the Church Fathers for Jewish remnants that had been lost to the Jewish textual tradition and borrowed by the Church. He also knew of Ginzberg's hundreds of entries written for the *Jewish En-*

cyclopedia, one of the major educational projects committed to the efforts of American Jewish renewal. Both the dissertation and the encyclopedia entries highlighted Ginzberg's commitment to Jewish textual retrieval and broad cultural dissemination. Ginzberg shared Schechter's commitment to what came to be characterized as JTS's two-tiered approach to scholarship: the retrieval and (re)interpretation of past Jewish texts, on the one hand, and the transmission of Jewish wisdom to the widest possible audience, on the other.[14]

In an essay on the JTS charter, Schechter described the scholarship of his institution as sacred and sustaining work: "Every discovery of an ancient document giving evidence of a bygone world is, if not undertaken in the right spirit—that is, for the honor of God and the truth and not for the glory of the self—an act of resurrection in miniature. How the past rushes in upon you with all its joys and woes! And there is a spark of a human soul like yours come to light again after the disappearance of centuries crying for sympathy and mercy."[15] Ginzberg came to hold Schechter in the highest esteem precisely for his life-giving interests, and attributed Schechter's gift to bring Judaism to life to his having a "big Jewish soul."[16] He lavished praise on Schechter's academic mission to resurrect and reconstruct the Jewish past for the sake of the present. Above all he envied and admired Schechter's ability to "make people feel," which he contrasted with what he considered to be his own lesser talents "to reason well."[17]

However, like Schechter, Ginzberg knew that the accurate reading of the Jewish past demanded Jewish scholarship. Jews must read their sources in order to read accurately. As Schechter put it, "We cannot have our love letters written for us. We must write them ourselves, even at the risk of bad grammar."[18] Jews need to provide Jewish readings of their sources to illuminate them properly. Schechter's JTS therefore called for a Jewish reading of the Bible. He held Jewish scholars particularly responsible to read this foundational text for themselves, to write Jewish commentaries to the Bible and to respond to the anti-Jewish implications of biblical criticism. Schechter viewed the Bible as the Jews' "gift to the world . . . and our *raison d'etre.*" He argued as such that Jews must defend the Bible against Christian attacks. "We have stormed heaven to snatch [it] down . . . [and] threw ourselves into the breach and covered it with our bodies against every attack. . . . We bore witness to its truth and watched over its purity in the face of a hostile world." And thus Jews must defend the Bible against "the Higher anti-Semitism," Schechter's phrase for biblical criticism, which he argued sought "to destroy" us by "denying all our claims for the past, and leaving us without hope for the future."[19] Without a past, no future could transpire.

In *Legends,* Ginzberg responded to the wide-ranging efforts to deny the Jews their past. As Schechter knew well, contemporary academic and religious arguments over the past carried in their midst arguments about the present. Christian academics used biblical criticism to read Jews out of the covenantal promise of the Hebrew Bible. Jewish reformers also turned to the results of biblical criticism to leave much of traditional Judaism in the past. At the same time, there were political implications to the arguments over the nature of the Jewish past and the viability of Jewish history. Those who defined history as political history considered Jews to possess no history. European nationalist arguments over citizenship considered Jews without a tenable history to have no viable present and no ability to contribute positively to the emerging nations in which they resided. *Legends* stood in the midst of these numerous efforts to mobilize a reading of the Jewish past and Jewish canonical sources in the service of contemporary political and religious arguments. Through *Legends* Ginzberg attempted to demonstrate that Jews indeed have a history. Not political history or a history of the sword, but a history of culture, of the pen, and one marked by great moments of canonization. Jewish history as recounted from the closure of the Bible through the editing of the Mishnah through medieval and early modern halakhic codes to *The Legends of the Jews* is vibrant.[20] A modern moment of Jewish history, *Legends* canonized over a thousand years of aggadah as Jewish legend. Ginzberg's grand legendary narrative gathered in encyclopedic fashion sources spanning over a thousand years.

Beyond demonstrating the mere reality of the Jewish cultural past, Ginzberg demonstrated a particular view of Rabbinic culture in *Legends.* In six volumes of narrative and notes he told an ancient and contemporary story, narrating the legendary account of the birth of Israel from creation into the Second Temple period, as well as the story of Rabbinic Judaism of late antiquity. Ginzberg the scholar, antiquarian collector, and traditionalist anthologizer strove to have "the legendary material as complete as possible."[21] Ginzberg the storyteller, the modern-day creator of Jewish lore, the contemporary melammed, strove to weave the manifold material into "a readable story and . . . an interesting tale."[22] He never wanted the story to undermine his concern for preservation, intending throughout the project to stay as close as possible to the original nature of the material.[23] Ginzberg thus chose to present midrash in the synthetic form of a grand folkloric epic of national origins for a people the Christian scholarly world and the Jewish reformers considered to have no national identity. And he chose to add the notes so that all could see the high cultural ideas underlying Jewish lore.

In the notes, Ginzberg rabbinized the folk. In these annotations Ginzberg correlated the creations of the common folk with the high ideals of normative Rabbinic Judaism. Though folklore differed in form from Rabbinic hermeneutical or theological formulations, Ginzberg considered the different modes of expression as insignificant differences. Folklore and normative Rabbinic Judaism merely expressed themselves differently according to their different audiences. Folklore resembled the Jewish essence, a singular, continuous, and uniform development beginning with the Bible and extending throughout Jewish history. The Rabbinic or Jewish culture Ginzberg depicted responds to critics of this culture as antiquated, overly legalistic, non-spiritual, and irrelevant. Ginzberg presented Judaism as universal and national, individual and social, legal and mystical, dogmatic and practical, which nonetheless featured a "unity and individuality just as a mathematical curve has its own laws and expression."[24] Ginzberg underscored this continuity and uniformity structurally by insisting on pairing the narrative and the notes. Jewish culture comprised the Bible, Midrash, law, liturgy, and folklore, as well as material in the extra-biblical Apocrypha and Pseudepigrapha. Judaism remained fastened to its biblical past in this portrait, while its normative canvas extended beyond what anyone had thought heretofore. In

Ginzberg's hands even the Church Fathers emerge as rich source of Jewish culture.

Ginzberg's *Legends* displayed a complex and somewhat paradoxical use of folklore. Ginzberg turned to the category of folklore to highlight Jewish uniqueness and Jewish universality. A rabbinic and national portrayal of the Jews emerged. Even as Ginzberg underscored a common national identity of Jews and their European counterparts, he maintained a strong commitment to Jewish originality and particularity. Although Ginzberg employed the category of folklore to translate Rabbinic midrash into more universal terms, he presented talmudic culture throughout *Legends*. A war raged against rabbinic culture, and Ginzberg took up the pen to depict talmudic Judaism sympathetically by highlighting the harmony between Jewish mass and elite culture and the true nature of talmudic culture. The folk give voice to the values of the Rabbis. They articulate high religious ideals in accessible and popular form; for example, "Creation, the election of Israel, the Torah, the merits of the Fathers, reward and punishment, and many similar problems. . . ."[25] Ginzberg strove to counter the many misimpressions of Rabbinic Judaism. He wrote to combat the impression that "the Talmud, or at least the greater portion of it, together with Rabbinical literature in general, contains nothing but questions concerning eating and drinking, which things are forbidden and which are allowed, what is clean and what is unclean," by showing the extensive religious concerns held by the folk in common with the Rabbis. He wrote to combat those who think that the Talmud produces nothing but skepticism and should therefore "be kept at a distance from innocent youth"; toward this end he offered a talmudic Judaism of the folk espousing profound religious ideals. He wrote against the many American Jews who think the Talmud is "entirely superfluous," for "everything that is pleasant is permitted, everything that is attractive is clean," and even the Rabbis "do not show any excessive eagerness for the study of the Talmud"[26] by demonstrating how inseparable talmudic Judaism is to the proper understanding and account of Judaism.

But even while he rendered the folk rabbinic, Ginzberg knew well the cultural value in arguing that Jews possessed a folklore (however elite the folk appear). In this claim, Ginzberg was partaking in a broader movement to turn to the folk to make a case for Jewish peoplehood in the wake of religious and non-Jewish claims to the contrary. The turn to the folk, the gathering of oral tales, and the search for folklore served to foster national identity among many European nationalist efforts. Ḥ. N. Bialik and Y. Ḥ. Ravnitzki's *Sefer ha-aggadah* and M. J. Berdyczewski's *Mimekor Yisrael* similarly turned to Jewish aggadic traditions as sources of folklore. Unlike Ginzberg, however, they decidedly did not harmonize Rabbinic and popular traditions. Berdyczewski turned to non-normative sources to expand and ultimately lay claim to a new canvas upon which to view Jewish culture, and Bialik and Ravnitzki deliberately sought to whittle away the elite rabbinic culture into its non-rabbinic classic *aggadic* body.[27] Still, all three of these projects shared the belief that the turn to folklore demonstrated a universal feature of Jewish life: Jewish national identity. Ginzberg portrayed Judaism as both distinctly rabbinic but also as a participant in the national human drama. By utilizing the universal category of folklore for Rabbinic midrash and aggadah, Ginzberg translated a traditional Jewish genre, and a largely interpretive and elite genre, into one with universal cultural currency.

Ginzberg's use of folklore to launch universalistic and particularistic arguments about Jewish culture emerged strikingly in his famous Harvard tercentenary lecture on the topic. In 1936 Harvard celebrated its tercentenary with two weeks of public lectures and symposia attended by scholars from around the world. Ginzberg, the only scholar of Judaica to receive an honorary doctorate, lectured on Jewish folklore. Ginzberg deliberately chose this lens through which to respond to the request from Harvard's president to speak about the Jewish connection to the Middle East. Through folklore, Ginzberg demonstrated how Jewish legends reveal the broad cultural connections between the Jews, the people of the Middle East, and the Europeans. "American Indians, the Hindus, and many other peoples who never heard of the Bible" indeed shared many common folkloric traditions, such as those describing the creation of Adam as a hermaphrodite.[28] Jews shared in the broad culture of the peoples of the West and East. However, even at Harvard, Ginzberg emphasized Jewish originality and uniqueness. In contrast to the interests of some folklorists to turn to evidence of folkloric parallels to demonstrate broad cultural similarities, Ginzberg emphasized highlighted Jewish origins and influence. Even as he spoke of Jewish commonality with the cultures of the East and West, he delineated a portrait of Judaism impervious to outside influences. Much as he does throughout the notes in *Legends,* he emphasized "that the Talmudic-midrashic legends fail to show any dependence whatever upon non-Jewish literary sources."[29] Though Ginzberg never adequately substantiated this presumption, it served a clear cultural purpose. Ginzberg relegated the Babylonian influence to biblical times, and, with the exception of a few examples of Persian, Egyptian, and Indian influence, Ginzberg limited the foreign influences on Jewish folklore to Greek culture. Jewish biblical legends, Ginzberg claimed, were rather more influential on the legends of Christianity and Islam than the other way around.[30] Continuing the work he began for his dissertation, Ginzberg furnished multiple examples of Jewish legends appearing in the writings of the Church. Ginzberg thus took the opportunity of this international forum at Harvard to speak of Jewish originality and influence. Folklore, in this rendition, underscored the autochthonous Jewish culture at the heart of talmudic-midrashic Judaism. Folklore, in Ginzberg's hands, a Janus-faced category, revealed the broad, cross-cultural, and national dimensions of Jewish culture while preserving its distinguishing features. For Ginzberg, this broad category both linked the Jews to western culture and ultimately revealed their primary influence upon this history. Ginzberg heralded this non-exclusivist Jewish national identity as a hallmark of ancient and modern Judaism. Modern Jews resembled the Judaism espoused by Israel's biblical prophetic forebears: "The Prophets . . . were strongly nationalistic but their nationalism was of a spiritual kind. The Messianic hopes of the Pharisees were, as we have seen, universalistic, yet at the same time national."[31] This most palatable form of Jewish nationalism, with its universal impulses yet original features, did not preclude broad affiliation with humanity. Indeed, Jews understood in this way could clearly be imagined to continue to contribute favorably to the history of the West.

Like the nationalist projects of collection of Bialik and others,

Ginzberg held broad aspirations to gather in all the shards of tradition. A work of *kinnus,* a work of cultural ingathering, Ginzberg's project could be characterized in much the same language as Bialik understood his own work, and as Schechter understood the work of JTS. In his inaugural address for the Hebrew University of Jerusalem, Bialik captured the spirit and holy work of these efforts: "Of all the disciplines of our literature, from every corner and angle, wherever a trace of the nation's 'holy spirit' lurks, wherever a little of the creative force of its finest people resides, we must extract and fan the dying and distant flickers of them all, connect and unify them, and make them a whole in the nation's hands."[32] Ginzberg gathered and attempted to unify. Readers of *Legends* characterized his achievement as unifying individual cells into "finished wholes, into bodies of well-defined shape and form."[33]

However, this commitment to gather exhaustively all the sparks of biblical legend undermined Ginzberg's other desire—to make people feel. Ginzberg's traditionalist compulsion to record comprehensively constrained his capacity to offer a work fully capable of nourishing the people through original artistry and creativity. In the effort to be exhaustive, the narrative never fully transcended its stitched-together quality, its weave of many disparate, often contradictory, and unconnected midrashic sources. Given the contradictory nature of the sources, the enormity of the material, and his commitment to authenticity and comprehensiveness, Ginzberg deliberately limited his creativity. In the end, rather than create something entirely new, a new midrash, a new legend of biblical and national origins, a new artistic piece, Ginzberg preferred to be beholden to the old, for, as he characterized himself, "I am not one of those who like 'new things.'"[34] Ginzberg the encyclopedist willingly worked in tension with Ginzberg the storyteller.[35]

Uninterested in the new, Ginzberg turned to the anthology, a genre ostensibly invested in collecting rather than creating.[36] The traditional vehicle for the gathering and editing of Rabbinic midrash, the anthology allowed for the simultaneous preservation and reconfiguration of the past. It promised therein to redeem the literature of the past for the sake of the perpetuation of Judaism while not creating something entirely new. Bialik argued for creation:

"The concept of culture in its comprehensive and pan-human sense, has now overtaken the theological concept of Torah in the nation's consciousness. We have come to acknowledge that any people that wishes to exist without shame and disgrace must create culture; not just to use it but to create it, literally to create it with its own hands, with its own tools and materials, and under its own imprimatur."[37] Ginzberg, in contrast, presented his *Legends* as the mere reproducing of the past. In this, once again, Ginzberg resembled Schechter. Rather than write a work of systematic theology, Schechter preferred to allow the Rabbis to speak for themselves. He ostensibly gathered their voices to share in his theological anthology *Some Aspects of Rabbinic Theology.*[38] Ginzberg utilized the category of folklore, a new definition for late antique Rabbinic Judaism to shed light on the traditional culture of Rabbinic Judaism in general. The genre of the anthology suggested minimal tampering, the work of collecting, gathering, and editing rather than creating. This genre enabled Ginzberg to launch his project of cultural ingathering as though merely reproducing. For Ginzberg, the only people capable of true understanding were those who lived the past and were truly capable of inhabiting it. To enter the soul of the past required inhabiting it sympathetically. Once again, Schechter embodied this for Ginzberg: "Only our soul fathoms the depth of life," and "Dr. Schechter's big Jewish soul penetrated into the soul of the Synagogue; where others saw only forms and ceremonials, he saw spirit and life. His theology is not only a restatement of the facts of the religious life of the Jews, but also a new appreciation of them."[39] Much like prayer, scholarly arguments, and biographical sketches, the anthology of *Legends* allowed Ginzberg to bring the tradition forward for a sympathetic rendering of the Jewish past.

The most recent reissuing of *Legends*, a two-volume set published in 2003, takes a new format: the notes appear at the end of each subsection rather than in separate volumes.[40] Without distinct volumes readers can hardly avoid seeing Ginzberg's narrative and notes together. Though today's world of scholarship on Jewish folklore and Rabbinic midrash differs from Ginzberg's in many significant ways, in this new two-volume format the notes remain integral to his original vision. Ginzberg's preservation of the traditions of the past through the notes, perhaps the work's most lasting contribution, remains invaluable. In the end, the grand legendary narrative serves to point the way toward the vast treasure trove of sources Ginzberg amassed for *Legends.* The narrative may still offer a readable tale, but one wonders if it still or ever actually did offer much more to the masses. Did it ever offer spiritual nourishment or a respite from the weariness of the present? It is hard to say whether or not the work moved the people as Ginzberg wanted.

Ginzberg's influence upon the academic world continues. As demonstrated by this rich collection of articles dedicated to Ginzberg's monumental work and translated from the Hebrew annual publication of the World Union of Jewish Studies, *Madaey ha-Yahadut* with some additions, the significance of *Legends* endures. As the present volume also highlights, however, contemporary Rabbinic and folkloric scholarship has also moved beyond Ginzberg's methodological assumptions and conclusions in many ways. Praise and acknowledgment coincide with critique and expansion throughout this impressive collection of articles. Both the continuity and the distance that contemporary scholarship has traveled since the time of Ginzberg's monumental project becomes entirely clear upon reading the articles presented here. For example, Daniel Boyarin's chapter argues for a shared cultural influence between Christianity and Judaism in late antiquity rather than Ginzberg's one-directional assumption of Jewish origins and influence upon Christianity. Boyarin writes of shared cultural milieus and mutual influences rather than Jewish originals influencing Christianity.[41] Contemporary Rabbinic scholarship also differs with Ginzberg on the understanding of many aspects of aggadah and folklore, such as the nature of its transmission and the proper distinctions between biblical legend and non-biblical legend.[42] Ithamar Gruenwald argues, for instance, for the need to expand Ginzberg's original conception of the parameters of biblical legend to include such cases as Ḥoni the Circlemaker, which undoubtedly finds its inspiration in the biblical wonder-workers and rainmakers Elijah and Elisha.[43] While critiquing the unity Ginzberg alleged for the Bible, Gruenwald makes the case to further break down the divide between the world of the Rabbis and the world of biblical legends. And, as Galit Hasan-Rokem's chapter indicates, contemporary understandings of the relationship between midrash and folklore continue to share many of the presumptions of Ginzberg, such as the need to dismantle the facile divide between the world of the folk and the world of the rabbis, between popular and elite culture, even while paying closer attention to hermeneutics and textual contexts of midrashic production.

Ginzberg boldly imagined folklore at the heart of traditional Judaism, setting the stage for the erasure of the lines dividing high and low culture. Through folklore he expanded the canvas for the study of the history of Judaism beyond normative Jewish lines as well as beyond the contours of Judaism. Such a broad conception of the territory continues to shape Jewish studies, however changed our assumptions are about the very question of influence and the boundaries under consideration. But perhaps most importantly, his work continues to enable a return to the sources for their ongoing analysis by academics and perusal by the populace, inviting a return to their consideration from all vantage points. Without the notes Ginzberg's work might have remained relegated to the past. Ginzberg might have appreciated, above all else, the continued commitment to bringing the past forward. As a result of his foresight and commitment to preserving tradition, the notes continue to enable readers to review his sources, expand upon them, redefine them, and reimagine them, as the present volume on Ginzberg's *Legends* powerfully attests.

Notes

1. Jonathan D. Sarna, *A Great Awakening: The Transformation That Shaped Twentieth Century American Judaism and Its Implications for Today* (New York: Council for Initiatives in Jewish Education, 1995), 13, 15.
2. Ibid., 30–31.
3. Ibid., 13, 15.
4. Mel Scult, "Schechter's Seminary," in *Tradition Renewed: A History of the Jewish Theological Seminary of America—The Making of an Institution of Jewish Higher Learning,* ed. Jack Wertheimer (New York: Jewish Theological Seminary of America, 1997), 86–87.
5. Louis Ginzberg, *The Legends of the Jews* (Philadelphia: Jewish Publication Society, 1909–1938). *Legends* was subsequently translated into Hebrew as Louis Ginzberg, *Aggadot ha-Yehudim,* trans. and ed.

Mordekhai ha-Kohen (Ramat Gan: Masadah, 1966); reprinted (in English) by the Jewish Publication Society in 1967–1969; published in paperback by Johns Hopkins University Press in 1999; and issued in a two-volume set by JPS 2003. For a full version of this introductory essay and a study of the various components and influences on *Legends,* see my "The Making of a Legend: Louis Ginzberg's *Legends of the Jews*" (Ph.D. diss., University of Chicago, 2003). [Editors' note: A new Hebrew edition is discussed in David Golinkin's chapter of the present volume.]

6. Ginzberg,"Rabbi Israel Salanter," *Students, Scholars and Saints* (Philadelphia: Jewish Publication Society, 1945), 147.
7. Ginzberg, "Isaac Hirsch Weiss," *Students,* 237.
8. Ginzberg, "Rabbi Israel Salanter," *Students,* 155.
9. Ginzberg,"The Jewish Primary School," *Students,* 28.
10. *Legends,* 1:ix–x.
11. Ginzberg,"The Rabbinical Student," *Students,* 63.
12. Louis Finkelstein, quoted in David Golinkin, "Introduction," in *The Responsa of Professor Louis Ginzberg,* ed. David Golinkin (New York: Jewish Theological Seminary of America), 10–11.
13. Ginzberg, *Students,* ix.
14. Jonathan Sarna, "Two Traditions of Seminary Scholarship," in Wertheimer, *Tradition Renewed.*
15. Solomon Schechter, "The Charter of the Seminary," in *Seminary Addresses and Other Papers* (New York: Burning Bush Press, 1959), 17–18.
16. Ginzberg, "Solomon Schechter," *Students,* 249.
17. Eli Ginzberg, *Louis Ginzberg: Keeper of the Law* (1966; reprint, Philadelphia: Jewish Publication Society, 1996), 118
18. Schechter, "His Majesty's Opposition," *Seminary Addresses,* 242.
19. Schechter, "Higher Criticism—Higher Antisemitism," *Seminary Addresses,* 37.
20. Ginzberg, "Rabbinical Student," *Students,* 59–60.
21. *Legends,* 1:ix–x.
22. *Legends,* 5:vii.
23. *Legends,* 1:xi.
24. Ginzberg, *Keeper of the Law,* 159–60.
25. *Legends,* 1:vii–viii.
26. Ginzberg, "Disciple of the Wise," *Students,* 38.
27. See Galit Hasan-Rokem's chapter in the present volume.
28. Ginzberg, "Jewish Folklore East and West," in *On Jewish Law and Lore,* ed. Louis Ginzberg (1955; reprint, New York: Atheneum, 1970), 63.
29. Ibid., 63.

30. Ibid., 66–67.
31. Ginzberg, "The Religion of the Pharisees," *Students*, 98–99.
32. Israel Bartal, "The Kinnus Project: *Wissenschaft des Judentums* and the Fashioning of a 'National Jewish Culture' in Palestine," in *Transmitting Jewish Traditions: Orality, Textuality, and Cultural Diffusion*, ed. Yaakov Elman and Israel Gershoni (New Haven, Conn.: Yale University Press, 2000), 316.
33. Solomon Goldman, "The Portrait of a Teacher," in *Louis Ginzberg Jubilee Volume* (New York: American Academy for Jewish Research, 1945), 5.
34. Golinkin, "Introduction," 28.
35. For her emphasis on this storytelling aspect of Ginzberg's work, see Hasan-Rokem's chapter in the present volume.
36. See in this volume the chapter by Jacob Elbaum.
37. Bartal, "The Kinnus Project," 316. [Editors' note: Bialik's work in *Sefer ha-aggadah* did not follow these guidelines, and the sources remained discernable and separate.]
38. Solomon Schechter, *Some Aspects of Rabbinic Theology* (New York: Macmillan, 1909), xviii.
39. Ginzberg, "Solomon Schechter," *Students*, 249.
40. Louis Ginzberg, *The Legends of the Jews* (Philadelphia: Jewish Publication Society, 2003).
41. See Daniel Boyarin's chapter in this volume.
42. See Hasan-Rokem's preface in this volume; also see Daniel Boyarin's and Hillel I. Newman's chapters in this volume.
43. See Ithamar Gruenwald's chapter in this volume.

1

The Legends of the Jews in the Eyes of Louis Ginzberg and in the Eyes of Others

David Golinkin

To mark the one hundredth anniversary of the publication of the first volume of *The Legends of the Jews* in English and the publication of a second Hebrew edition with a new index, I would like to examine three issues related to this work: the history of *Legends; Legends* in the eyes of others; and *Legends* in Ginzberg's eyes.

The History of *The Legends of the Jews,* 1901–2009

Louis Ginzberg arrived in the United States in 1899 at the invitation of Rabbi Isaac Mayer Wise, who invited him to teach biblical interpretation at Hebrew Union College in Cincinnati. When Ginzberg arrived in New York, his brother handed him a letter from Wise canceling the appointment because the Board of Trustees had not approved it. We now know that Wise himself canceled the appointment because Ginzberg accepted Higher Criticism, something Wise objected to; paradoxically, Wise was concerned that Ginzberg was too observant and would try to influence the college's students.[1]

As a result, Ginzberg began to support himself by writing articles for *The Jewish Encyclopedia.* After the first volume appeared, the publisher announced that he could not continue because it had cost $50,000. Ginzberg thus realized he had no way to earn a living in the United States and decided to return to Europe. This is what he relates:

> I was consequently out of a job so I thought that I would return to Europe. In preparation for this, I went to Philadelphia to

> say goodbye to my friend, Judge Mayer Sulzberger. In addition to his other jobs, he was then the president of the Jewish Publication Society and he said to me, in horror at the thought of my leaving, that I should write a book encompassing the legendary material which appeared in the encyclopedia. He suggested a book of about three hundred pages, including introduction, text, notes and index and he offered me $1,000 for the job.[2]

A short time later, Ginzberg received a letter from Henrietta Szold, the secretary of the Jewish Publication Society's publication committee, dated November 6, 1901:

My dear Sir:
Your letter of September 18 submitting your plan for the proposed work on "Jewish Legends relating to Biblical Matters" was put before the Publication Committee by the Chairman early in October, and by it approved and recommended for adoption by the Board of Trustees. The latter has now had its meeting, and I am instructed to write to you that your proposition has been accepted, together with the terms you suggest. The understanding is that you will write, in German, a book on the lines laid down in your proposition, to contain approximately one hundred thousand words, and to be available for the use of the Society in the year 1903, all rights in the book to be ceded to the Jewish Publication Society of America, for a Honorarium of $1000.

The Committee suggests that, as the manuscript must be handled by a translator, it be written in ink and only on one side of the paper.[3]

In 1903, Ginzberg realized that the book would be much longer and asked for a larger honorarium, but JPS rejected his request.[4]

Indeed, from 1901 to 1909 Ginzberg worked on the first volume of *The Legends of the Jews*—which eventually became two volumes—with Szold. He wrote the book in German and she translated it into English. Many details of this collaboration were preserved in Szold's journal and in letters published in Baila Shargel's book about Szold and Ginzberg.[5]

This fruitful collaboration ended in 1909, when Ginzberg suddenly married Adele Katzenstein. Szold, who was in love with Ginzberg, was devastated and unable to continue working with him. As a result, the third volume was translated by the linguist and anthropologist Paul Radin and was published in 1911. The latter was offended when he was not asked to translate the fourth volume,[6] which appeared in 1913, although it is unclear who did so.

Sometime around 1919, Sulamith Ish-Kishor published a book of children's stories based on *The Legends of the Jews.*[7]

In 1924, eleven years after the fourth volume of text was published and one year before the publication of the first volume of notes, Ginzberg wrote to JPS and asked the publisher to underwrite a volume of indices with three large appendices and a bibliography totaling some 600 pages. They agreed without hesitation and suggested to Ginzberg that he also prepare a one-volume abridged version of the book, similar to the abridged version of Sir James Frazer's *The Golden Bough,* prepared by his wife.[8]

In the summer of 1925, before the notes appeared, Ginzberg received a call from the attorney Clarence Darrow, who at the time was defending the right to teach evolution in the public schools—the famous Scopes Monkey trial. Ginzberg did not like speaking on the phone and the conversation took place via his wife. Darrow asked if, according to the Bible, Cain had married his sister. Ginzberg replied that he didn't like to discuss scandal and certainly not on the phone, but he would send Darrow several references to *The Legends of the Jews*![9]

After a number of attempts from 1916 to 1919 to find translators for the notes, Ginzberg carried out the translations himself between 1919 and 1924, and they appeared in two volumes in 1925 and 1928.[10]

In his well-known biography of his father, Eli Ginzberg relates that there were quite a few doctoral students from Germany who built their dissertations on the notes in volumes 5–6. One young man whose plagiarism was conspicuous wrote to Louis Ginzberg and drew his attention to the theory advanced in his dissertation. Ginzberg thanked him for his dissertation and told the student that, in the meantime, he had changed his opinion regarding what he had written in *Legends*![11]

In 1938, Boaz Cohen's detailed 612-page index was published, ten years after the release of the book's last volume. According to a letter written in 1935 from Frank Schechter, Solomon Schechter's son,[12] it appears that Cohen prepared his huge index on index cards and submitted them directly to JPS for printing.[13]

During the 1940s and up until his death in 1953, Ginzberg gave away quite a few copies of the book to nephews and others as bar mitzvah presents, as well as to his numerous doctors, who did not manage to cure him or relieve his pains.[14] He related to the latter with his characteristic sense of humor in a letter to Dr. Solomon Grayzel, the editor of JPS: "I know one might maintain that my book is a poor compensation for the work spent on me by the physician. In view, however, that he did not succeed in his efforts, and hence can only claim reward for good intentions, and as to good intentions, I put claim to them in writing *The Legends*."[15]

In 1948, Mrs. Lillian Freehof, the wife of well-known Reform Rabbi Solomon Freehof, published *The Bible Legend Book*, a children's book based on volume 1 of *Legends*.[16]

In 1951, two years before his death, Ginzberg wrote to a Rev. Jack Lewis that he planned an eighth volume of *Legends* that would contain six long appendices and that they were ready for publication, but he was doubtful whether the book would appear given his age and poor health.[17]

In 1956, three years after Ginzberg's death, his son carried out the idea raised in the above-mentioned letter from 1924 and published an abridged version of *Legends* in one volume, with an introduction by Shalom Spiegel. The abridged version contained 80 percent of the first four volumes without the notes and was reprinted several times.[18]

The six-volume Hebrew version of *The Legends of the Jews* was published between 1966 and 1975. The book was translated and edited by Rabbi Mordechai Hacohen, with the help of his son, Prof. Pinḥas Peli, Mordechai Aharoni, and Asher Bar-Tana. A four-volume Italian edition, *Le leggende degli ebrei*, ending with Moses in the desert, was translated by Elena Loewenthal and published by Adelphi from 1995 to 2003. An abridged Dutch edition appeared in 1991, and the complete French version was translated by Gabrielle Sed-Rajna and appeared as *Les légendes des Juifs* from 1997 to 2006.

New English editions were published by Johns Hopkins University Press in 1998 and by JPS in 2003, and the book was issued on a CD by Davka in 1998. The second edition of the Hebrew version was published by the Schechter Institute of Jewish Studies with a new index of names and subjects in 2009.

Finally, a group of researchers from Germany, including Johannes Sabel, are now preparing for publication the original unpublished German manuscript, written by Ginzberg himself.[19]

The numerous editions, translations, and abridged versions over the course of 100 years indicate that *The Legends of the Jews* has become one of the standard reference works of Jewish studies and of comparative folklore.[20]

The Legends of the Jews in the Eyes of Others

Surprisingly, there were no reviews of *The Legends of the Jews* at the time the various volumes were published, perhaps because they were waiting for the publication of the book in its entirety (see below). Nonetheless, the archive of Ginzberg's papers in New York does contain letters from various scholars which indicate that the book was well received from the start by scholars from various disciplines.

Prof. Theodor Nöldeke, Ginzberg's teacher and mentor, wrote to him in 1910, thanked him for the second volume of the book, and asked when the book would be published in its German original. He said the book would interest researchers in Germany and Russia not fluent in English.[21]

In 1913, Ginzberg received a letter from a Prof. Emerson of Western Reserve University in Cleveland. The latter was an expert in Middle English Poetry. Since the notes to *Legends* had yet to be published, he asked Ginzberg to provide him with sources on Lot's wife that had perhaps influenced a Middle English poem.[22]

Two years later, Ginzberg received a letter from the well-known scholar Rabbi Moses Gaster of England. Gaster thanked him for the last two volumes of *Legends* and asked when the volume of notes would appear in print.[23]

The Protestant scholar George Foot Moore from Harvard thanked Ginzberg in December 1925 for the first volume of the notes and regretted the fact that it had not appeared before Moore had written *Judaism in the First Centuries of the Christian Era* because he could have vastly improved his book with the help of the notes.[24]

In 1933–1934, the noted folklorist Bernhard Heller published a detailed serial review in the *Jewish Quarterly Review*, the only in-depth review of the book ever published. At the outset, he expressed his enthusiasm about the book: "But withal, what thoroughness! What grasp! It is hardly conceivable how one man could create this work. Every biblical character, every occurrence, every motive is investigated, as to how the Apocrypha, Pseudepigrapha, Tannaites, Amoraim, Hellenists, Church Fathers, Gaonim, Darshanim, Kabbalists, Chassidim conceived of them. The comparison leads also to ancient Egypt, Babylon, Persia, even to Hellas and Rome."[25]

Saul Lieberman referred to *The Legends of the Jews* in several places in his writings and letters. In an article in honor of Ginzberg's sixtieth birthday that appeared in *Haaretz* in December 1934, Lieberman wrote: "In the study of Aggadah, Ginzberg laid a cornerstone in his mammoth six-volume work, *The Legends of the Jews.* A gigantic work that is a revelation of sorts even to non-expert readers, but at the same time he made many comments which can solve mysteries even for scholars and researchers."[26]

Four years later, on 17 Tevet 5698 (December 21, 1938), Lieberman wrote to Ginzberg as follows:

> Mrs. Ginzberg promised at one time to send me his *The Legends of the Jews,* but I have not yet had the opportunity all of this time to purchase the book (aside from Volume I which I bought by chance), and it is very uncomfortable for me to ask it of him, but I would be grateful if he were to notify me where I can obtain the other volumes and I would pay the full cost.
>
> With much love and respect,
> S. Lieberman[27]

In 1940, Lieberman published his book *Midreshei Teiman.* There he incidentally expressed his opinion regarding *The Legends of the Jews.* After citing the aggadah about Hiel hiding beneath the altar (from *Yalkut Shimoni* to *Melakhim,* paragraph 214, in the name of a midrash), Lieberman writes that it "is not found in its complete form anywhere in Talmudic literature (see R. L. Ginzberg's wonderful anthology, *The Legends of the Jews,* volume 6, p. 319, note 15)."[28]

Finally, in 5733 (1973), Lieberman began his article "*Zeniḥin*" with these words:

> Scholars of Aggadah and lovers of Jewish folklore search for every little crumb in the aggadic sources in order to redeem them and make them accessible to the reading public. From the day we were privileged to receive R. L. Ginzberg's comprehensive anthology, *The Legends of the Jews,* unfurled and revealed before us are all the scrolls of the Aggadah woven around the biblical stories, and the only thing that remains for us to do is to add pebbles and small stones to his vast building.[29]

Returning to 1938, we find that Boaz Cohen wrote in his introduction to the index volume of *The Legends of the Jews:* "Suffice it to say that this work represents the greatest single contribution to the study of the *Agada* within a century. Its significance lies not only in its unsurpassed collection of materials from all out-of-the-way sources, but also in the fact that it paves the way for numerous monographs in the various fields of theology, folklore, superstition, customs and legends.[30]

Seven years later, Solomon Goldman, another student of Ginzberg, described *The Legends of the Jews* almost poetically:

> The general observer loitering in the long corridors and great halls of the first four volumes of the monumental *Legends* and viewing the famed frescoes and beautiful friezes on their mountain walls, will hardly suspect that the architect of this imposing and magnificent structure was himself its builder, and himself had gathered straw for bricks not only along the banks of the Jordan, Nile and Euphrates, but in the remotest places, whithersoever the winds had wafted the faintest echo of a Jewish tale or fancy. The design of the work is all his own, new and unconventional, no one before him having thought of reshaping the Haggadah according to a pattern of

biblical events and personages. His predecessors in the field were satisfied merely to compile the scattered and dispersed folklore of their people into motley anthologies, performing hardly any greater service than making its perusal and study more convenient. Professor Ginzberg, on the other hand, recognizing in the welter of homiletical and fictitious material in which the *Talmudim* and *Midrashim* abound the protoplasm of organic creations which, though they existed in isolated cells and unstable combinations, he understood had sprung from the large Biblical totalities, took the task of the student of the Haggadah to be the combining of the cells and building them up into finished wholes, into bodies of well-defined shape and form. Proceeding on this assumption, he traced out in the Haggadah, the grand themes of the Bible and its more illustrious men and women, and gave us in his *Legends* coherent accounts of the former and vivid portrayals of the latter. To make his presentation as complete as it was humanly possible to do so, he traversed not only the highways of his subject, a journey his predecessors had found sufficiently arduous, but explored its hidden bypaths and obscure alleys as well. The immense riches he brought back, the infinite number of odds and ends he accumulated, the perpetual variations in the old texts, and the diversity of languages attending the research sufficed to rear another Babel. The master, however, never comes to confusion. Nothing ever gets out of his hands. As we read his pages, we have a feeling of watching an Ictinus or Callicrates restore the ruins of the Parthenon. He goes about his work methodically, skillfully, with the artist's warmth and concentration, and with uncanny familiarity. It is as if he were putting together parts of an object he had himself designed and were rejoicing at the reconstitution of his handiwork. Every detail is fitted into its proper place and the whole emerges full-sized, living, an old-new creation.[31]

In his introduction to *Legends of the Bible,* the above-mentioned abridged version of *The Legends of the Jews* which appeared in 1956,

Shalom Spiegel stated: "Ginzberg's *Legends* easily rank as the most significant work on Jewish lore ever published in the English language."[32]

Joseph Heinemann stressed the importance of *The Legends* in his book *Aggadot ve-Toldoteihem* in 1974. At the beginning of his book, he cites the pioneering work by Leopold Zunz "and among the major milestones of the last generation, L. Ginzberg's vast anthology stands out."[33]

In an undated article, E. E. Urbach noted that "the book opened up an entire world to general research and to the study of folklore and the science of religion and many scholars have started to pay attention to Jewish folklore thanks to Ginzberg's work, even if they do not always cite it as a source."[34]

In his introduction to the Johns Hopkins paperback reprint in 1998, James Kugel presented *Legends* as a classic:

> Long before the last volume was completed, Ginzberg's work had already become a classic. Its success is perhaps best indicated not by its overall sales—though more than half a million books have been printed in English alone—but by the simple fact that, for several decades now, *The Legends of the Jews* has been cited in scholarly works as if it were a primary source ("Ginzberg, *Legends,* 2:235," or the like), rubbing shoulders with the other, considerably older members of the "classical" Jewish library alluded to earlier. Read for pleasure by millions of Jews and Christians, consulted by students, scholars, and ordinary folk, *The Legends of the Jews* has itself become legendary, the master work of one of the twentieth century's greatest and most original Jewish scholars.[35]

There was, however, also criticism of *The Legends of the Jews.* Even though Bernhard Heller, mentioned above, heaped praises on the book, he also included in his article four pages of corrections as well as a critique of the division of *The Legends* between the text and notes.[36]

Lieberman, cited above, noted that *Palaea Historica,* an important work published from manuscripts in 1893, was overlooked by Ginzberg and others.[37]

Urbach also criticized the book and especially its structure, arguing that Ginzberg should have reversed the book's structure by making the notes the inside of the book and putting the aggadot in the notes.[38]

Finally, Yonah Fraenkel criticized Ginzberg's attempt to separate popular, original, or true aggadah and midrashic aggadah that includes learned additions of the scholars of the beit midrash. Frankel argues that *The Legends of the Jews* is "a very strange hybrid." The narrative section in the first volumes "in and of itself is not of much value," but the two volumes of notes "are a basic work for the study of Aggadah to this day."[39]

The Legends of the Jews in Ginzberg's Eyes

It is quite clear that most of the scholars cited above considered *The Legends of the Jews* to be Ginzberg's magnum opus. The question is: how did Louis Ginzberg himself view *The Legends of the Jews* in comparison to his other works?

On one hand, he understood the importance of the work and he was undoubtedly also proud of it. In the introduction to the first volume in 1909, he wrote: "In the present work, 'The Legends of the Jews,' I have made the first attempt to gather from the original sources *all Jewish legends*, in so far as they refer to Biblical personages and events, and reproduce them with the greatest attainable completeness and accuracy."[40]

In 1923, before the publication of the two volumes of notes to *Legends,* Ginzberg published an article entitled "Haggadot Ketu'ot" in *Ha-Goren.* He explains in the introduction there the importance of gathering all the fragments and remnants of popular aggadah "and for over fifteen years I have been working on this task, and my books in this field will attest to the fact that I did not toil in vain nor labor for naught, but it is not enough for us to gather the material needed from printed books" but also from manuscripts. In note 1, he refers to his books on Jewish aggadah in the works of the Church Fathers, "and in the four parts of my book *The Legends of the Jews* I gathered *all the haggadot of the Jews* found in printed books and related to the Bible."[41]

In 1925, in the introduction to the first volume of notes, Ginzberg reiterates this with a touch of humility: "What I strove to achieve, and I hope I have not failed, was to have the legendary material as complete as possible. *There are very few Jewish legends bearing on biblical events or persons that will not be found, or at least referred to, in the seven volumes of this work.*"[42]

Finally, in an autobiographical fragment taken from interviews with his daughter-in-law in 1952, he spoke of *The Legends of the Jews* with a characteristic mix of modesty and arrogance laced with humor:

> As a matter of fact, memory is not an indication of intellectual ability. Memory is useful, but in modern times it is not nearly as important as it used to be. In my *Legends*, I have 36,000 references, all of which I kept in my head. I did not gain very much by this since I might easily have written them down, but if one has a good memory, he hates to bother and, secondly, my handwriting is so bad that I wouldn't have been able to read it.[43]

Nevertheless, despite Ginzberg's appreciation of *The Legends of the Jews,* he apparently felt that his lengthy commentary on the Jerusalem Talmud—*Perushim ve-ḥidushim ba-Yerushalmi*—was his most important work. There are several proofs of this assertion. First, he said so to David Druck in a series of Yiddish interviews that appeared in *Der Morgen Zhournal* in 1933–1934 and subsequently in Druck's Hebrew biography of Ginzberg:

> When Dr. Schechter discovered the Genizah in Cairo and later on found among the texts fragments of the Jerusalem Talmud, it is told that he asked R. Levi if there was any value in these fragments. R. Levi responded at the time that they would be of value after he writes his commentary on them. And so it was. These faded leaves . . . have now been brought back to life by R. Levi's magic touch in his important work *Seridei ha-Yerushalmi.*[44]

Druck's last comment is not accurate. Louis Ginzberg did indeed write a brief commentary on the volume of Yerushalmi fragments that he published in 1909 and that was supposed to have appeared in a separate volume, but Eliezer Diamond has proved that this commentary is still in a manuscript in New York.[45] In any case, the story does indicate that Ginzberg wanted to publish a commentary to *Seridei ha-Yerushalmi.*

Druck's last paragraph on this subject is even more relevant to our topic:

> He also wrote a new commentary on the entire Yerushalmi and in it he also cites the early commentators' opinions, which he sometimes contradicts and sometimes agrees with. The world has yet to see this commentary. It is, for the time being, lying in a box in a closet. But it is possible that the world will see it in the future if the scholars of the generation will take to heart the incredible value of this work. R. Levi himself is proud of this commentary and his honor rests on it. He even goes so far as to say that everything he wrote before, about Aggadah, Halakhah and the Geonim, is null and void in comparison to this commentary on the Yerushalmi.[46]

As for the breadth of this commentary, Druck once again exaggerated. Louis Ginzberg wrote a lengthy commentary on Yerushalmi Berakhot, chapters 1–5, and on Yerushalmi Pesaḥim, chapters 1–5. The first was published in four volumes between 1941 and 1960, while Eliezer Diamond is preparing the second for publication. Furthermore, Diamond has proved that Louis Ginzberg was working on this lengthy commentary precisely in the mid-1930s, when Druck interviewed him.[47] And as for the quote from Ginzberg that this is his major commentary, more important than everything he had previously written, it should not be doubted. It finds support in the following facts.

Eli Ginzberg, Louis Ginzberg's son and biographer, also refers to his father's commentary on Yerushalmi Berakhot as "the most important fruit of his scholarly labors."[48] Eli Ginzberg was not a talmudist and barely knew how to read Hebrew.[49] There is no doubt that he heard this line from his father. Sol Stroock, an important donor to the Jewish Theological Seminary of America who was not a talmudist, wrote to Louis Ginzberg in 1941, a short time before the publication of the book, about "the publication of your monumental work." He apparently heard the phrase from Prof. Louis Finkelstein or from Ginzberg himself.[50]

But why? Why did Louis Ginzberg consider his commentary on the Yerushalmi, which covered only a small portion of the Yerushalmi, more important than *The Legends of the Jews,* which covered, according to his own testimony, all of the aggadot on the Bible and which he worked on for over twenty-seven years?

In my opinion, there are four answers to this question:

1. *The Legends of the Jews* was intended for laypeople (the first four volumes) and for academic scholars (the last two volumes), whereas his lengthy commentary on the Yerushalmi was intended for *talmidei ḥakhamim,* for talmudic scholars.
2. *The Legends of the Jews* was written in German and published in English, whereas his lengthy commentary on the Yerushalmi was written in Rabbinic Hebrew.
3. *The Legends of the Jews* deals with aggadah, while his lengthy commentary on the Yerushalmi deals with the Talmud and halakhah.
4. *The Legends of the Jews* belongs to the world of Jewish studies that Louis Ginzberg entered at the age of sixteen, whereas his lengthy commentary on the Yerushalmi belongs to the world of his ancestor the Vilna Gaon and to that of his father, the pious Rabbi Yitzḥak Eliyahu Ginzberg, in which he grew up.

Solid proofs of the above I have not found, but hints to that effect I have found in his letters and in his son's testimony.

When Louis Ginzberg visited his father in Amsterdam in the summer of 1907, he was working at that time simultaneously on *The Legends of the Jews* and on *Seridei ha-Yerushalmi*—and, indeed, both books were published in 1909. He talked with his father about *Seridei ha-Yerushalmi,* but there is no hint that he talked to him about *The Legends of the Jews.*[51]

Ginzberg testifies in three places that both his father and his teacher, Rabbi Eliezer Gordon, the head of the Telz Yeshiva, were both very disappointed that he had not become a *gaon* (genius) and head of a yeshiva.[52] On the other hand, Louis Ginzberg told his son in 1948 that he could not have published his commentary on the Yerushalmi while his father was still alive.[53] This apparently was because it dealt, according to its subtitle, "with the development of Halakhah and Aggadah in Eretz Yisrael and Babylonia" and with source criticism, and these are things that his father, apparently, would not have agreed with.

In other words, Ginzberg's commentary on the Yerushalmi was more important to him than *Legends*[54] because it linked him to his ancestor the Vilna Gaon and to his heritage in eastern Europe, but, on the other hand, he understood that this commentary was too critical to be acceptable to his pious father.[55] This is, in my opinion, the reason why Louis Ginzberg stopped publishing the commentary in the middle of the tractate of Berakhot and why the second part on Yerushalmi Pesaḥim is only now being prepared for publication from his handwritten manuscript.[56]

In any case, to each his own, but I believe that most scholars of Rabbinic literature during the last century would agree that *The Legends of the Jews* is Louis Ginzberg's magnum opus, which remains as relevant today as it was when it was written.

Notes

1. See David Golinkin, ed., *The Responsa of Professor Louis Ginzberg* (New York: Jewish Theological Seminary, 1996), 18–19, and the literature cited there.
2. "Autobiographical notes dictated by Louis Ginzberg to his daughter-in-law, Ruth Szold Ginzberg during the last year of his life," Louis Ginzberg Archive, Jewish Theological Seminary Library, Archive 42: Louis Ginzberg, Box 16, p. 45. For a list of the articles Ginzberg published in volume 1 of *The Jewish Encyclopedia,* see the Ginzberg bibliography by Boaz Cohen in Alexander Marx et al., eds., *Louis Ginzberg Jubilee Volume* (New York: American Academy for Jewish Research, 1945), English section, 36–40.
3. Baila Shargel, *Lost Love: The Untold Story of Henrietta Szold* (Philadelphia: Jewish Publication Society, 1997), 37; and cf. Eli Ginzberg, *Louis Ginzberg: Keeper of the Law* (1966; reprint, Philadelphia: Jewish Publication Society, 1996), 73–74. It should be noted that Solomon Schechter invited Ginzberg to serve as a professor of Talmud at

the Jewish Theological Seminary in 1902. Thus, Ginzberg was no longer dependent on the honorarium from JPS for his livelihood.

4. Shargel, *Lost Love*, 37–38; Ginzberg, *Keeper of the Law*, 102–3.
5. Shargel, *Lost Love*, 154, 191, 193, 194, 195, 199, 218, 226, 251, 260, 268–69, 270, 274–75, 290, 295–96, 298. Regarding the German manuscript of *Legends*, see Sabel's essay in the present volume.
6. Ginzberg, *Keeper of the Law*, 74. He stresses that this was the decision of JPS and not of Louis Ginzberg himself.
7. Sulamith Ish-Kishor, *Friday Night Stories Adapted for Children* (New York: Women's League of the United Synagogue of America, ca. 1919–1925).
8. Eli Ginzberg summarizes this in *Keeper of the Law*, 180–81, and the letter is in the Ginzberg Archive, Box 6 or 7.
9. Ginzberg, *Keeper of the Law*, 216.
10. See Sabel's chapter in the present volume, based on the proceedings of the JPS Publication Committee.
11. Ginzberg, *Keeper of the Law*, 308. It is not clear when this episode took place.
12. Frank Schechter (1890–1937) was a talented lawyer and a good friend of the Ginzberg family who died young of a terminal illness. About him see Ginzberg, *Keeper of the Law*, 88, 151; Daniel S. Schechter, *Our Family History and My Life Story* (Glencoe, Ill.: n.p., 2008), 4–6.
13. Ginzberg Archive, Box 6 or 7. On Boaz Cohen's virtues as a researcher and bibliographer, see my article, "A Bibliography of the Writings of Professor Boaz Cohen," *Jewish Law Annual* 13 (2000), 65–85.
14. Ginzberg Archive, Box 6, "Jacobs, Maurice," and Box 5, "Grayzel, Solomon."
15. Ibid., Box 5, "Grayzel, Solomon."
16. Ibid., Box 4, "Freehof, Solomon." Volumes 2 and 3 of Freehof's book appeared in 1952 and 1956.
17. Ibid., Box 8, "Lewis, Rev. Jack."
18. Ginzberg, *Keeper of the Law*, 75, 181.
19. See Sabel's essay in the present volume.
20. On Ginzberg's contribution to the study of Jewish folklore, see Galit Hasan-Rokem's essay in this volume. On *Legends* as a classic, see below, note 35.
21. Ginzberg Archive, Box 10, "Nöldeke." I am grateful to Dr. Johannes Sabel, who sent me a typed version of five letters in German from Nöldeke to Ginzberg that he copied from there. On Ginzberg's relationship with Nöldeke, see Ginzberg, *Keeper of the Law*, 45, and David Druck, *R. Louis Ginzberg: Yaḥaso, ḥayav, u-sefarav* (New York, 5694 [1933/34]), 52–53.

22. Ginzberg Archive, Box 4, "Emerson, O.F."
23. Ibid., Box 4, "Gaster, Moses."
24. Ibid., Box 9, "Moore, George Foot."
25. Bernhard Heller, *Jewish Quarterly Review* 24, no. 1 (July 1933), 52. [Editors' note: Heller's first name is given variably in this book, as "Bernhard" (when publishing in English or German), "Bernard" (sometimes in French, sometimes in English), and "Bernát" (in his native Hungarian).] The article was printed in five parts and covers some 120 pages! For other shorter review articles, see David J. Galter, *Jewish Exponent,* January 14, 1938, 1, 7; *New York Herald Tribune,* July 3, 1938; Abraham Halkin, *American Hebrew,* July 29, 1938, 8, 12; Shalom Spiegel, *New York Times,* August 21, 1938; Robert Pfeiffer, *Journal of Bible and Religion,* August 1939, 139–41 (all located in the Ginzberg Archive, Box 14); Herbert Danby, *Journal of Biblical Literature* 58/4 (1939), 389–91.
26. Saul Lieberman, "La-yovel shel Ha-prof. R. Levi Ginzberg," *Haaretz,* 20 Kislev 5794 (December 8, 1933), which was reprinted in *Meḥkarim be-torat Eretz Yisrael,* ed. David Rosenthal (Jerusalem, 5751 [1990/91]), 613.
27. Ginzberg Archive, Box 8, „Lieberman, Saul."
28. Saul Lieberman, *Midreshei Teiman* (Jerusalem, 5700 [1939/40]), 11.
29. Saul Lieberman, „*Zniḥin,*" *Tarbiz* 42 (5733 [1972/73]), 42 which was reprinted in *Mehkarim*, 97.
30. Boaz Cohen, introduction to Louis Ginzberg, *The Legends of the Jews* (Philadelphia: Jewish Publication Society, 1938), 7:ix.
31. Solomon Goldman, in *Louis Ginzberg Jubilee Volume*, 4–5.
32. Shalom Spiegel, in Louis Ginzberg, *Legends of the Bible* (Philadelphia: Jewish Publication Society, 1956), xix.
33. Joseph Heinemann, *Aggadot ve-toldoteihem* (Jerusalem, 1974), 1.
34. E. E. Urbach, „Al Levi Ginzberg," *Mehkarim be-madaei ha-yahadut,* vol. 2 (Jerusalem, 5758 [1997/98]), 874.
35. James Kugel, foreword to *The Legends of the Jews* (Baltimore: Johns Hopkins University Press, 1998), 1:xii. Also see David Stern's introduction to the 2003 edition (Philadelphia: Jewish Publication Society, 2003), xv–xxiv.
36. Bernhard Heller, "Ginzberg's Legends of the Jews," *Jewish Quarterly Review* 25/1 (July 1934), 42–51.
37. Lieberman, "Zniḥin," and also in *Tosefta ki-fshutah,* volume 5, *Seder Moed* (New York, 5722 [1961/62]), 1097, and there he refers to *Legends* as "R"L Ginzberg's monumental work."
38. Urbach, "Al Levi Ginzberg."
39. Yonah Frankel, *Darkhei ha-aggadah ve-ha-midrash* (Givatayim: Masada, 1991), 554–55. And see recently Rebecca Schorsch, "The

Making of a Legend: Louis Ginzberg's *Legends of the Jews*" (Ph.D. diss., University of Chicago, 2003).

40. Louis Ginzberg, *The Legends of the Jews* (Philadelphia: Jewish Publication Society, 1909), 1:xi. Emphasis added.
41. Levi Ginzberg, *Ha-Goren* 9 (5683 [1922/23]), 33, which was reprinted in *Al halakhah ve-aggadah* (Tel Aviv, 5720 [1959/60]), 222 and 295n.4. Emphasis in the original.
42. Louis Ginzberg, *The Legends of the Jews* (Philadelphia: Jewish Publication Society, 1925), 5:ix. Emphasis added.
43. Autobiographical notes, Ginzberg Archive, Box 16, p. 24.
44. Druck, *R. Louis Ginzberg*, 89.
45. Eliezer Diamond, "Darko shel R''L Ginzberg be-ferush ha-Yerushalmi: Ha'arakhah rishonah" (unpublished). He prepared that article on the basis of Ginzberg's unpublished commentaries on the Yerushalmi, which I discovered in the Rare Book Room of the JTS Library in New York.
46. Druck, *R. Louis Ginzberg*, 92.
47. Diamond, "Darko shel R. L. Ginzberg."
48. Ginzberg, *Keeper of the Law*, 9.
49. So he told me several times in the years when I knew him (1987–2002); and cf. Ginzberg, *Keeper of the Law*, 248–49.
50. Ibid., 154. Stroock says in the same letter that he heard from Finkelstein that the book would appear soon.
51. Shargel, *Lost Love*, 27.
52. Ibid., 112, 126, 135, and cf. Ginzberg, *Keeper of the Law*, 99, which is based on Druck, *R. Louis Ginzberg*, 68–69.
53. Ginzberg, *Keeper of the Law*, 265.
54. Dr. Menahem Katz pointed out to me a similar phenomenon regarding A. M. Luncz. He published many books, but his daughter, Hannah Luncz-Bolotin, notes in her book, *Meir Netivot Yerushalayim: Hayyei Avraham Luntz* (Jerusalem, 5728 [1967/68]), 78: "My father saw as the highlight of his life's work, his new edition of the *Talmud Yerushalmi.*"
55. On the piety of Ginzberg's father, Rabbi Yitzhak Eliyahu Ginzberg, see Golinkin, *The Responsa of Professor Louis Ginzberg*, 6–9.
56. In a 1947 letter, he mentions that the manuscript of volumes 4 and 5 of his commentary on Yerushalmi Berakhot is sitting on his desk, but he is too weak to progress (Ginzberg Archive, Box 6, "Jacobs, Maurice"). Between 1940 and his death in 1953 he did not publish another volume of his commentary on Yerushalmi Berakhot, nor any of his other commentaries on the Yerushalmi mentioned above.

2

Louis Ginzberg, *The Legends of the Jews*, and the Church Fathers

Hillel I. Newman

Louis Ginzberg was born in Kovno, Lithuania, in 1873. A direct descendant of the brother of the Gaon of Vilna, he received both a traditional rabbinic and a secular education. He proved to be a student of prodigious talent and attended university in Berlin, Strasbourg, and Heidelberg. After immigrating to America in 1899, he was appointed professor of Talmud in 1902 at the fledgling Jewish Theological Seminary of America in New York. For more than half a century, until his death in 1953, he devoted himself to almost every aspect of talmudic scholarship and was recognized as one of the giants of his generation. His classic study of biblical aggadah, *The Legends of the Jews*, has been reprinted numerous times and has been translated into several languages. This essay addresses the place of the study of Christianity in Ginzberg's work on the history of aggadah.[1]

In hindsight, it is clear that Ginzberg began to lay the scientific foundations for *The Legends of the Jews* while still a student, first in Strasbourg and later in Heidelberg, where he submitted a dissertation on aggadah in the writings of the Church Fathers—*Die Haggada bei den Kirchenvätern.* In Strasbourg Ginzberg studied under Theodor Nöldeke, the outstanding Orientalist of his generation. Ginzberg's son Eli noted that four photographs adorned the wall beside his father's desk in his study: one of Nöldeke, one of George Foot Moore of the Harvard Divinity School, one of Solomon Schechter (the first president of the Jewish Theological Seminary), and one of the tombstone marking the grave of Ginzberg's own father, Rabbi Isaac Ginzberg, in Amsterdam.[2] We do not know what role Nöldeke played in Ginzberg's choice of a dissertation topic, but his influence is apparent not only in the latter's philological-historical method, but also in his expansive perspective and the elegance with which he nimbly bridged the distances separating languages and faiths of antiquity. Though Ginzberg did not often cite his teacher's works in his own writings on the Church Fathers and the aggadah, we find a revealing comment in his article on Aphraates in the first volume of *The Jewish Encyclopedia,* published in 1901. Ginzberg alludes there to Nöldeke's remarks in a review from 1869 of William Wright's edition of Aphraates' homilies. In Nöldeke's words: "A church author of the fourth century . . . who in the midst of a polemic against the Jews, against whose contentions the greater part of his book is directed, remains almost entirely free of hatred and keeps throughout to the factual, such a man truly deserves our esteem."[3] This passage suggests something of the scholarly disposition of the nineteenth-century Christian Orientalist of Strasbourg, as well as of his Jewish disciple. The ideal of inquiry *sine ira et studio* is, in the nature of things, increasingly elusive the more highly charged the topic. But the young Ginzberg, displaying erudition and sobriety well beyond his years, dealt with the subject of Jewish-Christian relations, a topic as highly charged as any, with the purpose of investigating not only what separated Jews and Christians but also what they shared in common, and even when writing about polemics, he did not do so for the sake of polemicizing.

Ginzberg published his dissertation and related studies in a series of monographs entitled *Die Haggada bei den Kirchenvätern,* comprising two books and four articles, whose publication extended over many years. The relationship between these monographs and *The Legends of the Jews* warrants a closer look, inasmuch as many of the notes in the magnum opus cover similar territory. The first part of the series, which appeared in 1899, is a small volume devoted primarily to the aggadah in the *Quaestiones* of Pseudo-Jerome on Judges, Samuel, Kings, and Chronicles.[4] While Pseudo-Jerome serves as a platform for the study, Ginzberg cast his net much further and brought relevant material from a wide variety of Patristic sources. Though Ginzberg rejected the hypothesis that Pseudo-Jerome was a Jew by birth, in more recent years Avrom Saltman has demonstrated that the author was probably indeed a Jewish convert to Christianity from the Frankish empire of the late eighth or early ninth century, perhaps assisted by a Christian collaborator.[5] At any rate, this problem does not detract from the lasting value of Ginzberg's comparisons and analyses of Jewish and Christian sources. At the end of his study Ginzberg stated that the second part of his dissertation, dealing with aggadah of the Pentateuch, had already been submitted. Chapters on Genesis appeared in the *Monatsschrift für Geschichte und Wissenschaft des Judentums* in 1898 and 1899 and a year later were collected in a single volume.[6] Another twenty-seven years passed, however, before Ginzberg published the next installment, presumably from his dissertation, on Exodus.[7] In the interim, the first five volumes of *The Legends of the Jews* appeared in print, including the first volume of notes. The next chapter in the series, on the aggadah of Numbers and Deuteronomy, was published in 1929—after the appearance of the sixth volume of *The Legends of the Jews.* Ginzberg explained that due to personal considerations as well as for reasons of substance he chose not to alter the contents of what he had written thirty years earlier, except for adding references to relevant notes in *The Legends of the Jews.*[8] He prefaced the last two papers in the series with the same remark. The first of these, which appeared in 1933, is devoted to Jerome's commentary on Ecclesiastes and the second, from 1935, is a study of Jerome's commentary on Isaiah.[9] In the final paper he expressed his regret at not having had an opportunity to engage further in research of the topic. In other words, despite the fact that his bibliography creates the impression that he spent decades scouring Patristic literature in search of Jewish aggadah, it is clear that the foundations for his research—including that reflected in the sixth volume of *The Legends of the Jews* (the second volume of notes)—were for all intents and purposes laid at the very beginning of his career, before his immigration to America. This is a striking intellectual achievement by any standard. Though one occasionally encounters corrections in the notes to *The Legends of the Jews* to what the author himself had written in the first two parts of *Die Haggada bei den Kirchenvätern,* these are exceptional,[10] and a comparison between the notes in the book and the substance of the monographs which appeared in print only later reveals clearly that in the former he already makes use of the latter. On the other hand, Ginzberg published no monograph corresponding to the final chapters of volume 6—those dealing with the Exile, "The Return of the Captivity," and Esther—though there, too, he makes reference to Patristic sources. Could he have had at his disposal an unpublished draft of a study covering this material? This strikes me as a likely possibility, one that warrants further archival research. The question is not merely biographical or bibliographical, for the chapters of *Die Haggada bei den Kirchenvätern* supplement and illuminate what we find in the notes to *The Legends of the Jews.*

The study of aggadah in the writings of the Church Fathers did not, of course, begin with the work of Louis Ginzberg. Among his predecessors Ginzberg himself lists Heinrich Graetz, who published several papers on the topic; Alexander Heinrich Goldfahn, who wrote on the aggadah in the work of Justin Martyr; Salomon Funk, who studied Aphraates; David Gerson, who wrote on Ephraem; and Moritz Rahmer, who made important contributions to the study of aggadah in the writings of Jerome and Pseudo-Jerome.[11] Ginzberg, however, aspired to much more than any of those who came before him. His intention was "to provide for the first time a complete overview of the mutual relations between the church fathers and the aggadists, in which we bring into the scope of our research all that they have in common, whether legendary or hermeneutical in nature."[12] The categories of the "legendary" and the "hermeneutical"—crucial for an understanding of his conception of the genres and historical development of the aggadah—are his terms for expressing the distinction between what might otherwise be described as narrative aggadah on the one hand and aggadic midrash—formally linked to Scripture, which it explicitly interprets in sequence—on the other.[13] In his grand project Ginzberg sought to embrace everything: all of Patristic literature and all of Scripture. In what follows we shall see that the final product was far from complete, a failing that was, however, inevitable considering the tremendous scope of the undertaking.

From the outset, Ginzberg contrasted his work on the aggadah to that of Leopold Zunz: Zunz sought to write the history of collections of redacted aggadah, whereas Ginzberg sought to write the history of aggadah per se. He emphasized that the testimony of the Church Fathers often demonstrated the antiquity of aggadic traditions found only in later Jewish sources.[14] But the use of Patristic literature in Ginzberg's work in general and in *The Legends of the Jews* in particular can hardly be reduced to attempts to push back the dating of later aggadic traditions. Ginzberg also collected Patristic parallels to aggadah well documented in contemporary Rabbinic literature. He sought to identify in Christian sources remnants of aggadic traditions not otherwise attested in Jewish sources of any period; some of these "lost" traditions are attributed explicitly to the Jews by Christian sources, while others were presumed by Ginzberg to be Jewish because of their contents. He discussed adaptations by Christians of Jewish aggadah in accordance with their own theological notions. He uncovered parallel motifs in the two corpora that in his opinion originated in a common pool of folk tradition that should not be construed as evidence of borrowing by one group from the other. He found traces—particularly in the later aggadah—of Christian beliefs appropriated by the Jews. He also wrote, as one might expect, of polemics: of aggadah as a vehicle of Jewish polemics against Christianity and of Christian polemics against the Jews and their aggadah.[15]

Note which topics are absent from Ginzberg's agenda in *The Legends of the Jews:* he does not seek systematically to present a history of the relations between Jews and Christians or between Judaism and Christianity, nor does he address the question of how the Church Fathers perceived the fundamental nature of aggadah or what role aggadah plays within Patristic literature.[16] Evidence in his other writings for his opinions on these matters is scanty as well. By the time the fourth volume of *The Jewish Encyclopedia* appeared in 1903, Ginzberg had already been enlisted by Solomon Schechter as a faculty member of the Jewish Theological Seminary and so was able to contribute "only" twenty articles. Among the close to four hundred entries he composed for the first three volumes are articles on Ambrose, Aphraates, Athanasius, and Augustine.[17] The entry "Church Fathers" in the fourth volume was written, unfortunately, by Samuel Krauss, a scholar of outstanding erudition who was, however, prone to sloppiness. Had the topic been assigned to Ginzberg, the final product would undoubtedly have looked very different, and we might have learned of his views on broader historical issues.

What may be gleaned, nevertheless, from Ginzberg's writings concerning his conception of the manner in which Jewish tradition was transmitted to the Church Fathers? In his introduction to volume 5 of *The Legends of the Jews* he describes the reception of Jewish elements in Patristic literature via two routes. The first was through exposure to Jewish apocryphal literature and Hellenistic Jewish literature. Of the second route he writes that

> cognizance must also be taken of the oral communications made by Jewish masters to their Christian disciples. Not only the Church Fathers, Origen, Eusebius, Ephraem and Jerome, of whom it is well known that they studied the Bible under the guidance of Jewish teachers, have appropriated a good deal of Jewish legendary lore, but also Tertullian, Lactantius, Ambrosius, Augustine and many other teachers and leaders of the Church have come under direct influence of the Jews.[18]

In a lecture given in 1936 at the tercentenary celebrations of Harvard University, he was more specific: "There is no evidence for the direct use of rabbinic literature by the Christian world before the twelfth century. Despite the theological differences between the Fathers of the Church and the doctors of the Synagogue, personal relations continued intermittently, providing thereby a medium for the diffusion of rabbinic legends."[19] For Ginzberg, the oral transmission of aggadah to the Church Fathers was almost axiomatic. As early as 1899, in his first monograph, he stressed twice that Pseudo-Jerome received talmudic traditions orally.[20] This principle is even more apparent in the notes to *The Legends of the Jews,* where we encounter it repeatedly.[21] Why this emphasis on oral transmission? In the case of Pseudo-Jerome, Ginzberg's purpose is to explain the author's errors, which are mustered as evidence for his conviction that Pseudo-Jerome was no *Hebraeus,* but a gentile Christian who inadvertently corrupted that which he heard from his Jewish informant. Clearly, there is also an apologetic edge to his description of the intellectual and social contacts between "Jewish masters" and their "Christian disciples." In the final analysis, however, Ginzberg makes an important historical point. On the one hand, some Christian authors do refer explicitly to direct contacts with Jewish informants; on the other hand, there is—to the best of my knowledge—no Patristic evidence for the existence of written talmudic literature before the sixth century.[22] In his discussion of Jewish traditions in the writings of Augustine, Ginzberg cites a famous passage in Augustine's *Contra aduersarium legis et prophetarum*: "Besides the legal and prophetic Scriptures, the Jews have certain traditions of their own, which they do not possess in written form but preserve by memory and transmit orally one to the other, which they call *deuterosis*." Ginzberg remarks: "This would indicate that the Jews of Africa in the beginning of the fifth century possessed only an unwritten Mishnah (Deuterosis), and Rabbi's Mishnah could not therefore have been written down."[23] When, why, and how the Oral Torah was committed to writing has long been a topic of scholarly debate. Hence Ginzberg's comments on the Jewish sources of the Church Fathers are of some consequence for the study of more far-reaching issues. Indeed, in other contexts Ginzberg often stresses the abiding importance of the oral transmission of tradition in the Amoraic and Geonic academies.[24]

In his introduction to the first volume of *The Legends of the Jews*, Ginzberg declared that his purpose was to assemble "all Jewish legends," not merely "rabbinic" legends; he did not wish to limit the collection to that which could be found solely in talmudic sources.[25] Ultimately, his goal was to recover what he perceived to be the "folk" core not only of Rabbinic aggadah, but of all Jewish aggadah preserved in extra-Rabbinic sources. The second category includes material deemed Jewish by Ginzberg even in cases where this is not made explicit in the source. A discussion of Ginzberg's conception of aggadah as Jewish folklore falls beyond the scope of this essay.[26] I would like, however, to illustrate by means of two examples the inherent complexity of exploiting Christian sources for the purpose of recovering aggadah unattested in talmudic literature.

I open with a passage from the itinerary of the Bordeaux Pilgrim.[27] Describing the Temple Mount in Jerusalem, the author refers to a "pierced stone" anointed each year by Jews mourning the destruction of the Temple.[28] This is taken by many, probably correctly, to refer to the so-called *even shetiyyah* (foundation stone) on the site of the ruins of the Jewish Holy of Holies. I would like to draw attention, however, to the passage that follows: "The House of Hezekiah, king of Judah, is there too." From this brief report it is impossible to tell precisely where the author believed he saw the House of Hezekiah, though the context implies that it stood somewhere on the Temple Mount. The structure is mentioned once again in Eusebius's *Commentary on Isaiah,* in his discussion of the "Steps of Ahaz." Eusebius writes with undisguised skepticism of "the house shown until today in Jerusalem around the Temple courtyard, which till today they call [the House] of Hezekiah."[29] The site was known also to Jerome, who writes in his own *Commentary on Isaiah:* "The guides to the holy places in this province routinely point to the steps of the House of Hezekiah or of Ahaz within the fence of the Temple . . . but I would never believe that the house of any righteous king—I do not mean Ahaz, who was a wicked king—stood in God's Temple."[30] The evidence from the early fourth century to the early fifth century thus points to a popular belief propagated among Christian pilgrims, who identified certain remains on the Temple Mount with the House of Hezekiah. On the other hand, our two intellectuals, Eusebius and Jerome, consider the presence of a royal palace on the site of the Temple implausible. I have suggested elsewhere that the remains in question were those of the walls and chambers which originally enclosed the inner courtyards surrounding Herod's Temple.[31] Be that as it may, one more testimony—roughly contemporary with those already cited—must be mentioned: the Latin version of Josephus's *Jewish War*, attributed to "Hegesippus." Through it the House of Hezekiah enters Hebrew literature. Describing the battle for the western portico of the Temple Mount at the climax of the Great Revolt, Josephus writes: "The flames consumed the portico as far as the tower which John, during his feud with Simon, had erected over the gates leading out above the Xystus."[32] Hegesippus renders this as follows: "And so the portico was burnt as far as the tower which John built when he waged war against Simon, above the gates of the royal house which King Hezekiah built for himself as a residence."[33] This is the source of the parallel passage in the medieval Hebrew work attributed to "Yosippon," where we read: "The fire proceeded to burn the entire portico as far as the House of Hezekiah, king of Judah, which was beside the Temple."[34]

Yet the question remains: how did the palace of King Hezekiah find itself adjacent to the Temple in the first place? Is there an element of biblical exegesis that could have given rise to this local tradition? We do read in Kings and Isaiah of Hezekiah's occasional visits to the Temple,[35] but nothing in the Bible suggests that he established his permanent residence there. Who, then, was responsible for the creation of this local tradition, current among Christian pilgrims, which apparently is not found in a Jewish source prior to Yosippon? Might it be a remnant of a lost Jewish aggadah that, like other Jewish traditions, became ensconced in the landscape of Christian holy places? Or is it rather a local tradition of purely Christian provenance?

A Jewish midrash preserved only in Christian sources (and recorded by Ginzberg in his collection) may shed some light on the problem.[36] In his *Dialogue with Tryphon,* Justin Martyr contends with his Jewish opponent over the proper interpretation of Psalm 110, which opens with the verse: "The Lord said to my Lord, 'Sit at my right hand while I make your enemies your footstool.'"[37] According to Justin, it is Jesus who sits at God's right hand. But, he writes, Jewish teachers have interpreted the psalm with respect to King Hezekiah, "as if he were instructed to seat himself at the right of the Temple."[38] According to Justin, the Jews believe God's right hand in the psalm signifies the right side of God's Temple. Tertullian, too, is familiar with this interpretation, perhaps through Justin. He writes: "They [the Jews] say that [David] chanted this psalm with respect to Hezekiah, for he sat to the right of the Temple."[39] We should consider the possibility that this Jewish interpretation inspired Jewish visitors to the Temple Mount to seek Hezekiah's palace among the ruins adjacent to those of the Temple, and it was from such Jews that Christian pilgrims learned to identify the site. Of course, even if this hypothesis is correct, the House of Hezekiah ultimately entered medieval Jewish literature—as we have seen—only by virtue of a Latin Christian version of Josephus.

The second example is taken from a work of a different sort altogether: *The Polemic of Nestor the Priest,* or more precisely its Judaeo-Arabic source, *Qiṣṣat Mujādalat al-Usquf.* This anti-Christian polemic purports to be a letter composed by a Christian priest who has converted to Judaism. Its most recent editors, Daniel J. Lasker and Sarah Stroumsa, believe that the author was a Jew of the mid-ninth century; they are uncertain where the text was written.[40] At the end of the work, the author challenges his opponent by asking if he does not know that God spoke to Moses 570 times, whereas in the Gospels God did not speak to Jesus even once.[41] Where does the notion that Moses spoke directly with God 570 times come from? Ginzberg makes no mention of it, and it does not seem to be found in any Rabbinic source. At first glance, this could easily pass for a "lost" Jewish aggadah. Nevertheless, to the best of my knowledge the only parallels older than the Jewish text are found in Christian sources, all of them Coptic texts written over a period of approximately two hundred years before the composition of *Qiṣṣat Mujādalat al-Usquf.* The same tradition is found in a seventh-century homily (apparently from 644/45) of the Coptic patriarch Benjamin I.[42] It appears in the Coptic apocalypse of Pseudo-Athanasius, probably from the eighth century,[43] and in a Coptic hymn "On the prophet Apa Shenoute" found in a ninth-century manuscript.[44] Eventually it makes its way into the Arabic synaxarium of the Coptic Church.[45] One case seems to be exceptional: the same tradition appears in a homily about the archangel Michael attributed to Severus, patriarch of Antioch in the early sixth century.[46] Youhanna Youssef has argued, however, that the homily, known only in Coptic, is in fact an eighth-century pseudepigraphon.[47] It appears that we are dealing with an exclusively Coptic tradition (whose rationale remains obscure) adopted by a Jewish anti-Christian polemicist writing in Arabic, who may or may not have recognized its Christian origins. The Arabic text was then translated, with minor changes, into Hebrew. If this reconstruction is accurate, it has implications for the larger question of the work's provenance, which would seem to be Egyptian.

These two examples, chosen at random, illustrate an inherent limitation of Ginzberg's undertaking: the frequent obscurity of the aetiology of aggadah within the matrix of Jewish and Christian tradition. It is by no means obvious in all cases whether a given element originated among Jews or among Christians—or perhaps among both simultaneously. They also suggest how great the territory still uncharted by scholarship is. True, much of the material that Ginzberg mined from Christian sources of late antiquity is explicitly identified there as Jewish, yet even with respect to this category we must ask how close he came to achieving his goal of completeness. By pointing to this or that failing, we risk falling into the trap of hubris, but only by confronting the question directly can we responsibly plot the course of future scholarship. In the spirit of constructive criticism, I offer the following statistics, which give some indication of how much remains to be done. In the index volume to *The Legends of the Jews,* Boaz Cohen lists citations in Ginzberg's notes of 110 passages from the works of Jerome—arguably the most important of the Church Fathers in this regard.[48] I, too, once scoured Jerome's writings in search of aggadah, and though limiting myself to passages explicitly attributing traditions and interpretations to the Jews, I came up with a list of 388 items.[49]

It is not Ginzberg's occasional failures in collecting Christian sources for *The Legends of the Jews* that should surprise us, but rather his staggering achievements. Today it is clear that no individual could singlehandedly complete such a project. Instead, we find many scholars engaged in the examination of the works of a particular author or in the study of the exegetical history of a particular biblical book or theme. But specialization, too, has its price.

Ginzberg himself was aware that, in general, Patristic literature remained an insufficiently exploited resource for Jewish studies. In 1921, in his capacity as president of the American Academy for Jewish Research, he wrote to Jewish community leader and civil rights lawyer Louis Marshall to solicit funds for four research projects, also specifying which scholars he recommended to undertake them. The largest sum—$15,000—was earmarked for the following: "The Jews in Patristic Literature—a work to consist of five volumes to contain all the material in Greek, Latin and Oriental literature."[50] The funds were not forthcoming, and the work was never written. Today, by the way, it is clear that five volumes would have been sufficient merely to scratch the surface of the mass of available material.

A century after the publication of the first volume of *The Legends of the Jews*, we can appreciate both Ginzberg's accomplishments and the magnitude of the tasks he left for us to complete.

Notes

This English version was previously published, with minor variations, in Görge K. Hasselhoff, ed., *Die Entdeckung des Christentums in der Wissenschaft des Judentums* (Berlin: De Gruyter, 2010), 183–94.

1. See Eli Ginzberg, *Louis Ginzberg: Keeper of the Law* (Philadelphia: Jewish Publication Society, 1996); David Golinkin, "Introduction," in *The Responsa of Professor Louis Ginzberg* (New York: Jewish Theological Seminary of America, 1996), 1–34; Rebecca Schorsch, "The Making of a Legend: Louis Ginzberg's *Legends of the Jews*" (Ph.D. diss., University of Chicago, 2003).
2. Ginzberg, *Keeper of the Law*, 45–56, 269.
3. Theodor Nöldeke, "Review of *The homilies of Aphraates, the Persian sage* . . . by W. Wright," *Göttingische gelehrte Anzeigen* Stück 39 (September 29, 1869), 1525–26 (the bibliographical reference in *The Jewish Encyclopedia*, 1:665, is hopelessly corrupt).
4. Louis Ginzberg, *Die Haggada bei den Kirchenvätern. Erster Theil: Die Haggada in den pseudo-hieronymianischen "Quaestiones"* (Amsterdam, 1899).
5. Avrom Saltman, ed., *Pseudo-Jerome. Quaestiones on the Book of Samuel* (Leiden: Brill, 1975), 11–17.
6. Louis Ginzberg, *Die Haggada bei den Kirchenvätern und in der apokryphischen Litteratur* (Berlin, 1900). For complete references to the articles in the *Monatsschrift für Geschichte und Wissenschaft des Judenthums* see Boaz Cohen, "Bibliography of the Writings of Prof. Louis Ginzberg," in *Louis Ginzberg Jubilee Volume*, ed. Alexander Marx, Saul Lieberman, Shalom Spiegel, and Solomon Zeitlin (New York: American Academy for Jewish Research, 1945), 19.
7. Louis Ginzberg, "Die Haggada bei den Kirchenvätern: Exodus," in *Livre d'hommage à la mémoire du Dr. Samuel Poznański* (Warsaw: O. Harrassowitz, 1927), 199–216.
8. Louis Ginzberg, "Die Haggada bei den Kirchenvätern: Numeri–Deuteronomium," in *Studies in Jewish Bibliography and Related Subjects in Memory of Abraham Solomon Freidus* (New York: Alexander Kohut Memorial Foundation, 1929), 503–18.
9. Louis Ginzberg, "Die Haggada bei den Kirchenvätern: V. Der Kommentar des Hieronymus zu Koheleth," in *Abhandlungen zur Erinnerung an Hirsch Perez Chajes* (Vienna: Alexander Kohut Memorial Foundation, 1933), 22–50; Ginzberg, "Die Haggada bei den Kirchenvätern: VI. Der Kommentar des Hieronymus zu Jesaja," in

Jewish Studies in Memory of George A. Kohut, ed. Salo W. Baron and Alexander Marx (New York: Alexander Kohut Memorial Foundation, 1935), 279–314.

10. Louis Ginzberg, *The Legends of the Jews* (Philadelphia: Jewish Publication Society, 1909–38), 5:126, 133, 384; 6:196, 197.
11. Ginzberg, *Die Haggada bei den Kirchenvätern. Erster Theil*, iv; Ginzberg, *Die Haggada bei den Kirchenvätern und in der apokryphischen Litteratur*, 1. For further bibliography see Judith Baskin, "Rabbinic-Patristic Exegetical Contacts in Late Antiquity: A Bibliographical Reappraisal," in *Approaches to Ancient Judaism*, ed. William S. Green (Atlanta: Scholars Press, 1985), 5:53–80; Adam Kamesar, "The Church Fathers and 'Rabbinic Midrash: A Supplementary Bibliography, 1985–2005," *Review of Rabbinic Judaism* 9 (2006), 190–96; Görge K. Hasselhoff, "'Sapientes docent traditiones': Der Rabbiner Moritz Rahmer und der Kirchenvater Hieronymus," in *Die Entdeckung des Christentums in der Wissenschaft des Judentums*, ed. Görge K. Hasselhoff (Berlin: De Gruyter, 2010), 147–63.
12. Ginzberg, *Die Haggada bei den Kirchenvätern und in der apokryphischen Litteratur*, 1.
13. See for example Ginzberg, *Legends*, 1:x–xi; Louis Ginzberg, *Genizah Studies in Memory of Doctor Solomon Schechter* (New York: Jewish Theological Seminary of America, 1928), 1:xv.
14. Ginzberg, *Die Haggada bei den Kirchenvätern. Erster Theil*, i–iii.
15. For hundreds of examples see Bernhard Heller, "Ginzberg's Legends of the Jews," *Jewish Quarterly Review* 24 (1934), 281–307.
16. These questions have taken on greater importance in modern scholarship. See Adam Kamesar, "Rabbinic Midrash and Church Fathers," in *Encyclopedia of Midrash*, ed. Jacob Neusner and Alan J. Avery-Peck (Leiden: Brill, 2005), 20–40.
17. For a complete list see Cohen, "Bibliography," 36–47.
18. Ginzberg, *Legends*, 5:ix.
19. Louis Ginzberg, *On Jewish Law and Lore* (New York: Atheneum, 1977), 67.
20. Ginzberg, *Die Haggada bei den Kirchenvätern. Erster Theil*, 7, 44.
21. For example, Ginzberg, *Legends*, 5:92, 222, 242; 6:21,114, 373, 375; cf. the remarks on Celsus, 5:89.
22. This is implied in the *Commentary to Ecclesiastes* of Olympiodorus of Alexandria (Patrologia Graeca 93:625).
23. Louis Ginzberg, "Augustine," *Jewish Encyclopedia*, 2:313, with reference to Augustinus, *Contra aduersarium legis et prophetarum* 2, 1 (2) (Corpus Christianorum Series Latina [CCSL] 49:87–88).
24. Yaakov Sussmann, "'Oral Torah' Plain and Simple" [in Hebrew], in *Meḥqerei Talmud*, ed. Yaakov Sussmann and David Rosenthal

(Jerusalem: Magnes Press, 2005), 3:226n.1. See also Louis Ginzberg, *Geonica* (New York: Jewish Theological Seminary of America, 1909), 1:73–75; Ginzberg, *On Jewish Law and Lore*, 11.

25. Ginzberg, *Legends,* 1:xi.
26. The question is addressed at length by Schorsch, "Making of a Legend." See also the essay of Galit Hasan-Rokem in this volume.
27. On this text see Oded Irshai, "The Christian Appropriation of Jerusalem in the Fourth Century: The Case of the Bordeaux Pilgrim," *Jewish Quarterly Review* 99 (2009), 465–86.
28. See CCSL 125:16. A similar reference to Jewish practices is found in the writings of Theodore Abū Qurrah, an Arab Christian author of the early ninth century, in his tract on the veneration of icons. Theodore alludes to a Jewish custom, prohibited in his own day, of kissing the stone that is beneath the Dome of the Rock and of anointing it with oil. See Sidney H. Griffith, "Theodore Abū Qurrah's Arabic Tract on the Christian Practice of Venerating Images," *Journal of the American Oriental Society* 105 (1985), 62; Griffith, *A Treatise on the Veneration of the Holy Icons Written in Arabic by Theodore Abū Qurrah, Bishop of Harrān (c.755–c.830 A.D.)* (Louvain: Peeters, 1997), 76. For a proposed connection between the Jewish custom described by the Bordeaux Pilgrim and the Moslem practice in the Umayyad period of anointing the sacred stone with scented oil see Julian Raby, "In Vitro Veritas. Glass Pilgrim Vessels from 7th-century Jerusalem," in Jeremy Johns, ed., *Bayt al-Maqdis, II: Jerusalem and Early Islam* (Oxford: Oxford University Press, 1999), 171–77.
29. Eusebius of Caesarea, *Commentary on Isaiah* 38:4–8 (*Die Griechischen Christlichen Schriftsteller der ersten Jahrhunderte* 57:242).
30. Jerome, *Commentary on Isaiah* 38:4–8 (CCSL 73:445).
31. Hillel I. Newman, "Jerome and the Jews" [in Hebrew] (Ph.D. diss., Hebrew University of Jerusalem, 1997), 246–47.
32. Josephus, *Jewish War,* 6, 191, trans. Henry St. J. Thackeray in *Josephus* (Cambridge, Mass.: Harvard University Press, 1928), 3:431.
33. Hegesippus, *Historiae* 5, 39 (Corpus Scriptorum Ecclesiasticorum Latinorum 66:381).
34. David Flusser, ed., *Sefer Yosippon* (Jerusalem: Bialik Institute, 1978), 1:406.
35. 2 Kings 19:1, 14 = Isaiah 37:1, 14.
36. Ginzberg, *Legends*, 6:366n.70. Ginzberg nowhere refers to the sources mentioning the House of Hezekiah.
37. Thus the translation of the Jewish Publication Society.
38. Justin Martyr, *Dialogue with Tryphon* 83, 1, ed. Miroslav Marcovich, 213.
39. Tertullian, *Against Marcion* 5, 9 (CCSL 1:690).

40. Daniel J. Lasker and Sarah Stroumsa, eds., *The Polemic of Nestor the Priest* (Jerusalem: Ben-Zvi Institute, 1996), 1:13–22.
41. Ibid., 88 (cf. note on 169). In the Hebrew version 570 becomes 576 (ibid., 129–30).
42. Maged S. A. Mikhail, "On Cana of Galilee: A Sermon by the Coptic Patriarch Benjamin I," *Coptic Church Review* 23/3 (2002), 93.
43. Francisco Javier Martinez, "Eastern Christian Apocalyptic in the Early Muslim Period: Pseudo-Methodius and Pseudo-Athanasius" (Ph.D. diss., Catholic University of America, 1985), 475, 561–62.
44. Karl H. Kuhn and William J. Tait, *Thirteen Coptic Acrostic Hymns from Manuscript M574 of the Pierpont Morgan Library* (Oxford: Griffith Institute, 1996), 137.
45. *Synaxarium Alexandrinum,* vol. 1 (Corpus Scriptorum Christianorum Orientalium 78 [Scriptores Arabici 12]), 17 (eighth of Tout).
46. E. A. Wallis Budge, *Saint Michael the Archangel: Three Encomiums* (London, 1894), 72*. For a variant text see Budge, *Miscellaneous Coptic Texts in the Dialect of Upper Egypt* (London: Longmans and Co., 1915), 759.
47. Youhanna Nessim Youssef, "The Homily on the Archangel Michael Attributed to Severus of Antioch Revisited," *Bulletin de la société d'archéologie copte* 42 (2003), 103–17.
48. Ginzberg, *Legends*, 7:591–93 (for the Vulgate cf. 529).
49. Newman, "Jerome and the Jews," 207–19. Note that in his articles Ginzberg occasionally discusses sources lacking in the notes of *Legends*, where his criteria for inclusion are more restrictive.
50. Ginzberg, *Keeper of the Law,* 166–67.

3

An Unimagined Community

Against *The Legends of the Jews*

Daniel Boyarin

When Louis Ginzberg wrote his monumental *Legends of the Jews,* his project, *mutatis mutandis* like those of this rough contemporaries I. Heinemann and M. Y. Bin-Gorion, was to produce a virtual *Volkspoesie* for the Jews. Without such an epic, no people could be properly constituted as a folk at that late moment in the romantic nationalism of the late nineteenth century. His monument should be understood as the Jewish *Kulevala.* It had to be close to the earth (Heinemann's language) and also somehow authentically Jewish in spirit and origin. Accordingly, the project was to virtually strip these narratives of their historical and hermeneutical contexts as well as of their connections with other cultural entities. In this essay, I propose an entirely different model for understanding two sets of relations: on the one hand, the relations between the so-called folk and high literatures, and, on the other, the relation between Jewish and other literatures. Moving beyond Ginzberg's two breaks, on the one hand, I propose folklorist modes of transmission and even production of "high" theological concepts and narratives within rabbinic literature; while on the other hand, I propose the mobility of these concepts and the modalities by which they migrate à la folklore from ethno-religious group to others.

This article argues for—or, better, hypothesizes—a cultural relationship, not merely a typological parallelism, between the Greek Christian West and the Babylonian Talmud. This is a controversial point. It is commonly held among scholars and learned lay folk alike that while the Palestinian Rabbis were in dialogue (and dispute) with Christians and other Hellenists, the Rabbis of Babylonia were only in cultural contact with them secondarily through the medium of their interaction with Palestinian Rabbis and their literature and traditions.[1] I am proposing, however, that the Babylonian Rabbis had a Hellenism of their own.

At this point a caveat must be entered, lest I be misunderstood. By asserting that Babylonian rabbinic culture was a Hellenistic culture, I am not in the least denying profound Iranian impact on the culture as well. Recent work in this field, primarily by Yaakov Elman and under his aegis, is exploring and exposing the richness of reading the Bavli (the Babylonian Talmud) through Iranological lenses as well.[2] Insofar as a Hellenism is by definition a "mixed" culture, there is, however, not the slightest contradiction in reading the Bavli as one articulation of Hellenism. Nor would Elman think so either. As he has noted, following James R. Russell, "influences" from one culture do not preclude in any sense "promiscuous intermingling with material from another tradition."[3] Sasanian Babylonia was a Babel of cultures, including the Persian, Eastern Christian, Mandaean, and Jewish, as well as Manichean cultures and religions. The argument for a Babylonian Rabbinic Hellenism is especially compelling with respect to matters not known from Palestinian Rabbinic traditions. These, at least arguably, only enter the Rabbinic textual world at a period and in a stratum of the Babylonian Talmud in which impact from Palestine is considerably less likely than interaction with the local milieu of trans-Euphratian Christian Hellenism.

In a very important discussion, Shaye Cohen has pointed to the Hellenism in Jewish Babylonia, noting that the very structuration of the Rabbinic academies there, resembling the Hellenistic philosophical schools with their successions of "heads," is not to be found in Rabbinic Palestine, and, therefore, "perhaps then the parallels between patriarchs and scholarchs tell us more about the Hellenization of Babylonian Jewry in the fourth and fifth centuries than about the Hellenization of Palestinian Jewry in the second."[4] My arguments tend to support Cohen's position fairly vigorously, albeit not in terms of Hellenistic "influence," nor even yet in terms of "Hellenization"; rather, I suggest we consider Babylonian Jewish culture as itself a Hellenism, or more nuanced, as a vibrant participant in Richard Kalmin's "rudiments of a partly shared elite culture [which] may have been emerging in Syria and Mesopotamia, perhaps a refinement of a rudimentary shared non-elite culture which had existed earlier."[5] This emergence involves the development of a shared intellectual culture that flows through the Roman East and the Sasanian West—an International Style, if you will.[6]

The ways that I imagine such cultural exchange, namely between Christian or "pagan" Greek-writing intellectuals and Babylonian Jewish intellectuals, are drawn from the models and methods of folkloristic research.[7] Diffusion among cultures of motifs, stories, sayings, proverbs, and legends is, of course, a very well known phenomenon, intensively studied since the nineteenth century. I certainly do not imagine Babylonian Rabbis reading Platonic dialogues—there just isn't evidence for that from the seventh century, even though a century or two later they certainly were reading them—but rather that literary modes and religious ideas reached them via the modes of diffusion of the kinds of literatures that we design as folklore. This does not mean, of course, that they were not elite products. Recent folkloristic scholarship assumes that "folkloristic" modes of production and dissemination occur at all levels of society and culture capital. This would provide a model to explain at least partially Kalmin's "shared elite culture." Such disseminated products are then subject to another well-studied process known as ecotypification, in which they undergo transition and are modified to fit better the cultural situation of their new environment.[8]

Finally, it is important to realize that written culture becomes transmuted into oral culture and then back again by such means over and over and over again. Some recent work on early Islam will also help to demonstrate this point. In a lucid and compelling account, Uwe Vagelpohl has discussed the problems attending "the philological outlook," defined by him as "a tendency to look at the translation movement as a philological phenomenon in isolation from its political and intellectual contexts,"[9] or, in other words, the exclusive attention to written texts. As Vagelpohl makes clear, "One consequence of the 'philological outlook' is the centrality accorded to the *textual* transmission of Greek thought."[10] Vagelpohl goes on to explain that in addition to actual texts translated from Greek into

Syriac and into Arabic, there are other means by which Greek wisdom was transmitted to the East. Arguing that "we cannot explain every Grecism and every instance of terms and ideas apparently inspired by a Greek source, whether directly or indirectly," he claims that we must postulate "a certain amount of oral communication across linguistic boundaries and 'para-translational' phenomena which leave less conspicuous traces in a literary tradition than the outright translation of texts."[11] Since the particular historical, linguistic, and cultural system of which Vagelpohl writes is substantially the same one as that of the Babylonian Talmud (with Greek materials diffusing eastward via Syriac-speaking Christians),[12] albeit a couple of centuries later, the phenomena of which he speaks are, in my view, very plausibly postulated for the later layers of the textual/cultural processes that gave rise to the Bavli also. As Louise Marlow has stated, "The assimilation of Hellenism into the culture of the eastern Mediterranean in the course of the sixth and seventh centuries foreshadowed the permeation of Islamic thought by Classical Greek and Neo-Platonic social ideas."[13]

Dimitri Gutas points out that it is extremely difficult to prove oral transmission, since, almost necessarily, it has not left a written record.[14] Gutas also makes the excellent point that what would be transmitted by such posited or hypothesized oral means is not full philosophical doctrines but rather short and poignant sayings and anecdotes, precisely the sort of material I see as revealing the Bavli's Hellenism.[15] Some scholars wish to deny any explanatory value to that which cannot be demonstrated positively[16] (in this camp among Jewish scholars would be E. E. Urbach),[17] assuming always internal cultural development until proven otherwise. For my taste, in contrast, it is quite enough that we have parallels to such transmission avenues to make the explanatory value of hypothesizing them rich and telling when particular puzzling textual phenomena in the Bavli are illuminated thereby.[18]

An example that seems quite compelling to me is the idea of *anamnesis*. For Plato, famously, the fetus knows all truth but forgets it upon birth, so learning is remembering (*Meno* 86b). For the rabbis, equally famously (if in more limited circles), an angel teaches the fetus the whole Torah and then makes him/her forget it on birth, so all learning of Torah is remembering (Niddah 30b). For another example of the same consonance, witness the Seventh Letter in which Plato writes: "I do not . . . think the attempt to tell mankind of these matters a good thing, except in the case of some few who are capable of discovering the truth for themselves with a little guidance" (341b). One should compare this to the famous clause in the Mishnah that one only teaches esoterica to "one who is wise and understands of himself," on which the Bavli remarks that "we give into his hands the chapter headings alone" (Ḥagigah 13a). These are too specific parallels to be mere chance, and they bespeak some cultural channels, by no means necessarily written, by which Platonic stories and maxims reached the Rabbis of Babylonia. Thus, it is not implausible to imagine by this means that even Platonic motifs, let alone Lucianic or Petronian ones, became part of oral culture, were transmitted to the Babylonian Rabbis through the media of oral transcultural transmission, and then reappeared in writing within the Bavli itself, having undergone a sort of sea change (or perhaps desert change) en route.[19]

Another significant factor in the increased "Hellenizing" of the Babylonian rabbis may very well be the increased movement of Syriac Christian sages after 489 A.D., after the bishop of Edessa was given permission to close down the theologically suspect "School of the Persians" in that city. Its adherents thereupon fled over the Persian border and founded their school at Nisibis.[20] Gafni has argued that the founding of this East Syrian (formerly known as Nestorian) school in Nisibis had a big impact on the formation of the Rabbinic schools in that area.[21] This perspective has the potential to lead to revolutionary new ways of conceiving the history of Babylonian Rabbinic Judaism,[22] insofar as one of the outstanding features of these Syriac-speaking and -writing Christian scholars and teachers was their concern with Greek (and especially Neoplatonic) philosophy. It is important to note that in areas very close to the centers of production of late ancient Babylonian Rabbinic culture, an Aramaic-speaking and -writing Christian community was increasingly articulating its religious thought on the basis of Greek philosophy, just as Christian writers had been doing, if somewhat earlier, in the Greek-speaking West. These Christians were also passionately devoted to the scholarly and even the scholastic life with their foundations of study institutions much like the Geonic yeshiva.[23] The geographical center of authority for the Babylonian Jews is in Maḥoza (Syriac Maḥoze, a section of Seleucia-Ctesiphon, the Sasanian capital), the site of the Catholicos of the East Syrian church. As Becker has put the point, "Jews and Christians in Mesopotamia spoke the same language, lived under the same rulers, practiced the same magic, engaged in mystical and eschatological speculation, and shared scriptures as well as a similar fixation on the ongoing and eternal relevance of those scriptures. They developed similar institutions aimed at inculcating an identity in young males that defined each of them as essentially a *homo discens,* a learning human, or rather, a *res discens,* a learning entity, since learning was understood as an essential characteristic of their humanity."[24] Given these considerations, Becker adumbrates—but in concert with the scope of his project does not develop the particulars of—the importance of this shared culture for the formation and content of the Babylonian Talmud. Vagelpohl, moreover, has identified Seleucia-Ctesiphon and Nisibis as being "at the time of the Islamic conquest" two of "the centers of Greek scholarship in the eastern part of the Roman Empire and western Persia."[25]

My considerations above of the plausibility of a joint cultural milieu, or at least of the possibility of cultural contact between the authors of the Bavli and late Hellenistic literary and thought forms, are meant to be just that, an argument for the inherent plausibility of such a milieu, not a proof for its existence. Given this inherent plausibility of such a cultural environment, my question is this: Does positing it help me produce a hypothesis to account for previously unexplained anomalies in particular texts or in the entire corpus? If I can account for anomalies small or large, in a text, small or large by relating them to a particular historical-literary context, and if there does not seem to be an alternative explanation that can explain such anomalies, then I will deem the exercise worthwhile. I will offer this reading as a hypothesis. Should someone find another way of reading the text that accounts for more of the text on fewer assumptions, that interpretation would be preferable to the one I offer here. Failing that, my readings should provide evidence for the hypothesis of extensive cultural contact and interaction between the Rabbis of late Babylonia and the Greco-Christian cultural world. The "method" is to imagine a different place, a hypothesized Republic of Letters, in which a series of textual readings can be imagined to lodge. It is vital, of course, that this new metanarrative not violate the more or less assured results of historians to date, but it surely can go beyond the hypotheses and conclusions that they draw upon these findings.

A Case in Point

In his excellent monograph on Eunomius, a late fourth-century "neo-Arian" theologian, Richard Vaggione discusses an important point of theological resonance for his hero having to do with the nature of human souls, a point that has powerful implications for any theology of the Incarnation. The eponymous hero of Vaggione's book holds what appears to be a very strange and unique doctrine. All human souls were created at the time of the first creation of humanity itself, when Adam came into being. There are, accordingly, a preestablished and finite number of souls. The condition for the end of the world is that all the pre-created souls will have lived a life in bodies. Fascinatingly, the "paradigm" of the creative act by which God created the souls is the infusion of breath into Adam's body.[26]

Piecing the doctrine together from the various sources cited by Vaggione,[27] I would take the analysis (synthesis) a bit further. A hostile witness to the Eunomian doctrine, Nemesius of Emessa presents its foundation in the following manner: "Eunomius, then, defined the soul as a bodiless essence created in a body [agreeing with Plato and Aristotle]. For, on the one hand, the 'bodiless essence' came from the 'truth' [Plato], on the other hand, the 'created in a body' is learned from Aristotle. He did not see, despite being clever, that what he was trying to bring together was incompatible."[28]

Vaggione himself remarks "that there is no need to try to 'unpack' Nemesius' criticism here or go into the background of the doctrine." For my purposes, at least, a partial "unpacking" and "going into" is the essence of what is needed, for Eunomius's doctrine is fully explicable and Nemesius's objection answerable when comparison is made to an important Rabbinic holding. Moreover, as we shall see, the talmudic saying is illuminated by the comparison to Eunomius as well. At four places in the Babylonian Talmud[29] (and only in the Babylonian Talmud), we find the following somewhat puzzling statement: "Rabbi Assi said, 'The son of David will not come until all of the souls in the body are finished, as it says, "For I will not contend for ever, neither will I be always wroth: for the spirit shall fail before me and the souls that I have made" [Isaiah 57:16].'" Rabbi Assi's midrash reads the verse to mean the Messiah will come only when the spirit and the souls that God has made run out, as it were, before him. When the spirit and the souls "fail before me," when they are gone and finished, then, says Rabbi Assi, God will not contend or be wroth, for the redemption will have come. In other words, we find here in a midrashic word the entire content of Eunomius's controversial doctrine that there is a finite number of human souls from the beginning and that the redemption will only come when all of them have been born into bodies. This is not to deny Vaggione's elaborate reconstruction of the philosophical theology underlying Eunomius's position but to elaborate its homelier sources in traditional biblical interpretation common to some Jews and Christians. Although some antecedents to part of this doctrine—namely, the theologoumenon that all the pre-created souls need to be used up before the redemption—can be found in the apocalyptic literature, the late ancient forms of the tradition share details not found before.[30] I find it entirely plausible to imagine this doctrine (rather rare in the Talmud itself, as we have seen) circulating between and among Babylonian Jews and Cappadocian Christians in the fourth century. (Lest the connection seem too far-fetched, let me remark that the Talmud itself knows of many connections between its Rabbinic heroes and Cappadocia; according to Babylonian legend none less than Rabbis Akiva and Meir found themselves in Cappadocia on occasion.) No wonder, then, that one Christian author, the so-called Pseudo-Athanasius, regards at least some elements of this doctrine as "secundum fabulatores Judaeos," and, pace Vaggione, these fabulatores would hardly be Philo, who would never be referred to in such dismissive terms by Patristic writers.[31] There is further evidence for a Rabbinic provenience for this theologoumenon/interpretation, pointed out by Vaggione but, in my opinion, not fully appreciated by him. In the *Clementine Recognitions* 3.26, we find the doctrine as well: "And on this account the world required long periods, until the number of souls which were predestined to fill it should be completed, and then that visible heaven should be folded up like a scroll, and that which is higher should appear, and the souls of the blessed, being restored to their bodies, should be ushered into light."[32] Vaggione implies that this is, perhaps, an Anomoean interpolation in the pseudo-Clementine text, remarking that this is "a work with at least one substantial Anomoean interpolation."[33] When we consider, however, the well-established connections between the authors of the pseudo-Clementina and Jews,[34] and even Rabbinic Jews, a much more attractive hypothesis emerges through which the *Recognitions* may have been the source for Eunomius, rather than the opposite, or at any rate that the *Recognitions* provide precious evidence for the circulation of this idea, *secundum fabulatores Judaeos* in fourth-century Christian circles. The very fact that the putatively "orthodox" writer of the Pseudo-Athanasian text also knows the tradition and that its provenance is Jewish suggests too that knowledge of this doctrine was widespread in early Christian circles.

While I thus agree with Pseudo-Athanasius, on fairly plausible chronological grounds, that it is not unlikely that this doctrine has come to Eunomius following Jewish aggadists (fabulatores), Eunomius, in turn, helps us unravel a puzzle in the Rabbinic text as well. The medieval Jewish commentators (chiefly Rashi) certainly understand that "in the body" here is a reference to a mystical doctrine of a treasury of souls, but they seem unable to explain why it is called "in the body." The scholar of Rabbinic ideas E. E. Urbach held that the "body" here referred to the individual bodies into which the souls would be born,[35] an opinion rightly rejected by Sysling out of hand.[36] Sysling, however, is no more able to explain the use of the term "body" here than is Rashi himself. Eunomius's connection, however, between this doctrine and the breathing of God's spirit into Adam solves this exegetical conundrum nicely. The "body" here is the body of the supernal Adam, and what was breathed into that body was all the souls that would ever exist, all created at that moment, precisely as Eunomius would have it. Perhaps it is not going too far to suggest that Nemesius has (willfully?) misread Eunomius as well, and that Eunomius's reference to the soul as being "created in a body" (*en sōmati ktizomenēn*) should rather be read "in *the* body," referring to the Adamic body, and there is no self-contradiction between "the truth" and Aristotelianism in Eunomius, either. The remarkable thing remains, in any case, that we have what is to my mind compelling evidence here of cultural and religious connection of a deep, specific, and recognized sort between the Christian world of fifth-century Cappadocia and the Babylonian Rabbinic world to the east and south and over the *limes* of the Roman Empire.[37]

Lest I be misunderstood at this point, I wish to offer another methodological reflection. I do not write here as a historian but as a historicist interpreter of texts. There is an enormous difference.[38] Aristotle said that "it is the mark of a trained mind never to expect more precision in the treatment of any subject than the nature of that subject permits." It is demanding more precision than the nature of the subject permits to expect proof of a specific connection between a given text and another, and in my opinion the right level of precision is to establish the plausibility of such a connection. Given such an inherent plausibility of such a cultural environment, my question is this: Does positing it help me produce a hypothesis to account for previously unexplained anomalies in particular texts or in the entire corpus? Because I don't wish my *interpretative* hypotheses to be founded on nonsense (as, for instance, in the recent case of a scholar who explained the art at Dura Europos as a response to the Christian Empire), I have tried not to make them violate any known historical data; that is, I will not explain an earlier text by referring to later conditions or the like. If I can account for anomalies in a text, small or large, however, by relating them to a historical context (by which I don't mean specific events but general tendencies and movements), and if there does not seem to be an alternative explanation that accounts for as much in the text, I will offer this reading as a hypothesis. Once again, it is important to emphasize: Should someone find another way of reading the text that accounts for more of the text on fewer assumptions, that interpretation would be preferable to the one I offer here. The hypothesis thus is, in principle, falsifiable. I cannot, then, claim in any sense to prove my readings but offer them as elegant solutions—or so I hope—to outstanding problems in the reading of Greek (in this case Christian) literature and of the Talmud.

Conclusion: Replacing Romantic "Folklore"

In the introduction to this essay, I raised the question of the motivation and ideology behind the folkloristic research of Louis Ginzberg and his contemporaries. I suggested that the motivating force for their work was the construction of a Jewish nation on the model of the European nations that had been invented in the nineteenth century, the imagined communities, to use Benedict Anderson's now-classic formulation. This Ginzbergian move required two processes of separation, a separation of an implicitly denatured elite literature from that of the folk, and the insistence on a uniquely "Jewish" set of themes and narratives. From this followed Ginzberg's practice of abstracting midrashic legendary material from its biblical hermeneutic context and treating it as an independent corpus of folk narrative, attached artificially to the biblical text by a kind of Rabbinic scholasticism. Hence my suggestion that for Ginzberg, *The Legends of the Jews* was a kind of *Kalevala* for the Jews, a *Volkspoesie* of their own, to justify, inter alia, a nation-state of their own. The text that I have examined here falsifies Ginzberg's approach in two ways. On the one hand, it shows that even the "elite" productions of the Jews are the product of folkloristic processes, such that it is impossible to separate off a Jewish folk from their elites.[39] On the other hand, it shows that Jewish cultural products have been intimately in communication with those of others as well, subject to processes of acculturation and especially ecotypification. A post-Ginzberg *Legends of the Jews* would, therefore, lead more easily to a picture of different cultural groups in contact, rather than to a system of supposedly discrete nation-states. In contrast, then, to Ginzberg's project (common in this sense to that of I. Heinemann and M. Y. Bin-Gorion) to construct the Jews as a nation among nations in a system of nation-states, I would imagine a Jewish culture embedded in multiple intercultural contexts.

Notes

1. For instance, even the very savvy Joshua Levinson considers only the question of the depth and intensity of the Hellenism in Jewish Palestine. "The Tragedy of Romance: A Case of Literary Exile," *Harvard Theological Review* 89/3 (July 1996), 227. See, however, Abraham Wasserstein, "Greek Language and Philosophy in the Early Rabbinic Academies," in *Jewish Education and Learning Published in Honour of Dr. David Patterson on the Occasion of His Seventieth Birthday,* ed. Glenda Abramson (Chur, Switzerland: Harwood Academic Publishers, 1994), 221–31. A very recent exception is Richard Kalmin, who treats other aspects of western connections for Babylonian Rabbinism, in *Jewish Babylonia between Persia and Roman Palestine* (Oxford: Oxford University Press, 2006). For a more extensive form of my argument here, see Daniel Boyarin, "Hellenism in Rabbinic Babylonia," in *The Cambridge Companion to Rabbinic Literature,* ed. Charlotte Fonrobert and Martin Jaffee (Cambridge: Cambridge University Press, 2007), 336–63.
2. Yaakov Elman, "Acculturation to Elite Persian Norms," in *Neti'ot le-David: Jubilee Volume for David Weiss Halivni,* ed. Yaakov Elman, Ephraim Bezalel Halivni, and Zvi Arie Steinfeld (Jerusalem: Orhot Press, 2004), 31–56; Yaakov Elman, "Middle Persian Culture and Babylonian Sages: Accommodation and Resistance in the Shaping of Rabbinic Legal Traditions," in Fonrobert and Jaffee, *Cambridge Companion to Rabbinic Literature*. See too Kalmin, *Jewish Babylonia between Persia and Roman Palestine*.
3. Elman, "Acculturation to Elite Persian Norms," 32.
4. Shaye J. D. Cohen, "Patriarchs and Scholarchs," *Proceedings of the American Academy of Jewish Research* 48 (1981), 85. See now, too, Adam H. Becker, *The Fear of God and the Beginning of Wisdom: The School of Nisibis and Christian Scholastic Culture in Late Antique Mesopotamia* (Philadelphia: University of Pennsylvania Press, 2006), 14–15. Further, Abraham Wasserstein has adumbrated such a result, arguing, "The Jews were as susceptible to the lure and influence of Hellenism as their gentile neighbours. This is no less true of the Aramaic-speaking Jews in Palestine and Babylonia than of those of their co-religionists who, living in Asia Minor or in Egypt, or in Greek-speaking cities in Palestine and Syria, had either adopted Greek speech or inherited it from their forebears." I thank Prof. Shamma Boyarin for bringing this essay to my attention. It is important to point out that Wasserstein emphasizes as well the common Hellenistic world of the Rabbis and of Syriac-writing Christians; Wasserstein, "Greek Language and Philosophy in the Early Rabbinic Academies," 223.

5. Kalmin, *Jewish Babylonia between Persia and Roman Palestine*, 174.
6. For a recent and very effective challenge to the notion of "influence" in the study of late ancient Jewish cultures, see Michael L. Satlow, "Beyond Influence: Towards a New Historiographic Paradigm," in *Jewish Literatures and Cultures: Context and Intertext*, ed. Anita Norich and Yaron Z. Eliav (Providence: Brown Judaic Studies, 2008), 37–53.
7. For such models in their richest application to Rabbinic texts, see Galit Hasan-Rokem, *The Web of Life—Folklore and Midrash in Rabbinic Literature*, trans. Batya Stein (Stanford, Calif.: Stanford University Press, 2000), and Dina Stein, *Memrah, magyah, mitos: Pirke de-Rabbi Eliezer le-or mehqar ha-sifrut ha-amamit* (Jerusalem: Magnes Press, 2004).
8. Daniel Boyarin, "Virgins in Brothels: Gender and Religious Ecotypification," *Estudios de Literatura Oral* 5 (Algarve, Portugal: Universidade do Algarve, 1999), 195–217.
9. Uwe Vagelpohl, *Aristotle's Rhetoric in the East: The Syriac and Arabic Translation and Commentary Tradition* (Boston: Brill, 2008), 1–2.
10. Ibid., 3.
11. Ibid., 5.
12. As Vagelpohl explains, "In pre-Islamic Palestine, Syria and Iraq, Greek learning was mainly transmitted through the various Christian churches of the area. Many of the Christian scholars trained in the convents and churches that were part of the local educational system(s) were familiar enough with Greek to read Greek literature in the original but their native language was Syriac, a dialect of Aramaic that had become the dominant language of scholars and merchants in the 'Fertile Crescent' in the wake of the spread of Christianity." Ibid., 15. Given, for instance, that the Targum to the Proverbs is simply the Peshitto transliterated into Hebrew characters, can we doubt that Jewish "scholars and merchants" found Syriac culture accessible? Further: "At the time of the Islamic conquest, the centers of Greek scholarship in the eastern part of the Roman Empire and western Persia were Edessa, Nisibis, Seleucia (near Ctesiphon) and Gundīšāpūr (all of them dominated by Nestorian denomination)." Ibid., 16.
13. Louise Marlow, *Hierarchy and Egalitarianism in Islamic Thought* (New York: Cambridge University Press, 1997), 44. Vagelpohl's book has been invaluable to me both for his own insights and for sending me to this reference and several others cited in these paragraphs as well.
14. Dimitri Gutas, "Pre-Plotinian Philosophy in Arabic (Other Than Platonism and Aristotelianism): A Review of the Sources," *Aufstieg*

und Niedergang der römischen Welt: Geschichte und Kultur Roms im Spiegel der neueren Forschung Teil 2, Bd.36, Tbd.7, Principat Philosophie, Wissenschaften, Technik Philosophie (systematische Themen; indirekte Überlieferungen; Allgemeines; Nachträge), von Wolfgang Haase / herausgegeben von Wolfgang Haase und Hildegard Temporini (Berlin: De Gruyter, 1994), 4947.

15. I am, as such, certainly not claiming anything like the "maximalist" version of a "hidden tradition," as anatomized by Gutas, ibid., 4945–46. But neither am I convinced that the "minimalist" position that Gutas dismisses (4945) is as trivial as he would have it be. Why indeed are "borrowed adages and similarities in outlook not among the constitutive elements of a high civilization"?
16. In this category falls Gutas himself. Ibid., 4944–49.
17. Ephraim E. Urbach, *The Sages: Their Concepts and Beliefs,* trans. Israel Abrahams (Jerusalem: Magnes Press, 1975), 246–48.
18. See Vagelpohl, *Aristotle's Rhetoric in the East,* 5n.13.
19. Cf. Michael G. Morony, *Iraq after the Muslim Conquest* (Princeton, N.J.: Princeton University Press, 1984), 7ff.
20. Becker, *Fear of God,* 2.
21. Isaiah Gafni, "Nestorian Literature as a Source for the History of the Babylonian *Yeshivot*" [in Hebrew], *Tarbiz* 51 (1981–1982), 567–76. For the significance of Nisibis (trans-Euphratian Antioch) as a center of Jewish learning, see Aharon Oppenheimer, Benjamin H. Isaac, and Michael Lecker, *Babylonia Judaica in the Talmudic Period* (Wiesbaden: L. Reichert, 1983), 328–31.
22. See Becker's remarks relating how changing legends of origin in Mesopotamia about Syrian monasticism were homologous with the institutional changes also taking place. So as the East Syrian monastic practices became Egyptianized, "the memories of early Syriac monasticism and its indigenous origins were completely erased. The culmination of this may be seen in the Mār Awgēn tradition, which held that monasticism was brought to Mesopotamia by Eugenius the Egyptian." Becker, *Fear of God,* 175.
23. Ibid.
24. Ibid., 5.
25. Vagelpohl, *Aristotle's Rhetoric in the East,* 16.
26. Richard Paul Vaggione, *Eunomius of Cyzicus and the Nicene Revolution* (Oxford: Oxford University Press, 2000), 119–20.
27. Any analysis I can provide here is owing to Vaggione's erudition and to the diligence of my research assistant, Ruth Haber, who tracked down and provided for me copies of every one of the many sources that Vaggione cites; perusal of his footnotes will show that both (erudition and diligence) are formidable.

28. Nemesius, *Nemesii Emeseni De Natura Hominis*, ed. Moreno Morani (Leipzig: B. G. Teubner, 1987), 30. For "the truth" as a name for Platonism, see Plotinus, *Ennead* II 9,6. 10–12.
29. Yevamot 62a, 63b; Avodah Zarah 5a; Niddah 13b. In all these cases, while the saying is used for very divergent purposes and arguments, its own form is absolutely stable and consistent.
30. Harry Sysling, *Teḥiyyat Ha-Metim: The Resurrection of the Dead in the Palestinian Targums of the Pentateuch and Parallel Traditions in Classical Rabbinic Literature* (Tübingen: Mohr Siebeck), 1996), 194, who points out as well the signal differences between the Rabbinic and the apocalyptic versions of the idea. I am grateful to Ishay Rosen-Zvi for calling this reference to my attention. For some further discussion, see below in the body of the text.
31. Vaggione, *Eunomius of Cyzicus and the Nicene Revolution,* 119n.255.
32. Clement, "Recognitions of Clement," *The Writings of Tatian and Theophilus and the Clementine Recognitions* (Edinburgh: T. & T. Clark, 1867), 121.
33. Vaggione, *Eunomius of Cyzicus and the Nicene Revolution,* 120n.257.
34. Albert I. Baumgarten, "Literary Evidence for Jewish Christianity in the Galilee," in *The Galilee in Late Antiquity*, ed. Lee I. Levine (New York: Jewish Theological Seminary of America, 1992), 39–50.
35. Urbach, *The Sages: Their Concepts and Beliefs,* 237.
36. Sysling, *Teḥiyyat Ha-Metim,* 207.
37. Adam H. Becker, "Beyond the Spatial and Temporal *Limes:* Questioning the 'Parting of the Ways' Outside the Roman Empire," in *The Ways That Never Parted Jews and Christians in Late Antiquity and the Early Middle Ages*, ed. Adam H. Becker and Annette Yoshiko Reed (Tübingen: Mohr Siebeck, 2003), 373–92.
38. This problem is one that has engaged me (and plagued me) from the very beginning of my intellectual and scholarly work on the Talmud.
39. Dina Stein, "'Let the People Go': The 'Folk' and Their 'Lore' as Tropes in the Reconstruction of Rabbinic Culture," *Prooftexts* 29/2 (Summer 2009), 206–41.

4

The Quiet Revolution

Louis Ginzberg's *The Legends of the Jews* and Jewish Anthological Literature

Jacob Elbaum

Among aggadic anthologies, *The Legends of the Jews* occupies a unique place of pride. Not only is it the most complete anthology following the sequence of the Hebrew Bible in our possession, it is also an invaluable and unparalleled research tool, acquainting the scholar with traditions that have accompanied the Hebrew Bible from the Second Temple period to the waning of the Middle Ages. In this latter respect, this composition differs from all its generic precursors in Jewish anthological literature (the yalqutim). Louis Ginzberg, the author of this work, approached this project first and foremost as a scholar of aggadic and related literatures. His scholarly acumen, attested to by the thousands of notes accompanying the text, in tandem with the rare literary talent he exhibited in weaving together disparate sources to create one flowing text—an impressive mosaic—provide the work with its defining character. On the one hand, the work is an original and impressive literary masterpiece, one which is essentially new; and, on the other hand, it is a unique work of scholarship, which every scholar of the Hebrew Bible, aggadah, midrash, and those works related to the Hebrew Bible and everything associated with it should have at his or her fingertips.

The Genre

In order to take the true measure of Louis Ginzberg's accomplishment and evaluate it from the proper perspective, several points need to be made concerning the anthological impulse in the field of aggadic and midrashic literature. This will allow us to delineate the unique characteristics of the anthology, a particular branch of literary creativity, within the general context of aggadah and midrash. Indeed, everyone agrees that aggadic and midrashic literature by their very nature possess the generic hallmarks of the anthological genre; therefore, it is crucial to differentiate between these two literary phenomena, which only appear to be similar: "For, do we weave them all in the same web?" (Berakhot 24a). This matter, however, will only be addressed indirectly.[1]

It is easy to see that not all of the rabbinic anthological works, whose focus is the Hebrew Bible, have the same aims, and it is also worth mentioning that this genre did not merit continuous, unbroken attention, as did other fields based on or related to the Hebrew Bible, including, for instance, biblical exegesis or the homiletical or sermonic literature. These have accompanied the Bible without surcease for over two thousand years, while the unique anthology genre has reared its head in certain periods and disappeared in others. Hundreds of years passed between the period of the aggadah's (even the late aggadah's) initial blossoming and the rise of the classical yalqut literature (which a rude approximation dates to the thirteenth and fourteenth centuries, when the following great anthologies were compiled: *Yalqut ha-Makhiri,* composed by R. Makhir ben R. Abba Mari, R. Jacob Sikili's composition known as *Talmud Torah,* and the most important of them all, *Yalqut Shimoni*). Several hundred more years passed between the period of the yalqut's initial flourishing and demise and the next period in which the yearnings for such a genre resurface; this time, the revitalized anthology takes a new form. This revival took place in the seventeenth century—the period in which the *Yalqut Reuveni* and *Yalqut Ḥadash* were composed, works that have been completely neglected by scholars in the various fields of Hebrew literature. I discuss these compositions in greater detail—albeit briefly—below. Here, I note only that these two works were the result of a trend dedicated to creating a new type of Hebrew anthology that had begun in the sixteenth century. While this trend had arisen in a different field of rabbinic literature, this process led to the composition of two anthologies of aggadic material from the Talmud: *Haggadot ha-Talmud* (the one and only printing of which took place in Constantinople in 5271 [1511]) and

Ein Ya'aqov (Salonika, 5276–5282 [1516–1522]). From this point on and until the modern period, the anthological impulse once again waned[2] only to revive again with the composition of the modern anthologies, the best known being M. J. Berdyczewski's *Mi-mekor Yisrael* and *Tsefunot ve-aggadot* (originally written in German), Ḥ. N. Bialik's and Y. Ḥ. Ravnitzki's *Sefer ha-aggadah,* and the focus of this essay, Louis Ginzberg's *Legends of the Jews.*

I must admit that the generalization I have made—which assumes that this genre developed in a linear fashion, and which dates the first appearance of this genre very late—is inaccurate. E. E. Urbach's assertion concerning the nature of *Pitron Torah*—that it is a "yalqut"—is well known (and he dates that composition to the eighth century, or, to be more precise, "not before the eighth century");[3] furthermore, my readers are no doubt astonished that I have not yet mentioned "R. Moses [Hadarshan's] midrash," composed by the famous scholar from Narbonne, who lived in the first half of the eleventh century. Based on what we can learn from *Numbers Rabbah* A (on *Bemidbar* and *Naso*), *Midrash Aggadah,* and Genesis Rabbati, R. Moses' literary creations bear the typical hallmarks of a yalqut;[4] similarly, R. Tobias ben R. Eliezer's *Leqaḥ Tov,* and the composition that followed in its footsteps, *Sekhel Tov* by R. Menaḥem ben R. Solomon (which was completed in 4999/1139), also have these hallmarks. Indeed, even though we cannot assert that the early yalqut literature necessarily took center stage immediately after the wells of aggadic creativity ran dry (since some of the aggadic literature's later exemplars were still in the process of being created at the time of some of the anthological compositions I have mentioned), we can still declare that a clear distinction may be drawn between the original midrashim—including the later ones—and the yalqutim. What seems to distinguish the yalqutim is their awareness of their belatedness, their acknowledgment that they are drawing upon texts that have already, in principle, been "closed" and become authoritative. Furthermore, even when the anthologists permit themselves to change (some more and some less) the original version, they still perceive the contents of these sources upon which they base themselves to be inviolate; they are texts whose essence must not be tampered with, insofar as their conceptual infrastructure, their intent, is concerned. In other words, the anthologists sometimes take upon themselves the responsibility of changing the text, abridging the wording, or reassembling a section in a novel way—after the original has been disassembled into its constituent parts (I would humbly suggest that the compiler of the *Yalqut Shimoni,* who is widely perceived to be one of the most conservative and cautious anthologists,[5] adopted this approach). However, they simultaneously stress in various ways (though never explicitly) that they do not claim ownership over the source text and that they are charged with preserving its original character (whatever that might be). (The anthologists of the *Yalqut Shimoni* and the *Yalqut ha-Makhiri* also highlight the source by explicitly noting the name of the composition "cited.") In so doing (though in other ways as well), the anthologists distinguish their mindset from the composers of the later midrashim (for instance, the *Tanḥuma* or *Seder Eliyahu*), for these authors believe themselves (insofar as we are capable of reconstructing their thoughts) to have acquired ownership of the ancient sources through the very act of reformulating them; they believe that the original deeds of ownership have been abrogated, and, thus, the earlier midrashim have become their own, as they have placed their own imprint on the ancient midrashic text.

Historical Perspectives

Having expressed these qualifications, I briefly resume discussing the genre's history. Before continuing, however, it is important to note that without a doubt the compilers of the yalqutim throughout history had many different reasons and goals for composing their works. This notwithstanding, certain common aspirations also definitely motivated the anthologists in the various ages. Had the early anthologists written prefaces to their anthologies, they almost certainly would have expressed sentiments similar to those of the *Yalqut ha-Makhiri's* author:

> And neither my wisdom nor the knowledge and insight in my heart are that from which I composed this book, and I have not made [it] for mine own honor or for the honor of my father's house, for this craft does not lend itself to distinguishing one's

> self, to be praised or to be glorified, for even the schoolchildren can do [this], and there is nary a person in the world who cannot do likewise, but the main purpose of my plans and my goal was to benefit an individual like myself, so that even the Torah-scholars might sometimes find pleasure in it because the midrashim and aggadot are scattered and dispersed all over, and most are not in their right places and because they [the Torah scholars] have taken great trouble [to study] the Talmud, the laws, and that which is forbidden and that which is permitted, [but] they will be unable to immediately lay their hands on the desired midrash[im] on each and every verse as they require them, so may this book function as a means to [help them] reach the trove of their thoughts and intentions.[6]

There are certainly those who would add that they composed their anthologies to aid those who did not have access to these works (which, of course, were only available in manuscript form at the time); and there were others who would provide even more complex explanations. And there were certainly anthologists, whose anthological goals were inherently exegetical, such as the *Leqaḥ Tov,* the *Sekhel tov,* and R. Samuel ben Nissim Masnut in his thirteenth-century "midrashim."

The accomplishments of the early anthologists (with *Yalqut Shimoni* leading the pack) apparently satisfied the needs of the masses. The influence of great books lives on long after they are written, until a tremendous need arises or until certain fundamental assumptions change, that rob even such coprehensive works as these of their relevance and vitality, leaving them open to being challenged.[7] *Yalqut Shimoni*—or, as hundreds of medieval scholars called it, either *Midrash Yalqut* (a sobriquet that certainly implies much) or even simply *Ha-yalqut* (the anthology)—provided all those who were searching for a midrash on the Hebrew Bible (from Genesis to Chronicles) with the source they were looking for. This continued to be the case until most if not all of the Torah scholars changed their minds about what books every educated Jewish reader must know. To be specific, no new anthologies were necessary until the lack of citations from kabbalistic literature—in particular, the Zohar—in the extant anthologies became so distressing that popular sentiment deemed them obsolete. Two compilations that I mentioned above in passing were compiled to fill this void. One—*Yalqut Ḥadash,* also known as *Yalqut ha-Yisraeli* (first printed in Lublin, 5408 [1648]), was a topically arranged anthology, and its author was (in all likelihood) R. Israel b. R. Benjamin of Belzits;[8] the other—*Yalqut Reuveni,* written by R. Abraham Reuben b. Joshua (or Heshki) (1605–1673), was published in two different formats: in 5420 (1660) in Prague, arranged by topic, and in 5441 (1681) in Wilhermsdorf, following the order of the Pentateuch. In order to distinguish the later edition from the first, the latter was called *Yalqut Reuveni [ha-]gadol al ha-Torah* in the subsequent printings. The *Yalqut ḥadash* does not have an author's preface; however, the wording on the title page is sufficient to provide us with a sense of how it surpasses earlier anthologies:

> [The] book
> Yalqut ḥadash
> Which was anthologized using clear language and with good sense from all books
> The Zohar [ha-]gadol: And [the] Zohar Ḥadash: And Tikkunei Zohar:
> And Yonat Elem: And Sefer ha-Kavvanot: And Asarah Ma'amarot
> And Galya Razaya and matters that are hidden [tsefunot]: All that one is permitted to
> preach in public for we have no dealings with esoterica: Also midrashic novellae
> found in Galanti: And in Megaleh Amukot: And supernal novellae from Sefer
> Ḥasidim: As well as astonishing midrashim from Yalqut ha-gadol and Pirqei R[abbi] E[liezer]
> And this is called *Yisraeli.*

R. Naftali Hertz ben R. Simeon Halevi Ashkenazi's publisher's introduction contains a more detailed survey of the sources used in compiling this composition, which I do not elaborate upon here. This yalqut received the approbation of two contemporary Torah giants: R. Naftali ben R. Isaac Katz (the Maharal's grandson) and R. Joshua Heschel.

The second anthology, *Yalqut Reuveni,* has a preface, and while the anthologist does not enumerate the kabbalistic sources cited in his work—of which there are many (in addition to the customary midrashim)—he reveals his own misgivings about his undertaking:

> [Whether] to make public hoary matters that are concealed from humanity, which the early sages decreed should only be said over in private, because not everyone who desires to take the name [of a kabbalist] may do so, and I was undecided whether to speak out or not to speak out, and I came to the logical conclusion that I should speak out, speak without shame; for indeed, the opposite is true—[I will stand] before kings and I will not be ashamed for "the paths of the Lord are smooth, the righteous walk on them" etc. [Hosea 14:10].

Later, the author explains that the name he chose for his composition also reflects his decision to reveal matters that are usually only revealed to the *tsenuim* (those who are modest): "and I have called the book *Yalqut Reuveni* [which] in gematria has the exact numerical value of 'with this I provide a service for the public.'"[9]

These two compilations seem to have attracted a large contemporary readership; they are often cited and were reprinted several times. *Yalqut ḥadash* was printed five times before the end of the seventeenth century, and *Yalqut Reuveni* was printed four times by 1712. *Shikhḥat Leqet,* a supplement to *Yalqut ḥadash,* edited by R. Nathan ben Isaac Jacob Bonn, was printed four times before the end of the seventeenth century (first printed in Prague in 5412 [1652]). It was even regularly printed as an appendix to *Yalqut Reuveni,* beginning with the *Yalqut*'s third printing (Amsterdam, 5460 [1700]).

I believe that two remarks should be made on this last topic. First, delving further into the nature of *Yalqut ḥadash* and *Shikhḥat Leqet,* its supplement, and taking a closer look at *Yalqut Reuveni*—all three of which undoubtedly belong to a different type of anthology than those previously mentioned—seem to lead the discussion away from "pure" anthologies into another generic context: to reference books on the Bible, to handbooks for preachers, and primarily to the genre of indices literature. Indeed, if we attempt to compare *The Legends of the Jews* (or Berdyczewski's anthologies and *Sefer ha-Aggadah*) to the earlier yalqutim, we will rapidly conclude that neither the "pure" exemplar of the genre, *Yalqut Shim'oni,* nor the other medieval yalqutim mentioned above (nor, for that matter, those I did not mention, such as those Yemenite midrashim *Midrash ha-gadol* and *Midrash ha-Ḥefets,* which possess unique identifying features that I do not discuss here), were the only anthological paradigms that offered themselves to the new anthologists. Rather, they opted to emulate those anthologies which, instead of following the sequence of the Hebrew Bible verse by verse, chose other organizational methods as they addressed a host of biblical topics (indeed, Ginzberg, whose extraordinary breadth of knowledge provided him with the opportunity of encompassing all that pertained to the matter at hand, mentions, though infrequently, *Yalqut ḥadash* [in his notes], and *Yalqut Reuveni* much more frequently). In order to ensure that my argument pertaining to *Yalqut Ḥadash* and *Yalqut Reuveni* has a solid foundation, I would like to draw attention to various types of anthologies that were feted in their eras, and whose relationship with each other is yet to be determined. One of these is exemplified by the influential alphabetical yalqut *Zikhron Torat Moshe,* compiled by R. Moses ben R. Joseph Figo, which, according to the title page of the work, "encompasses all the strands of the utterances in our Talmuds, the Babylonian and the Palestinian, [to allow the reader] to easily find the desired utterance and its source and the place where it is adduced in the commentators available to us." This yalqut was first printed in Constantinople, apparently in the year 5314 (1554), and later in Prague in 5383 (1623); it served as a model for several other index books.[10]

Second, the enormous (and additional) temporal gap between the flowering of this genre in the seventeenth century and its revival in the modern period may be an optical illusion—the result of our inability to locate such compositions and of the related fact that we lack a systematic and comprehensive bibliographical listing of the anthological literature;[11] indeed, it is quite possible that for these reasons certain important works have escaped attention. However, this notwithstanding, I believe that it would be fair to state that from the seventeenth century to modernity no yalqut was compiled that left an indelible stamp on the evolution of the genre. R. Jacob Culi's *Me-'am Lo'ez* (Constantinople, 5490 [1730] [on Genesis]; and Constantinople, 5493 [1733] [on Exodus, until *Terumah*]) is an exception that, in my humble opinion, merely proves the rule.[12]

Innovations

In addition to the light that I hope I have already shed above (by way of analogy and comparison) on Louis Ginzberg's methodology in *The Legends of the Jews,* I would also like to briefly summarize what I believe are the central insights arising from categorizing *The Legends of the Jews* as an anthology. I begin by reiterating my remarks above concerning the impact that the new works that were added to the educated Jew's required reading list seem to have had on the development of the later yalqutim literature. First, I admit that perhaps Ginzberg's inclusion in his notes and even in the body of the text of the following material is not a tremendous innovation: material originally found in medieval commentaries—such as the Tosafists' compositions (*Da'at Zekeinim, Hadar Zekeinim*); material drawn from the Spanish tradition, such as R. Joshua ibn Shueib's fourteenth-century writings, or the *Tseror ha-Mor* written by the Spanish exile R. Abraham Saba, a great biblical commentator (whose book is replete with midrashim, some found nowhere else); and, needless to say, passages from the *Zohar.* However, I would argue that Ginzberg's citation of lengthy passages from the following types of texts was unquestionably innovative: books whose authority many doubted and books that clearly rework earlier sources, such as *Sefer ha-Yashar* (which some scholars even date close to when it was first printed in Venice, 5385 [1625])[13] and *The Alphabet of Ben Sira* (about which Lieberman emphatically asserted: "Never was this book, which is replete with frivolity and obscene language, [considered] an authoritative book").[14] Finally and unquestionably, no one can argue that Ginzberg's greatest innovation was utilizing the material embedded in the apocryphal literature, the Hellenistic Jewish literature, and even the writings of the Church Fathers—material that he believed was derived from Jewish sources. This incredibly bold move even seems to outstrip that of Berdyczewski.

I now turn to another aspect of *The Legends of the Jews*—to what I believe seems to be an entirely new form for the biblical anthology. *The Legends of the Jews* is a sequential narrative that recounts the life stories of the figures and the events informing the biblical story from creation until Mordechai and Esther's era. As Ginzberg writes (in his preface to the notes), hundreds of legends from a vast literature spreading over two thousand years are presented in "connected form" in order "to offer a readable story and narrate an interesting tale." He does this without a priori bowing to the dictates of any extant source, without prejudicially privileging either early or late material (although he does list his sources in the notes in chronological order), and without accepting the fundamental presumption that certain texts are more authoritative than others. One historical instance of such a presumption is R. Hai Gaon's declaration "that everything which is set down in the Talmud is clearer than whatever is not set down therein."[15] (Maimonides seems to have also adopted this position, as did many of the medieval sages, among them anthologists.) Another instance of such a presumption would be the privilege—sometimes even before a particular set of sources was examined—that the scholarly community in Ginzberg's day granted (and which we still grant today) to the early Land of Israel traditions. Ginzberg's approach was certainly bolstered by the folkloristic underpinnings of his system, as is amply demonstrated by his programmatic article "The Legends of the Jews—East and West."[16] Certainly, he never thought that anyone would consider him oblivious to the fact that his synthesis of source texts created a new text (indeed, his meticulous documentation of the texts he drew upon proves this). However, without a doubt, neither did he denigrate such an act as inherently flawed. Though most compilers would certainly deny the following proposition, I would argue that all the compilers of yalqutim create—by the very nature of their quest to join many texts together—new texts, even when the original texts are not completely integrated with each other. Ginzberg, in any event, wanted to create a vital, living text, which would not function merely as a vehicle for conveying his notes. Had the latter been his goal, he presumably could have sufficed with writing a detailed index.

Whether I am correct or not, for perhaps I have overstepped the mark, since Ginzberg definitely wanted to provide his readers with a flowing narrative, those texts that contain expansive narratives in the first place are naturally granted greater weight. These essentially story-like texts may be found in the apocryphal literature and the early pseudo-epigraphic literature and in the later flowerings of midrashic and aggadic literature. Indeed, I would like to correct a mistaken impression that might arise from my characterization of the book as a narrative that recounts the life stories of the figures and the events informing the biblical story. The truth is that this description, based on Ginzberg's own remarks, fails to fully depict the riches to be found in the various chapters (not to mention in the notes). With true inspiration, Ginzberg inserted segments—some longer and some shorter—into the chapters, which discuss various facets of the sages' worldview. Even when other (modern) anthologies addressed such matters, they were set off from the narrative portion of the work (for instance, see *Sefer ha-Aggadah*). In choosing this approach, Ginzberg successfully adopted one of the characteristics common to Jewish works on the Hebrew Bible, works that strove to present the issues in diverse ways, eschewing generic (or any other form of) insularity.

A final remark: In portraying this work as an anthology two crucial chapters still remain to be written.

The first chapter concerns the aggadic anthologies of the last century and the place of *The Legends of the Jews* among them. That is to say, a comparison needs to be made highlighting the differences between *The Legends of the Jews* and *Sefer ha-Aggadah,* and perhaps even more interestingly between *The Legends of the Jews* and Berdyczewski's *Der Born Judas,* which was first printed between 1919 and 1923, and even made some use of Ginzberg's magnum opus. The comparison between these two works becomes even more of a desideratum given that both written in German. Ginzberg and Berdyczewski (and many others) worked and lived in a new cultural reality, in which it was a given that Jewish sources could be translated and even taught in translation, just as they had been in their original language. This novel assumption was a product of the

Enlightenment. As is widely known, Judaism's foundational works (excluding the Hebrew Bible) were not even translated into the Jewish languages (such as Yiddish and Ladino), and certainly not into the gentile vernacular, until the modern era. Indeed, investigating this cultural phenomenon—which indicates the profound change in the way texts once considered holy are now perceived—and establishing the extent of its influence on the way *The Legends of the Jews,* Berdyczewski's aforementioned book, and other anthologies (mostly in German) were formulated is a matter that needs to be examined independently. Within the context of this other study, an attempt should also be made to determine if the impact of modernity is indeed related to the modern anthologists' linguistic choices or if these aforementioned yalqutim merely continue and strengthen an earlier trend that began with anthologies like *Tsenah u-re'enah* (Yiddish) and *Me-'am Lo'ez* (Ladino), which do not seem to be mentioned in *The Legends of the Jews*' notes.[17]

The second chapter concerns the fact that Ginzberg lived in two worlds. Not only was he a vibrant, contributing member of the world of Jewish scholarship and a scholar deeply involved in the academic study of Judaism, he was also well aware of what was happening beyond Judaism's borders. Thus, his knowledge of and connection to anthological literature written in other languages and to the study of folklore in his day and age also needs to be addressed. Only by doing so can we complete the picture, providing the background necessary to understand and explain his groundbreaking masterpiece—*The Legends of the Jews.*

Notes

Translated by Meshulam Gotlieb.

1. On the anthological dimension of the aggadic and midrashic oeuvre as a whole, see David Stern's introductory remarks in David Stern, ed., *The Anthology in Jewish Literature* (New York: Oxford University Press, 2004), 1–31; the remarks of the authors cited there in the book; and my article therein, "Yalkut Shimoni and the Medieval Midrashic Anthology" 159–75, also published in *Prooftexts* 17/2 (1977), 133–51.
2. However, there was one exception, the indices (*maftehot*) literature. See below, and n. 10.

3. *Sefer pitron Torah, Yalqut Midrashim u-feirushim* (Jerusalem: Magnes Press, 5738 [1978]), introduction, 25; on the manner in which the compiler of *Pitron Torah* chose to bring his sources (none of which was ever cited by name), see especially 22–23.
4. On the approach of the compiler of *Bereshit Rabbati* to bringing sources, see Hanoch Albeck, *Genesis Rabbati* (Jerusalem: Wahrmann Books, 5700 [1940]), introduction, 2–5. On R. Moses Hadarshan (and his homiletical material embedded in the aforementioned midrashim), see Hananel Mack's recently published *The Secrets of Moshe ha-Darshan* [in Hebrew] (Jerusalem: Bialik Institute, 5770 [2010]).
5. On this, see Elbaum, *Yalqut Shimoni.*
6. Cited from the anthologist's preface to the anthologies on Isaiah, the Twelve Minor Prophets, and Psalms.
7. A similar observation may be made regarding the *Ein Ya'aqov.* This composition made an indelible impression both on the character of future anthologies devoted to the aggadic material of the Talmuds (the Babylonian and the Palestinian) and on the approach adopted by the aggadic commentaries on the Talmuds.
8. The author hid his identity but alludes to it by employing the sobriquet "Yisraeli." R. Israel of Belzits (d. 5415 [1655]) was the author of a book of sermons entitled *Sefer Tiferet Yisrael,* which may be found in manuscript form in Oxford. For further information about the author, *Yalqut Ḥadash,* and the book of sermons (and a translation of the sermon for the portion of *Balak* in the year 5408 [1648]), see Marc Saperstein, *Jewish Preaching 1200–1800* (New Haven, Conn.: Yale University Press, 1980), 286–303. Saperstein (286n.1) also remarks upon Adolf Neubauer's comments (regarding the *Yalqut Ḥadash* and the identity of its author) in *Maggid* 14 (December 1870; Tevet 5631), 397.
9. In order for the numerical values to be exactly the same, the title would have to be *Yalqut ha-Reuveni.*
10. The extent of its influence can be judged from the title page of the book *Beit Leḥem Yehudah* authored by Judah Aryeh of Modena (first printed in Venice in 5385 [1625]). *Beit Leḥem Yehudah* is characterized there as "a small gold key [enabling the reader] to find every utterance of our Rabbis, of blessed memory, from the Talmud, which were included in the book *Ein Yisrael* [Ein Yaaqov] and arranged topically in a splendid order, in the same manner as the book *Zikhron Torat Moshe.* However, it is briefer, easier [to understand], and better than that [work] for those who peruse it, and especially for the preachers, as experience will demonstrate." Similar words of praise for *Zikhron Torat Moshe* appear in R. Judah

Aryeh's preface, which is addressed to "the gentle reader." According to *Zikhron Torat Moshe,* a subject index was also included in a book entitled *Einei Avraham* (a book whose primary goal was to index all the verses homiletically interpreted in the *Midreshei Rabba*) written by R. Abraham de Fonseca (Amsterdam 5387–5388 [1627–1628]). For more on *Zikhron Torat Moshe* and its influence, see Meir Benayahu, "Rabbi Shmuel Yaffe Ashkenazi," *Tarbiz* 42 (5733 [1977]), 443–44.

11. Even though it is correct to state that we lack an inventory of the anthological works, a slight correction is in order. Those interested in this neglected genre will benefit from perusing S. Y. Agnon's preface to *Atem re'item* (Jerusalem: Schocken, 5718–5719) [1959]), which he entitled "*Ma'aseh ha-Sefer*" (the act of compiling the book). The preface and the act of compiling the book itself—that is to say, the method employed to determine what material was to be included in this topically arranged anthology (and in Agnon's other one, *Yamim Nora'im*)—still need to be studied. Investigating this matter, in and of itself, has intrinsic worth—or, to phrase it another way, determining the link between Agnon's authorship of these collections and Agnon's penning of his own original creative works would be a scholarly coup. To the best of my knowledge, this facet of Agnon's creativity has been completely neglected by the scholarly establishment. I have no doubt that such a course of inquiry would also retroactively shed light on the work of the new yalqutim, our primary concern here.

12. A review of seventeenth- and eighteenth-century compositions in manuscript form will almost certainly reveal the names of additional books generically similar to *Yalqut Ḥadash* and *Yalqut Reuveni.* In general, the works produced by the scholars in these centuries remain largely in the dark, obscure and unknown (this includes works that were printed, but not those dealing with Hasidism). Therefore, compositions like *Petaḥ ha-Ohel* (part 1) by R. Abraham ben Judah Leib of Premishla (Zultsbakh, 5451 [1691]) escaped the attention of those delving into this matter (including Agnon, *Atem Re'item*), even though this particular composition was (as the title page clearly states) "a truly wondrous yalqut [containing] all that is new, which has not been under the sun." This aggadic yalqut is arranged alphabetically and cites material from dozens of compositions related to its fields of interest (including from the aforementioned *Yalqut Reuveni* and the *Shihkḥat Leqet*). Another (unknown) composition belonging to this genre is *Leqet Yosef* by R. Joseph ben R. Mordecai Ginzberg (first printed in Hamburg 5448 [1688]; also printed under the title *Ḥiddushei ha-Torah*

[with supplements, first printed in Amsterdam, 5463 [1703]). This book was an alphabetically arranged topical index (it cites the aforementioned *Yalqut Ḥadash* several times). Another (unknown) alphabetically arranged topical index is a book entitled *Pi Shenayim* (Zultsbakh, 5462 [1702]) (it was based on *Yalqut Shimoni* and *Midrash Rabba*). Two individuals collaborated in producing this volume (as the title suggests): R. Simeon Aqiba ben R. Joseph and R. Isaac Zeligman ben R. Meir. The two quote passages from *Yalqut Shimoni* and the *Midreshei Rabba,* commenting upon them based on what they have discovered in many other works (including both oral and written insights proffered by contemporary Torah scholars). At the end of the book, a paragraph index (*mafteḥot simanim*) was printed. The final work that I mention in this context is *Leqet Shmuel* by Samuel Feibush ben Joseph Yozfe Hakohen (Venice, 5454–5455 [1694–1695]) (he also made use of the *Yalqut Ḥadash* and *Yalqut Reuveni*).

13. Y. Dan, "When was Sefer ha-Yashar composed?" [in Hebrew], in *Sefer Dov Sadan,* ed. S. Verses, N. Rotenstreich, and H. Shmeruk (Jerusalem: Magnes Press, 5737 [1977]), 105–10; Y. Dan, *Sefer ha-Yashar* (Jerusalem: Bialik Institute, 5746 [1986]), introduction, 12–17.
14. Saul Lieberman, *Sheki'in* (Jerusalem: Wahrmann Books, 5730 [1970]), 35.
15. See my book *Lehavin divre ḥakhamim* (Jerusalem: Bialik Institute, 5761 [2001]), 57, and see too Lieberman, *Sheki'in*, 30n.29.
16. A lecture delivered at Harvard University in 1938. See L. Ginzberg, *'Al halakhah ve-aggadah* (Tel Aviv, 5720 [1960]), 251–62.
17. In order to complete the picture, attention should also be paid to the innovations introduced into the new, though "traditional," anthologies, such as R. Barukh Halevi Epstein's *Torah Temimah* (first printed in Vilnius, 5662 [1902]).

5

Ancient Jewish Folk Literature

The Legends of the Jews and Comparative Folklore Studies at the Beginning of the Twentieth Century

Galit Hasan-Rokem

Very few are the books that openly profess to put forth a great vision—whether or not that vision is ultimately realized in the work. *The Cheese and the Worms,*[1] by the historian Carlo Ginzburg, is one such work; at its core lies an ethnographic image of an a-Christian subculture in the heart of Christian Europe, a subculture of fertility cults taking place, literally, in the dark. Another example is Michel de Certeau's work about the sixteenth and seventeenth centuries, *The Mystic Fable,*[2] in which a multi-dimensional mental image is etched: of a heavy cloud of loss and mourning hovering over Europe and penetrating every creative act therein. The colossal vision of Claude Lévi-Strauss, spanning his four-volume *Mythologiques,* encompasses, for its part, the entire Western Hemisphere and the complex narrative imagination of its original inhabitants.[3] *The Legends of the Jews* by Louis Ginzberg embodies a vision of this same type. In what follows, I attempt to describe this vision, the sources of its inspiration, and the way it is realized in the work itself. Ginzberg's vision strives to reconstruct, in text, the creative imagination of ancient Jews, the Jews of circa the first millennium C.E.

For scholars of Rabbinic literature who focus on the folkloristic, ethnographic, and, in particular, folk-literary aspect of this cultural phenomenon, Ginzberg's *Legends of the Jews* is a significant genealogical landmark.[4] This perspective allows one to regard Rabbinic literature as an all-encompassing cultural corpus: a literature in whose polyphonic texture one can identify not only well-established voices from the rabbinical schools and academies, but also voices from other social institutions within the Aramaic- and Hebrew-speaking Jewish society of the time, such as the home and the public sphere.

Ginzberg himself states, in the introduction to the first edition of this work (1909–1938), that Rabbinic literature did not emerge from the isolated erudite sphere of rabbinical schools, but through contact with all the spheres of Jewish cultural creativity of the period, including the domestic.[5] This statement anticipated and informed late twentieth-century scholarship that has highlighted the discursive and dynamic aspect of the production of Rabbinic literature, a process that took place between the home, the marketplace, the synagogue, and the rabbinic house of study.[6] The genealogical "dynasty" that originates partly in *The Legends of the Jews* continued in a direct though somewhat concealed fashion throughout the many studies of the late Avigdor (Victor) Aptowitzer, and from him to my own teacher, Dov Noy.[7] This scholarly family tree also stretches backward, to the tangled roots of Ginzberg's own intellectual context as he came to write *The Legends of the Jews.*

What follows is an examination of the role of nineteenth- and early twentieth-century folklore research as a theoretical and methodological groundwork for the approach adopted by Ginzberg in his work. Out of this entire scholarly discipline, two concepts or approaches stand out as keystones for Ginzberg's method: both are identified with folkloristic schools from his time, and both mark him, whether by his own admission or in scholarly hindsight, as a quintessential folklore scholar. The first concept is that of genre, with respect to which Ginzberg distinguishes between legend (*Sage*), folktale or fairytale (*Märchen*), and myth. This threefold distinction, which came to dominate folklore studies to such an extent as to be taken for granted and seen as ostensibly "natural,"[8] is unmistakably identified with the folkloristic tradition established by the Brothers Grimm at the beginning of the nineteenth century.[9] Their system of genres remained unchallenged in scholarship until the mid-twentieth century, and persists, to a certain extent, to this day. Another influential figure for Ginzberg, although they were practically contemporaries, was Hermann Gunkel, who applied the Brothers Grimm's system of genres to his studies of biblical literature.[10]

The other folkloristic-methodological approach applied consistently and with great sophistication and erudition by Ginzberg is the comparative method. Similar to many folklorists of his time, Ginzberg employed cross-cultural comparison of a geographical-historical nature. This method employs primarily philological and literary tools, among them the concepts of the motif and the type, which became standard in folklore studies from the second half of the nineteenth century under the influence of the Finnish geographical-historical school, which also prevailed until the mid-twentieth century.[11] Many other concepts have been added on top of these two fundamental concepts in folklore studies since the mid-twentieth century, in particular those having to do with socio-psychological factors, ecologies, and paradigms.[12] The older concepts of genre and comparative study still constitute important research tools, however, making Ginzberg's work relevant today even if there are points—in particular regarding some of his historical claims—that bear criticism in light of our knowledge and the current state of scholarship.

The goal of this essay is not to offer a comprehensive description of *The Legends of the Jews,* nor is it to provide an inventory of the things it included or omitted. This has been dealt with by many scholars.[13] I refrain here from making the obvious, albeit fascinating comparisons with contemporaneous works with similar goals to that of *The Legends of the Jews,* such as *The Legends of Israel* by Israel Benjamin Levner,[14] *Sefer ha-aggadah* (The Book of Legends) by Ḥaim Naḥman Bialik and Yehoshua Ḥana Ravnitzki,[15] and *Mimekor Yisrael* by Micha Joseph Berdyczewski (Bin-Gorion).[16] Notwithstanding the ostensible similarity between those anthologies and the work under discussion here, the difference in theoretical background between Ginzberg and his contemporaries is evident. Nonetheless, from all those mentioned above, it should be noted that the one closest in spirit to Ginzberg was Berdyczewski. Whereas Bialik and Ravnitzki emphasized the classical nature of the aggadic literature and thus anthologized exclusively classical Rabbinic works,[17] Berdyczewski, like Ginzberg, conceived of the aggadic literature first and foremost as "the Hebrew folktale," and therefore also included in his anthology later texts and works that were considered marginal.[18] Nevertheless, Ginzberg's scholarly concept of folklore diverged from the intellectual, rather Nietzschean, worldview of Berdyczewski. And, needless to say, it differed completely from Bialik's general, romanticized, and anti-intellectual "folklore."

Regarding Ginzberg's observation that the aggadah did not emerge solely from within the rabbinical academies—an observation whose inspiration I acknowledge in my own research[19]—a similar thing can be said of modern scholarship, which does not take shape exclusively through the influence of books and purely academic contexts.[20] I would like to suggest to try and understand the unique context in which Ginzberg's oeuvre came about, through two aspects: the scholarly repertoire at his disposal at the time of undertaking his oeuvre, and Louis Ginzberg the man, including the cultural context that inspired him in his scholarship and writing. I hope that this discussion will contribute to the understanding of the work in the relevant context—in particular the European academic-cultural context of the time—and to a more correct appreciation of its cultural status.

When Ginzberg arrived in the United States, he came with a German academic degree in ancient Near Eastern studies and philology, on top of a childhood education in the best rabbinical academies in his native Lithuania, where he was considered a prodigy.[21] He wrote his doctoral dissertation on the manifestation of aggadic literature in the writings of the Church Fathers; this was early evidence of the importance he would place throughout his academic career on the intercultural connections that exist in Rabbinic literature.[22]

In his preface to the notes volumes of the first edition of *The Legends of the Jews,* Ginzberg sets forth the double nature of his work: on the first level, the text volumes were aimed at a wide readership—Jews and non-Jews alike—to give them a glimpse into the imaginative and creative cosmos of ancient Jewry.[23] On another, apparently no less important level, Ginzberg's work is specifically addressed to scholars of antiquity, in particular scholars of folklore, through the erudite notes that appeared in separate volumes. In these notes, Ginzberg shares with his fellow scholars his vast philological and comparative knowledge. One cannot deny the tension, and even the contradiction, between these two goals.[24] The body of the text of *The Legends of the Jews* unravels the biblical drama as a single epic whose narrative branches continue to be organically interwoven and throughout the variety of genres and forms of the Rabbinic literature, just as the ancient stories of Greek heroes and gods continued to be woven in the narrative, poetic, philosophical, and especially dramatic arts of ancient Athens in its halcyon days. Ginzberg's epic is a tour de force of compilation, interweaving a vast number of independent narrative units of varying geographical and chronological origins from the vast corpus of Jewish literature: from the Hellenistic era in Palestine, Asia Minor, North Africa, and Mesopotamia; through the Rabbinic period in those same regions and, most distinctively, in Babylonia of the Roman, Byzantine, and Persian eras; and up to what is commonly known as medieval literature, with a geographical/cultural distribution that includes the Muslim world and Christian Europe. The work connects the so-called original stories and traditions to the overarching epic narrative. That being said, one must recall that in most of the places from which Ginzberg gleaned these tales for his work, the stories were already compiled with meta-narrative organizational principles in mind: for example, the order of the Torah verses in the midrashic literature of the exegetical or hermeneutical type (e.g., *Bereshit Rabbah* or *Eikhah Rabbah*) or of the narrative type (e.g., *Midrash Tanḥuma*); or some other structural principle based on the reading cycles of the Torah portions in the synagogue, as in the so-called homiletic midrashim (e.g., *Vayikra Rabbah* and *Pesiqta de-Rab Kahana*); or, according to halakhic principles, primarily the two Talmuds. Two exceptions to this rule are, on the one hand, ancient writings that themselves displayed a broad epic view of the history of the world and of the Jewish people, such as *Jewish Antiquities* by Josephus Flavius (Yosef ben Matityahu)[25] and *Biblical Antiquities,* which is attributed to Philo;[26] and on the other hand, and in a different way, the early Bible translations into Greek, Syriac, Aramaic, and later to Arabic. Further exceptions to the rule are the running Bible commentaries, and possibly also some groupings of the stories of the Babylonian Talmud, such as the tales of the destruction of the Temple at the end of tractate Gittin,[27] or the "Dream Tractate" at the end of tractate Berakhot.[28]

Some seventy years earlier, Elias Lönnrot, pioneer of the geographical-historical school in folklore studies and composer of the

Finnish folk epic *Kalevala*, produced a similar feat of compilation, weaving together a variety of sources into one continuous unit.[29] And yet the fact that Ginzberg's tales were drawn from ancient *written* sources singles out his oeuvre from the enterprises of transcribing oral traditions that emerged in European folklore studies, such as with the Brothers Grimm and their colleagues and counterparts von Arnim, Musäus, Lönnrot, and others. While Ginzberg took his ancient Jewish folktales and legends from sources that had been written down for hundreds of years, those folklorists sought out living storytellers, some of them illiterate, to collect their ancient stories.[30] In doing so, they realized the ideas of the philosopher Johann Gottfried von Herder, who suggested that the ancient culture of peoples is found in "their voices," to echo the title of his famous book *Stimmen der Völker in Liedern* (*Volksliedern* 1798–99/1807) (Voices of the people in their songs)—and Herder literally meant their voices, their speech, and, in particular, their oral poetry and stories.[31] As was common among scholars of his time, Herder knew Hebrew, and he even cited Hebrew aggadic and midrashic texts in some of his essays on ancient Hebrew literature, notwithstanding the fact that his declared definition of Hebrew literature included primarily the Bible.[32]

And yet one can also claim that Ginzberg's work was only seemingly different from the undertakings of the German Romantic folklorists. If we take a deeper look into the history of the study of folklore revolving around the Brothers Grimm, we can identify two phases—the "positivist" phase and the "critical" phase. The positivist stage in the study of the oeuvre of the Brothers Grimm tells about how they wrote down the stories transmitted by storytellers, in particular those told by Mrs. Katharina Dorothea Viehmann, a Huguenot farmer from Baden-Württemberg (in today's geographical terms) in southwestern Germany, in the region bordering on France and Switzerland. The similarity between many of the children's and domestic tales of the Brothers Grimm to French folktales has been explained by the French origin of the Huguenot family, which arrived in Germany following their persecution in Catholic France. The historian Robert Darnton also pointed out lines of national comparison—between the cruelty of the German tales, the optimism found in the French tales, and erotic and lewd elements found in their Italian counterparts.[33] The critical study of the Brothers Grimm, on the other hand, engaged in a close textual reading in order to prove that they did not always follow the spirit of their predecessor, Herder, and that large parts of the ostensibly orally transmitted stories were in fact adapted from written French sources, such as the well-known tales of Charles Perrault and other, lesser known, sources.[34] But whichever way we interpret the circumstances of the collection and compilation of the Brothers Grimm's tales, they had a decisive influence on other undertakings of compilation of oral traditions in societies where no such transcription had taken place, in particular on the periphery of Europe in places such as Finland, Scandinavia, and Ireland.[35] It was in such countries that the leading paradigms of folklore studies crystallized at the end of the nineteenth and beginning of the twentieth centuries, more or less concurrently with Ginzberg's vast enterprise.

In truth, neither the Brothers Grimm nor Lönnrot are the relevant comparison when we discuss *The Legends of the Jews.* A more apt comparison would be two contemporaries of Ginzberg, Johannes Bolte and Georg (Jiří) Polívka, who together wrote and edited five volumes of comparative notes to two hundred tales of the Brothers Grimm, based on the notes of Jacob Grimm himself.[36]

If we go by the publication dates of the two works—Ginzberg's and Bolte and Polívka's—one can clearly not portray the latter as a source of influence or inspiration for Ginzberg. Rather, I would like to point to a similarity between the two works, which drew contemporaneously on the same intellectual sources and from the same cultural repertoire.[37] Quite a lot has been written about Ginzberg's study of the ancient Near East at European universities.[38] Bolte, for his part, studied in Berlin and in Leipzig and wrote his doctoral dissertation about Homer, while Polívka studied in Prague and Vienna, focusing on Slavic, mostly medieval, philology. Among their partners in the compilation of the notes, in particular to the fourth volume of the general conclusions devoted to specific cultures, was the Hungarian Bernát (Bernhard, Bernard) Heller, one of the great Jewish folklorists of the beginning of the twentieth century. Besides the contributions he made from his fields of expertise to the specific notes of the stories, Heller also contributed to the fourth volume of Bolte and Polívka's notes a comprehensive article on Hebrew and Arabic tales, which remains as pertinent as ever. According to his unique cultural worldview, inspired by his great teacher, the scholar of Islam and of Arabic Ignác Goldziher, Heller's article treated the Hebrew and Arabic tales as mutually interrelated corpuses.[39] Heller also wrote a comprehensive survey and critique on the occasion of the completion and publication of the English edition of *The Legends of the Jews.*[40]

Also prominent in the fifth volume of Bolte and Polívka's notes are scholars from the outskirts and smaller cultures of Europe, such as the Estonian Walter Anderson, the Norwegian Reidar Christiansen, the Czech Jiří Horák, the Hungarian Robert Grager, and once again the Hungarian Jew Bernát Heller. The list also includes Max Böhm, the scholar of Latvian folklore (not to be mistaken with the Nazi folklorist of the same name),[41] and Elizabeth Kutscher, whose marginality is manifested, perhaps, in her being the only woman to take part in the project. The notes thus situate the German folktales in a broad and multicultural comparative perspective that transcends the borders of Europe, expanding the geographical-historical research method from a classification within the corpus of one people's stories (as Antti Aarne did in his study of Finnish stories) to a system of categorization of tale types that includes the entire body of international knowledge of the time. The tale-type classification system was enlarged to comprehensive international dimensions by the American scholar Stith Thompson some years after the appearance of Ginzberg's work.[42]

The volumes of notes to the Brothers Grimm seem to express a trend of de-territorialization, both by casting comparative light on the ostensibly German tales,[43] and through the active participation of scholars from the periphery and the smaller states of Europe, in particular from outside the Germanophone sphere. This trend, which, according to Deleuze and Guattari, characterizes "minor" literatures,[44] has the potential of countering the construction of a hegemonic all-German identity undertaken by the Brothers Grimm, in particular in the composition of their normative, supra-regional German language dictionary,[45] and also in blurring some of the dialectical characteristics of the stories that were written down from the oral tradition. Deleuze and Guattari identify de-territorialization as the primary trait of minor literatures.[46] Such de-territorialization takes place by the very attachment of the comparative apparatus of Bolte and Polívka et al.'s notes to the German folktales of the Brothers Grimm. The concept of de-territorialization should be as applicable to Ginzberg's oeuvre, which unites sources from a space of over one thousand years and three continents, as it is to the analysis of Kafka's works.[47]

Despite the many differences between the texts Bolte and Polívka addressed in their comparative work and those in Ginzberg, their tale-by-tale notes are identical in structure and character to Ginzberg's notes to the texts of the elaborated biblical legends. Yet, whereas in the notes to the Grimm tales there is a clear-cut distinction between the foundation text and the texts used for comparison, in Ginzberg's case the matter is a bit more complicated, due to the inherent complexity of the foundation text, which was gleaned from many different periods and written texts and also because of the eclectic and even to some extent syncretistic nature of the text.[48] But Ginzberg, too, it seems, had a certain yardstick for distinguishing between intrinsic and extrinsic in the construction of the textual corpus, since only Jewish texts were included in the foundation text, while the notes include also texts from neighboring cultures: polytheistic, Christian, and Muslim. The fact that Ginzberg alone did the research that yielded the comparative notes to *The Legends of the Jews*—a much larger and more complex corpus than the Brothers Grimm tales, which required an entire team of linguistic and cultural experts to write its notes—is a sign of his extraordinary talent but also accounts for some of the weak points of the book.

If we take a step back for a moment from the methodological aspect of the notes to the phenomenological aspect of the body of the text of *The Legends of the Jews,* it is quite clear that Ginzberg is not suggesting that we see his epic opus as a reconstruction of any sort of empirical narrative that existed in such a linear form, whether in the Rabbinic period or in any other earlier era. In my humble opinion, Ginzberg attempts to present a reconstruction of the Jewish narrative universe approximately from the completion of the Bible to the end of the Geonic period. The textual outcome constitutes a sort of potential database of the fruits or even the potentials, of the Jewish imagination of that time. The most apt concept for such an approach would be that of the *imaginaire,* which was coined by Jacques Le Goff when describing the cultural imagination of medieval Europe.[49]

In quite a few places in his writings, Ginzberg suggests that the elaborated biblical legends—as we have termed the dominant genre in the work—is the remnant of an ancient Israelite folklore that did not find its way into the Scriptures but which was part of the creative biblical imagination and continued to be transmitted orally. Thus, he alludes to a central concept extant in cultural evolutionism, in particular in Britain at the end of the nineteenth century and associated with names such as Edward B. Tylor and Andrew Lang: survival. As tempting as it might be, there is of course no way to prove that the name of Abraham's mother, Amathlai bat Carnevo, and the name of Haman's mother, Amathlai bat Urvathi,[50] are in fact traditions from the days of the events themselves, or, in a more cautious formulation, even from the days of the canonization of the Hebrew Bible. Moreover, sometimes the opposite is clearly the case, namely, that many of the legends betray the patently latter-day dating of their composition.[51] Indeed, this is Ginzberg's primary historical claim, on which I would like to shed critical light and to dispute.

Ginzberg wrote *The Legends of the Jews* entirely in the language of his academic studies, German,[52] but it was published in English for the target audience in his adopted country, the United States, where he arrived in 1899. Henrietta Szold's English translation gained fame because of the translator's central role in the Zionist movement and because of the piquant and bittersweet detail about the personal and possibly romantic friendship of the two.[53] Let us consider the dedication, which quotes the last two lines of a verse by Friedrich Schiller, and which appears only in German, thus signaling an intimate connection that may have passed unnoticed by the general, English-speaking, public:

[Alles wiederholt sich nur im Leben
Ewig jung ist nur die Phantasie,]

Was sich nie und nirgends hat begeben,

Das allein veraltet nie![54]

Evidently, the dedication does not hint only at the imaginary nature of the texts in Ginzberg's book (in Szold's translation), but also at the special and unrealized state of their relationship. Much less known than Szold's is the contribution of Paul Radin (1883–1959), a prominent German-born American anthropologist, who, following Franz Boas, cultivated Herder's legacy in American cultural studies and anthropology. Radin took upon himself the completion of the English translation when Szold stopped the work after her relationship with Ginzberg had ended. As an anthropologist, Radin became known for his research on the almost extinct language and culture of the Native American Winnebago tribe, and for his research on the figure of the trickster, which was done in close association with psychoanalysts.[55]

I would also like to examine Ginzberg's work from another angle that few have dealt with. I am referring to the personal perspective of Ginzberg as storyteller, which can be seen most vitally in his own writings and in those written about him, in particular after his death: the biography by his son, the economics professor Eli Ginzberg, and the eulogies delivered by his daughter, Sophie Ginzberg-Gould, and his student Louis Finkelstein. Finkelstein mentions in detail the anecdotes that are sprinkled throughout Ginzberg's academic and public lectures, and emphasizes that the fact that these stories stemmed from his childhood in Lithuania would make it difficult for someone who does not have a similar background to understand the full meaning of the stories.[56] He also praised his teacher's wonderful ability to listen, attributing this to the heritage of his (i.e., Louis Ginzberg's) teachers in the Mussar movement in Slabodka, a suburb of Kovno in Lithuania. In her eulogy, his daughter quoted her father as one who wondered if his students had learned something from his lessons and who hoped that at least they would remember his stories.[57] In citations of Ginzberg himself, there are many self-references as a storyteller. In particular, he liked to tell how much he loved telling stories to children. Unlike many others of his generation and renown, Ginzberg did not keep a diary, nor did he write memoirs, and thus his memories are dispersed throughout other people's writings. Large parts of his son's book are written as a son's memories of an adored father, and many periods are brought to life through letters written by Ginzberg the elder, leaving carbon copies for himself. In these letters, sometimes addressed to young friends or to the friends of his son and daughter, and sometimes to small children with whom it seems the aging scholar had strong personal connections, he mentions in particular his strong impetus to tell them stories (!). One of these letters, dated January 1947, in which he talks about telling stories to his beloved nephew Michael Ginzberg, highlights the connection between the personal act of storytelling and his great scholarly oeuvre: he offhandedly mentions that at the time of writing he had reached—in the series of stories he was telling to his nephew—the story of Jonah and the whale (using the erroneous popular English translation of the Hebrew words for "big fish"), which, by what he writes, was the boy's favorite story.[58] Out of the description of the storytelling act as a sequential act in which the story of Jonah's turn had come, one can understand that it was Ginzberg's custom to tell the child biblical and other stories in some sequential order. The boy's choice of this story as his favorite is understandable in the light of its folkloristic character and the fact that the miraculous tale of the biblical prophet was listed explicitly both in the index of international tale types and in the index of motifs.[59] From the above it is clear that conversations played a major role in Ginzberg's life. The bits of memories told in the first person by Louis Ginzberg himself in his son's book were written down by his daughter-in-law, the wife of the son-author, whose warm relationship with his father is affectionately and with pride described by the younger Ginzberg.[60] These notes make it clear that Ginzberg was happy to tell about his life to whoever struck him as a listening ear. And yet he did not seem to regard writing his own memoirs as something to which he would devote his time at the expense of his research and teaching.

Louis Ginzberg personally attributed his own storytelling drive to the world of the rabbinical academies in his native Lithuania and to the countless stories he had heard there from his teachers. On top of this was Ginzberg's powerful self-myth.[61] The self-myth is more than just the attribution of stories to an earlier link in the generational chain; it is an important component in the consciousness and artistic mission of the storyteller. Louis Ginzberg's self-myth focused on a single figure: the Vilna Gaon, Rabbi Eliyahu.[62]

This myth originated from a genealogical connection to the Gaon on his mother's side. One important tenet in Louis's childhood education was the constant demand to meet the standard set by the Gaon: not to engage in too much child's play and to devote oneself entirely to Torah study. As an adult, Ginzberg presented a more complex aspect of this emulation, namely, the Gaon's well-known path of combining Torah study with the sciences and in particular his interest in mathematics, which, it turns out, was also a scientific subject of interest for the young Ginzberg during a certain period.[63] The Vilna Gaon's particular appreciation for mathematics was also a part of Ginzberg's self-myth as his descendant. He himself recalled this, according to his son's book, in his descriptions of conversations on several occasions he had with Albert Einstein on matters regarding the Hebrew University of Jerusalem, as both were staunch supporters of its establishment from their seats in the United States.[64] To conclude this short discussion of the role of the Vilna Gaon as the keystone of Ginzberg's self-myth and its connection to Ginzberg's characterization of himself as a quintessential storyteller—a characterization supported in the testimonies of others—I would like to mention the memorial talk Ginzberg gave at the Jewish Theological Seminary of America in 1920, upon the bicentennial of the birth of the Gaon. He opened with some legends he had heard in his youth about the Gaon's great-grandfather, Rabbi Moshe Ben David Ashkenazi, who was appointed rabbi of the city of Vilna in 1670. Ginzberg, who aspired, and even succeeded to a large degree, in evoking the world of the narrative imagination of ancient Jews, was himself a link in the chain of Jewish storytellers.

I think it is appropriate to conclude with a discussion of Ginzberg's essay "Jewish Folklore: East and West."[65] In this essay, which Ginzberg delivered in 1936 in an honorary lecture for Harvard University's tricentennial celebration, an occasion where he served as the only representative of Jewish studies,[66] he presents himself most unambiguously as a folklore scholar. One can see this lecture as a summary of his great enterprise, both by its timing—upon the completion of *The Legends of the Jews*—and by its chosen subject matter. In the very first note to the article, Ginzberg lists the narrative genres that in his opinion can be found in the Bible: "stories, tales, legends, popular speech, proverbs, fairytales, riddles, and myths."[67] He devotes much of the introduction to his claim that there is no contradiction between seeing aggadah as the product of the Rabbinic academy and simultaneously as a popular folkloristic creation: "For most frequently scholastic ingenuity and popular fancy both contributed toward the production of these legends."[68] The main part of the essay deals with the question of the uniqueness of Jewish folklore and its reciprocal relations with the folklore of other cultures. The discussion seems to go astray when Ginzberg tries to reconcile what he calls, following Philo of Alexandria, the Bible's "unspoken aversion to mythology"[69] with the Canaanite influences on the text. Moreover, his principal claim, that only with the rise of Islam did the legends of the Jews begin to be influenced by the legends of other peoples, seems to contradict his accurate reference to the power of Greek influence on the Rabbinic lore, which he indeed does not deny. Neither does the claim regarding the Rabbis' aversion to myth correspond with the long list of mythical scenes from the textual corpus of the sages. And yet Ginzberg sounds most up to date when he announces that "Iranian influence upon Jewish folklore cannot be denied."[70] Returning to the subject of his dissertation, which preceded *The Legends of the Jews* by many years, he emphasizes: "Despite the theological differences between the Fathers of the Church and the doctors of the Synagogue, personal relations continued intermittently, providing thereby a medium for the diffusion of rabbinic legends."[71] Here, too, he heralds scholarly directions that have blossomed in recent decades.[72] As for the mutual influence of Jewish and Muslim legends, he at times disagrees with the view of the aforementioned Bernát Heller, who considered these two corpuses to be closely connected.[73]

By his own testimony and that of many of his students and colleagues, Louis Ginzberg's work was rooted in the rabbinical academy—yeshiva—going back to Lithuania and the leaders of the Mussar movement. His oeuvre is a complete and methodical reflection of the fact that this world was never only a world of study, and certainly not only a world of religious law, but, as David Weiss-Halivni writes in his memoirs from the Hungarian yeshiva, a world of study combined with a world of storytelling.[74] Ginzberg's representation of this storytelling world—alongside his scholarship and religious rulings, and also using the best of his contemporary scientific tools—is nothing other than a full reconstruction of the Rabbis'—and the rabbis'—creative universe—at the heart of which was an *imaginaire,* and a cultural context whose scholarly reproduction demands the active presence of the creative narrative imagination.

Notes

This article was written while I was a fellow at the Scholion Center for Interdisciplinary Research in Jewish Studies at the Mandel Institute of Jewish Studies at the Hebrew University in Jerusalem. It was inspired by the members of the research group "The Exegetical Imagination" and brought to fruition with the help of the staff of the Center. I thank Dan Ben-Amos, Paul Mendes-Flohr, and Eli Yassif for their insights. Special thanks to Sharon Katz and Lital Belinko-Sabah for their dedicated research assistance.

1. Carlo Ginzburg, *The Cheese and the Worms: The Cosmos of a Sixteenth-Century Miller,* trans. John C. and Anne Tedeschi (Baltimore: Johns Hopkins University Press, 1992). This fantasy is expanded even more in Ginzburg's subsequent books, in particular *The Night Battles: Witchcraft and Agrarian Cults in the Sixteenth and Seventeenth Centuries* (Baltimore: Johns Hopkins University Press, 1983); and *Ecstasies: Deciphering the Witches Sabbath* (London: Hutchinson Radius, 1991).
2. Michel de Certeau, *The Mystic Fable, I: The Sixteenth and the Seventeenth Centuries,* trans. M. B. Smith (Chicago: University of Chicago Press, 1992).
3. Claude Lévi-Strauss, *Mythologiques,* vol. 1, *The Raw and the Cooked*; vol. 2, *From Honey to Ashes*; vol. 3, *The Origin of Table Manners*; and vol. 4, *The Naked Man.* All were translated by Doreen and John Weightman, with volumes 1–2 published in 1983 and volumes 3–4 in 1990 by the University of Chicago Press.
4. Louis Ginzberg, *The Legends of the Jews*, 6 vols. (Philadelphia: Jewish Publication Society, 1909–1938), I: *From the Creation to Jacob* (1909); II: *From Joseph to the Exodus* (1910); III: *From the Exodus to the Death of Moses* (1911); IV: *From Joshua to Esther* (1913); V: *Notes to Volumes I and II* (1925); VI: *Notes to Volumes III and IV* (1928); *Index* (1938) (henceforth Ginzberg, *Legends* [English 1909–1938]).
5. Ginzberg, *Legends* (English 1909–1938), viii.

6. Dan Ben-Amos, "Talmudic Tall-Tales," in *Folklore Today: A Festschrift for Richard M. Dorson*, ed. Linda Dégh, Henry Glassie, and Felix Johannes Oinas (Bloomington: Research Center for Language and Semiotic Studies, Indiana University, 1976), 25–43; Ben-Amos, "Generic Distinctions in the Aggadah," in *Studies in Jewish Folklore*, ed. Frank Talmage (Cambridge, Mass.: Association for Jewish Studies, 1980), 275–301. Both works were based on his dissertation, "Narrative Forms in the Haggadah," which was completed at Indiana University in 1966–67. Eli Yassif, *The Hebrew Folktale: History, Genre, Meaning*, trans. Jacqueline S. Teitelbaum, with a foreword by Dan Ben-Amos (Bloomington: Indiana University Press, 1999); Galit Hasan-Rokem, *Web of Life: Folklore and Midrash in Rabbinic Literature*, trans. Batya Stein (Stanford, Calif.: Stanford University Press, 2000); and Galit Hasan-Rokem, *Tales of the Neighborhood: Jewish Narrative Dialogues in Late Antiquity* (Berkeley: University of California Press, 2003). Dina Stein focuses on the methodological aspect of folklore-influenced Midrash study but avoids expressing an opinion as to the institutional sources of Rabbinical literature. See Dina Stein, *Maxims, Magic, Myth: A Folkloristic Perspective of Pirkei de Rabbi Eliezer* [in Hebrew] (Jerusalem: Magnes Press, 2000); and Dina Stein, *Textual Mirrors: Reflexivity, Midrash, and the Rabbinic Self* (Philadelphia: University of Pennsylvania Press, 2012). Rebecca Schorsch, in her doctoral dissertation on Ginzberg's essay, focuses on Ginzberg's folkloristic worldview. See Rebecca Schorsch, "The Making of a Legend: Louis Ginzberg's *Legends of the Jews*" (Ph.D. diss., University of Chicago, 2003), and her Introduction to this volume.
7. For example, Victor Aptowitzer, *Kain und Abel in der Agada, den Apokryphen, der Hellenistischen, Christlichen und Muhammedanischen Literatur* (Vienna: R. Loewit, 1922); Dov Noy, "The Story of Abel's Burial: The Interrelationship of Myth and Custom," *Folklivsgransking* 21 (*Festschrift Olaf Bø*), 129–40. The significance of *The Legends of the Jews* for Noy's work is also evident in his "Motif-index of Talmudic-Midrashic literature" (Ph.D. diss., Indiana University, 1954), written under Prof. Stith Thompson. Noy compiled this index based on Ginzberg's *Legends* and *Mimekor Yisrael* by Micha Josef Berdyczewski (Bin-Gorion). Cf. Galit Hasan-Rokem, "Between Unity and Plurality: Dov Noy's Studies of Folklore in Talmudic-Midrashic Literature" [in Hebrew], *Jerusalem Studies in Jewish Folklore* 13–14 (1991/1992), 19–28.
8. William R. Bascom, "Four Functions of Folklore," in *The Study of Folklore*, ed. Alan Dundes (Englewood Cliffs, N.J.: Prentice Hall, 1965), 279–98; Lauri Honko, "Folkloristic Theories of Genre,"

Temenos 3 (1966), 48–66; and Dan Ben-Amos, "Analytical Categories and Ethnic Genres," in *Folklore Genres,* ed. Dan Ben-Amos (Austin: University of Texas Press, 1976), 215–42.

9. The scholarship on this issue is of course plentiful. The following are a few examples from different cultural contexts: Stith Thompson, *The Folktale* (New York: Holt, Rinehart and Winston, 1946), esp. 386–90; Max Lüthi, *Märchen* (Stuttgart: J. B. Metzler, 1974), esp. 62–82; Max Lüthi, *The European Folktale: Form and Nature,* trans. John D. Niles (Bloomington: Indiana University Press, 1986), esp. 112–15.
10. Hermann Gunkel, *The Folktale in the Old Testament,* trans. Michael D. Rutter, with an introduction by John W. Rogerson, ed. David M. Gunn (Sheffield: Almond Press, 1987); Hermann Gunkel, *Das Märchen im Alten Testament* (Tübingen: J. C. B. Mohr, 1917). And for Ginzberg's remarks on the genres, see Ginzberg, *Legends* (English 1909–1938), viii. Ginzberg dealt at greater length with the subject of the genre in the unpublished German version of his book, as can be seen in Johannes Sabel's essay in this volume, in which the author mentions an explicit citation of Gunkel in Ginzberg's writings.
11. Kaarle Krohn, *Folklore Methodology,* trans. R. L. Welch (Austin: University of Texas Press, 1971) (orig. *Die Folkloristische Arbeitsmethode* [Oslo: Instituttet for Sammenlignende Kulturforskning, 1926]); Giuseppe Cocchiara, *The History of Folklore in Europe,* trans. J. N. McDaniel (Philadelphia: Institute for the Study of Human Issues 1981); Dan Ben-Amos, "The Concept of Motif in Folklore," *Folklore Studies in the Twentieth Century,* ed. Venetia Newall (Woodbridge, Suffolk: Brewer, 1980), 17–36; Heda Jason, *Motif, Type and Genre: A Manual for Compilation of Indices and a Bibliography of Indices and Indexing* (Folklore Fellows Communications 273) (Helsinki: Suomalainen Tiedeakatemia / Finnish Academy of Science, 2000).
12. Galit Hasan-Rokem, "Aurora Borealis: Trans-formations of Classical Nordic Folklore Theories," in *Norden og Europa: Fagtradisjoner i nordisk etnologi og folkloristikk,* ed. Bjarne Rogan and Bente G. Alver (Oslo: Novus, 2000), 269–85.
13. James Kugel, "Foreword," in Louis Ginzberg, *The Legends of the Jews,* trans. Henrietta Szold (Baltimore: Johns Hopkins University Press, 1998), ix–xx (henceforth Ginzberg, *Legends* [English 1998]); David Stern, "Introduction to the 2003 edition," in Louis Ginzberg, *The Legends of the Jews,* trans. Henrietta Szold and Paul Radin (Philadelphia: Jewish Publication Society, 2003), 1:xv–xxiv (henceforth Ginzberg, *Legends* [English 2003]). A correction or deletion is necessary regarding the strange sentence that appears in Stern's introduction

(p. xx): "Where such a literature did not manifestly exist, it was invented, as in the case of the famous Icelandic epic *Laocoon.*" I have no idea what the author had in mind, since there is no such invented epic in Icelandic culture; on the other hand, Icelandic literature is indeed steeped in epic poetry that is by no measure "invented." Of course, Stern's conclusions stemming from this erroneous claim should be rejected, but that is not the matter at hand here. See also Golinkin's and Shinan's introductions to the second Hebrew edition of *The Legends of the Jews*: David Golinkin, "Introduction" and "Kavim li-dmuto shel Prof Levi Ginzberg," in Louis Ginzberg, *Legends of the Jews,* 2nd Hebrew ed., trans. from the first English ed. by Rabbi Mordechai Hacohen (Jerusalem: Schechter Institute of Jewish Studies, 2009), 7–12 (henceforth Ginzberg, *Legends* [Hebrew 2009]); and Avigdor Shinan, "Divrei mavo le-aggadot ha-yehudim," in Ginzberg, *Legends* (Hebrew 2009), 13–20.

14. Israel Benjamin Levner, *The Legends of Israel,* trans. Joel Snowman (London: J. Clarke, 1956), first published as *Kol aggadot Yisrael* (Warsaw: Tushia, 5658–5660 [1897/98–1899/1900]).
15. Ḥaim Naḥman Bialik and Yehoshua Ḥana Ravnitzki, *Sefer ha-aggadah: Mivḥar ha-aggadot she-ba-talmud uva-midrashim,* 1st ed., vols. 1–4 (Krakow: Ignacy Schiper, 5668 [1907/08]); vols. 5–6 (Odessa: H. N. Bialik and Sh. Borishkin, 5670–5671 [1910/11–1911/12]).
16. Micha Yosef Bin-Gorion (M. J. Berdyczewski), *Mimekor Yisrael: Selected Classical Jewish Folktales,* ed. Emanuel Bin-Gorion, trans. Israel M. Lask, prepared, with an introduction and headnotes, by Dan Ben-Amos (Bloomington: Indiana University Press, 1990) (orig. *Der Born Judas: Legenden, Märchen und Erzählungen* [Leipzig: Insel-Verlag, 1916–1921]).
17. Ḥaim N. Bialik and Yehoshua Ḥ. Ravnitzki, "Introduction," in *Sefer ha-aggadah: Mivḥar ha-aggadot she-ba-talmud uva-midrashim* (Tel Aviv: Dvir, 5727 [1966/67]), n.p.
18. See ibid., vii. Cf. Kugel, "Foreword," xiii. Rebecca Schorsch makes a systematic comparison between these anthologies, with the exception of Levner's work. See Schorsch, "The Making of a Legend," 92–102. Schorsch points to the fact that Ginzberg, the most religious and least secular of all these writers, paradoxically also had the greatest scientific education of all of them, and adopted the most scientific research methods. See Schorsch, "The Making of a Legend," 99–100.
19. Hasan-Rokem, *Web of Life,* 13 and esp. 15; Hasan-Rokem, *Tales of the Neighborhood,* 6.
20. See Mara Beller's insightful observations in relation to the history of science, inspired by Mikhail Bakhtin: Mara Beller, *Quantum*

Dialogue: The Making of a Revolution (Chicago: University of Chicago Press, 1999), 308–17.

21. Eli Ginzberg, *Keeper of the Law: Louis Ginzberg* (Philadelphia: Jewish Publication Society, 1966), 47–58.
22. Louis Ginzberg, "Die Haggada bei den Kirchenvätern. Die Haggada in den Pseudo-Hieronymischen-'Quaestiones'" (Ph.D. dissertation, 1899); Ginzberg, "Die Haggada bei den Kirchenvätern und in der Apokryphischen Litteratur," *MGWJ* (1898, 1899); as well as Ginzberg, *Die Haggada bei den Kirchenvätern und in der apokryphischen Litteratur* (Berlin: S. Calvary, 1900). For a discussion of the subjects of this work, see Hillel Newman's chapter in this volume.
23. See also Ginzberg, *Legends* (Hebrew 2009), 1:x (Introduction); Ginzberg, *Legends* (English 2003), 1:xxv–xxviii. Schorsch discusses this issue at length in several chapters of her "Making of a Legend."
24. Kugel, in his foreword to the 1998 English edition, which was written for a general audience, places more emphasis on the complementary nature of the two bodies of text. See Kugel, "Foreword," xviii. Schorsch expands on the matter of the tension. See Schorsch, "The Making of a Legend," 200ff.
25. English version: Josephus, *Jewish Antiquities* 5–13, trans. Henry St. John Thackeray, Ralph Marcus, Allen Wikgren, and Louis H. Feldman (Cambridge, Mass.: Harvard University Press; London: William Heinemann, 1930–1965); Hebrew version: Flavius Josephus, *Kadmoniyot ha-yehudim* 1–3, trans. Avraham Shalit (Jerusalem: Masada, 1944–1963).
26. Hebrew version: Philon, *Kadmoniyot ha-miqra, ha-sefarim ha-hitzoniyim,* vol. 7, translation and commentary by Elia S. Artom (Tel Aviv: Yavneh, 1967); French version: *Les antiquités bibliques par Pseudo-Philon,* introduction and critical text by Daniel J. Harrington, trans. Jacques Cazeaux, rev. Charles Perrot and Pierre-Maurice Bogaert; Latin version: *Pseudo-Philo's Liber antiquitatum biblicarum, Antiquitates biblicae* (South Bend, Ind.: University of Notre Dame Press, 1949); English version: *A Commentary on Pseudo-Philo's Liber antiquitatum biblicarum*, with Latin text and English translation by Howard Jacobson (AGAJU 31) (Leiden: Brill, 1996). Cf. Eli Yassif, "Sefer ha-zikhronot: Ha-antologia ha-sifrutit ke-historia universalit," in *Sifrut ve-historia,* ed. Raya Cohen and Yosef Mali (Jerusalem: Zalman Shazar Center, 2009), 89–108.
27. Eli Yassif, "The Story Cycle," chap. 4, sec. K, of *The Hebrew Folktale,* 209–44; Yassif, "The Hebrew Narrative Anthology in the Middle Ages," *Prooftexts* 17 (1997), 153–76 (reprinted in David Stern, ed., *The Anthology in Jewish Literature* [Oxford: Oxford University Press, 2004], 196–210).

28. Ḥaim Weiss, *"All Dreams Follow the Mouth": A Reading in the Talmudic Dreams Tractate* [in Hebrew] (Or Yehuda: Dvir and Ben-Gurion University Press/Heksherim, 2011); Weiss, "'Twenty-four Dream Interpreters were in Jerusalem . . .': On Dream Interpreters and Interpretation in the Talmudic *Dream Tractate*" [in Hebrew], *Jewish Studies* 44 (5767 [2007]), 37–77; Weiss, "Science, Folklore and Rationality in Dream Discourse during Late Antiquity" [in Hebrew], *Jerusalem Studies in Jewish Folklore* 26 (2009), 159–68.
29. Väinö Kaukonen, *Lönnrot ja Kalevala* (Helsinki: Suomalaisen Kirjallisuuden Seura / Finnish Literature Society, 1979); William A. Wilson, *Folklore and Nationalism in Modern Finland* (Bloomington: Indiana University Press, 1976). On the theoretical aspects of this question, see also Lauri Honko, ed., *Textualization of Oral Epics* (Trends in Linguistics: Studies and Monographs 128) (Berlin: W. de Gruyter, 2000). For reasons that I will not delve into in this essay, the *Kalevala* attained the status of a national epic—a status of which Ginzberg could only dream for his *Legends.* In the meantime, no evidence has been found, either in Ginzberg's own writings or in what has been written about him, of his familiarity with the Finnish epic, and certainly not of any influence from it. Neither could have Buber's article in praise of the *Kalevala*—which deals at length with the feat of compilation of texts from different epic streams and with the way in which it captures the "spirit of the nation"—served as a major inspiration for Ginzberg, due to its relatively late date, although it could have influenced his methods. See Martin Buber, "Kalewala, das Finnische Epos," *Das Literarische Echo* 14/23 (September 1, 1912), cols. 1611–22. This article would develop into Buber's introduction to Anton Schiffner's then new German translation of the epic, published in 1914. For a discussion of Buber's statements on the *Kalevala*, see also Paul Mendes-Flohr, "Editor's Introduction," in *Ecstatic Confessions: The Heart of Mysticism,* collected and introduced by Martin Buber, ed. Paul Mendes-Flohr, trans. E. Cameron (Syracuse: Syracuse University Press, 1996), xii.
30. See the bibliographical listings in notes 9 and 11, above.
31. First printed in 1778/79. I have recourse to the edition printed in Leipzig in 1978 for the 200th anniversary of the first publication: Johann Gottfried Herder, *Stimmen der Völker in Liedern. Eine Auswahl. Mit 35 Radierungen von J. Hegenbarth* [Voices of the people in their songs. A selection. With 35 illustrations by J. Hegenbarth], ed. H. Marquardt (Berlin: Verlag der Nation, 1978).
32. Johann G. Herder, "Vom Geist der Hebräischen Poesie," 2er Theil (Dessau, 1783) (reprinted in *Herders Sämmtliche Werke,* ed. Ber-

nhard L. Suphan [Berlin: Weidmann, 1880], 12:124–25); Herder, "Das Gesetz Gottes und Moses–Eine jüdische Dichtung"; Herder, "Parabeln; Jüdische Dichtungen und Fabeln," in *Herders Werke,* ed. Prof. Dr. Theodor Matthias (Leipzig and Vienna: Bibliographisches Institut, 1903), 67–122.

33. Robert Darnton, "Peasants Tell Tales: The Meaning of Mother Goose," chapter 1 of *The Great Cat Massacre and Other Episodes in French Cultural History* (New York: Vintage Books, 1985), 9–72.
34. An extreme example of such a critique can be found in John Martin Ellis, *One Fairy Story Too Many: The Brothers Grimm and Their Tales* (Chicago: University of Chicago Press, 1983).
35. Diarmuid Ó Giolláin, *Locating Irish Folklore: Tradition, Modernity, Identity* (Cork: Cork University Press, 2000), esp. 63–113; Pertti J. Anttonen, *Tradition through Modernity: Postmodernism and the Nation State in Folklore Scholarship* (Studia Fennica Folkloristica 15) (Helsinki: Suomalaisen Kirjallisuuden Seura / Finnish Literature Society, 2005).
36. Johannes Bolte and Georg (Jiří) Polívka, *Anmerkungen zu den Kinder—und Hausmärchen der Brüder Grimm* (Leipzig: Dieterich'sche Verlagsbuchandlung, 1913–1932); or see the 2nd unrevised ed. (Hildesheim: Georg Olms Verlag, 1963).
37. Dani Schrire has suggested to me another possibly significant cultural parallel: *The International Folk-Lore Congress of the World's Columbian Exposition,* Chicago, July 1893 (Chicago, 1898), vol. 3; Helen Wheeler Basset and Frederick Starr, eds., *Archives of the International Folk-Lore Association,* vol. 1 (Chicago, 1898)—see esp. Friedrich Salomon Krauss, "Why National Epics Are Composed: Some Reflections Illustrated by Song of Guslars of Bosnia and Herzegovina," 447–65. http://www.archive.org/stream/cu31924029886276#page/n13/mode/2up.
38. See, e.g., Schorsch, "The Making of a Legend," 69–74 and the references there.
39. Cf. Ignác Goldziher, *Mythology among the Hebrews and Its Historical Development,* trans. Russell Martineau (London: Longmans, 1877; reprint, Whitefish, Mont.: Kessinger Publishing Rare Reprints, 2006).
40. Bernhard Heller, "Ginzberg's *Legends of the Jews,*" *Jewish Quarterly Review,* n.s. 24/1 (1933), 51–66; 24/2 (1933); 165–90; 24/3 (1934), 281–307; 24/4 (1934), 393–418; 25/1 (1934), 29–52. The separate chapters of the article were devoted to (1) the ancient world; (2) Hellenistic Judaism; (3) the Church; (4) Islam, Arab culture, and general folklore; and (5) the reconstruction of "lost" midrashim according to later sources, additions, and corrections. In the

introduction to the first chapter of his critical survey, Heller bemoans the "diminution" (he is well aware of the irony of making such a critique for such a comprehensive oeuvre) of the elaborated biblical legends and the omission of the rich biographical and historical tales of the sages. It is somewhat paradoxical that he, the folklorist, asks to sharpen the distinction between the popular and the erudite (in chapter 5 of the article, p. 52).

41. I wish to thank my friends Prof. Regina Bendix and Prof. Ulrich Marzolph, both from Göttingen, for their help in clarifying this sensitive point.
42. *The Types of the Folktale: A Classification and Bibliography,* Antti Aarne's Verzeichnis der Märchentypen (Folklore Fellows Communications 3); second revision: Folklore Fellows Communications 184, orig. Folklore Fellows Communications 74. And now see Hans-Jörg Uther, *The Types of International Folktales: A Classification and Bibliography, Based on the System of Antti Aarne and Stith Thompson* (Folklore Fellows Communications 3) (Helsinki: Suomalainen Tiedeakatemia, Academia Scientiarum Fennica, 2004), 284–87.
43. As was mentioned in the works cited above, in particular in notes 33 and 34, the German-ness of the tales was questioned almost from the start due to the marginal identity of the transmitters (who were of French-Huguenot origin) and to research claims about the influence of written French anthologies.
44. Gilles Deleuze and Felix Guattari, "What Is a Minor Literature?," trans. R. Brinkley, *Mississippi Review* 11/3 (1983), 13–33. Originally published in French as *Kafka: Pour une littérature mineure* (Paris: Editions de Minuit, 1975), chap. 3. The group of terms "territorialization," "de-territorialization," and "re-territorialization" was developed for the first time in their book *Anti-Oedipus: Capitalism and Schizophrenia,* trans. Robert Hurley, Mark Seem, and Helen R. Lane (New York: Viking Press, 1977).
45. Jakob and Wilhelm Grimm, *Das Deutsche Wörterbuch* (Leipzig: Verlag von S. Hirzel, 1854–1961).
46. Followed by two additional central traits—the link between the individual and the political; and the link between those and the collective organization of speech, both of which certainly also fit the definition of folk literature.
47. It is worthwhile to mention that Deleuze and Guattari's definition of "minor literature" came about in the framework of their discussion of Kafka's Jewish Germanophone writings produced in Prague.
48. Other scholars, such as James Kugel ("Foreword") in fact emphasize the harmonistic trend in Ginzberg's redaction of the text.

This is evident also from Boyarin's characterization of Ginzberg in his paper in this volume, which includes the national-romantic aspect.

49. Jacques Le Goff, *The Medieval Imagination,* trans. Arthur Goldhammer (Chicago: University of Chicago Press, 1988); originally published in French as *L'imaginaire medieval* (Paris, 1985).
50. See the criticism about the connection of this name to the name of the adoptive mother of the Greek god Zeus, Amaltiya, in Heller, "Ginzberg's *Legends,*" chap. 1, p. 63.
51. See, e.g., Joseph Heinemann, "Anti-Samaritan Polemics in the Aggadah," *World Congress of Jewish Studies* 6/3 (1977), 57–69.
52. See Johannes Sabel's essay in this volume.
53. An entire chapter of Eli Ginzberg's book (chapter 6, "An Exceptional Friendship") is devoted to the subject. See Ginzberg, *Keeper of the Law,* 105–29. And see the comments of Ginzberg's daughter, who downplays both the relationship and Szold's contribution to the translation of the book, according to her father's testimony: Sophie Ginzberg-Gould, "Letters from My Father," in a special section, "Louis Ginzberg: A Centenary Tribute," *Conservative Judaism* 28/2 (1974), 18–24 ; Baila Round Shargel, *Lost Love: The Untold Story of Henrietta Szold: Journal and Letters* (Philadelphia: Jewish Publication Society, 1997), expounds on Szold's retrospective view of the events.
54. Friedrich Schiller, "An die Freunde" (1802) [not to be confused with the much more famous „An die Freude," the *Ode to Joy*], in *Schillers Werke-Nationalausgabe, Vol. 2, Part I: Gedichte in der Reihenfolge ihres Erscheinens. 1799–1805,* ed. Norbert Oellers (Weimar: Böhlau, 1983), 225–26. The poem praises the glorious past in contrast with the diminished present, although it notes: "We, we live!" (in the first verse), while Rome in all its glory is destroyed and buried under dust (fourth verse). For our purposes, one may note that this poem was published in 1803 in the publication *Taschenbuch für Damen.* Schiller's commentator, Heinrich Viehoff von Trier, notes that this poem was one of the favorite declamation poems in German schools. The original context of the poem is the intellectual and artistic circle that gathered around Johann Wolfgang von Goethe in Weimar, of which Schiller was one of the prominent figures. Heinrich Viehoff, *Schillers Gedichte erläutert* (Stuttgart: Franckh, 1872), 2:108–13. A contemporary Schiller scholar categorizes the poem among the "trifles" (*Lyrischen Kleinigkeiten*), of which Schiller wrote quite a few in this social context. See Georg Kurscheidt and Norbert Oellers, eds., *Schillers Werke-Nationalausgabe, Vol. 2, Part II B* (notes to vol. 2, part I)

(Weimar: Verlag Hermann Böhlaus Nachfolge, 1993), 161. It seems that Schiller himself came to appreciate the writing of the poems in due course: "Es ist eine erstaunliche Klippe für die Poesie, Gesellschaftslieder zu verfertigen—die Prosa des wirklichen Lebens hängt sich bleischwer an die Phantasie" (in Ernst Lautenbach, *Lexikon Schiller-Zitate: Aus Werk und Leben* [München: Ludicium, 2003], 557). (An anonymous online translation into English: "All in life repeats itself forever, / Young for ay is phantasy alone; / What has happened nowhere,—happened never,—That has never older grown." Project Gutenberg's Poems of The Third Period, by Frederich [*sic*] Schiller (http://www.gutenberg.org/files/6796/6796-h/6796-h.htm, accessed March 8, 2011).

55. Paul Radin, "The Winnebago Tribe," in *The Thirty-seventh Annual Report of the United States Bureau of American Ethnology* (Washington, D.C.: Smithsonian Institution, 1923), 35–550; Paul Radin, *The Trickster: A Study in Native American Mythology,* with commentaries by Karl Kerényi and Carl Gustaf Jung (New York: Philosophical Library, 1956); orig. *Der göttliche Schelm* (Zürich: Rhein-Verlag, 1954). See also Thomas Hauschild, "Christians, Jews, and the Other in German Anthropology," *American Anthropologist* 99/4 (1997), 746–53.
56. Louis Finkelstein, "Prof. Louis Ginzberg: An Appreciation," *Conservative Judaism* 28/2 (1974), 13–17, in a special section, "Louis Ginzberg: A Centenary Tribute."
57. Ginzberg-Gould, "Letters from My Father."
58. Ginzberg, *Keeper of the Law,* 280.
59. Antti Aarne and Stith Thompson, *The Types of the Folktales—A Classification and Bibliography* (Folklore Fellows Communications, 184) (Helsinki: Suomalainen Tiedeakatemia / Finnish Academy of Science, 1973), 511, type no. 1889G. Cf. Stith Thompson, *Motif-Index of Folk-Literature: A Classification of Narrative Elements in Folktales, Ballads, Myths, Fables, Mediaeval Romances, Exempla, Fabliaux, Jest-books, and Local Legends* (Bloomington: Indiana University Press, 1966), motif F911.6, 3:234; motif F913, 3:234–35; motif X1723.1, 5:535.
60. Ginzberg, *Keeper of the Law,* 264–65, 268.
61. In the past, in a discussion devoted to the Moroccan Jewish storyteller Abraham Lugasi—born in Asni and living in Kiryat Gat, Israel—I described what I called his "storyteller myth," in which he hyperbolically attributed "all of his stories" to his blind mentor (like the "Homerian" motif that praises blind storytellers in particular), Rabbi Joshua, in explicit contrast with the specific genealogies of specific stories, which he attributes to his grandmother or to other relatives. Galit Hasan-Rokem, "Cognition in

the Folk-Tale: Aesthetic Judgment and Symbolic Structures," *Scripta Hierosolymitana* 27 (1978), 192–204.

62. Ginzberg, *Keeper of the Law,* 17–18.
63. Louis Ginzberg, *The Gaon, R. Elijah, Wilna. Address Delivered in Commemoration of the Two Hundredth Anniversary of His Birth* (New York: Jewish Theological Seminary of America, 1920), 7.
64. Ginzberg, *Keeper of the Law,* 210. Ginzberg also served as the first visiting professor at the nascent Institute of Jewish Studies at the Hebrew University in 1928–1929. He received the position after Hanoch Albeck turned it down due to prior commitments in Berlin. Ginzberg, *Keeper of the Law,* 202–3.
65. Louis Ginzberg, "Jewish Folklore: East and West," in *On Jewish Law and Lore* (Philadelphia: Atheneum, 1955), 61–73.
66. Compare with what Shargel writes about Ginzberg as being the one primarily responsible for the academic prestige of the Jewish Theological Seminary of America. Baila Round Shargel, "Louis Ginzberg as Apologist," *American Jewish History* 79 (1989/1990), 210–20. Cf. Schorsch, "The Making of a Legend."
67. This sentence is taken from 307n.1 of the Hebrew translation of the essay (published as "Aggadot am yehudiyot: Mizraḥ u-maarav," in *Al halakha ve-aggadah: Meḥkar u-massa* (Tel Aviv: Dvir, 5720 [1959/60]). I must caution that there are several mistakes in this Hebrew translation, which distort the meaning of some central points of the essay.
68. Ginzberg, "East and West," 61. Cf. Schorsch's astute formulation: "With the *Legends* Ginzberg identifies the folk with the rabbis not via the folklorization of the rabbis, but through the rabbinization of the folk." See Schorsch, "The Making of a Legend," 17.
69. Ginzberg, "East and West," 63.
70. Ibid., 65. The point has been made by several scholars regarding the overall cultural influence of ancient Iranian culture on rabbinical culture. See, especially, works by Yaakov Elman, and subsequently Reuven Kiperwaser, Jeffrey Herman, and others, as well as Shai Secunda, *The Iranian Talmud: Reading the Talmud in Its Sasanian Context* (Philadelphia: University of Pennsylvania Press, 2013).
71. Ginzberg, "East and West," 67.
72. While Ginzberg is not explicit about the unique texture of these reciprocal relations, different approaches have come to coexist under this broad umbrella: e.g., Israel Yaakov Yuval's emphasis on the polemical aspect, Daniel Boyarin's on the blurring of boundaries, and my own emphasis on the popular channels of oral transmission. Especially worthy of mention is Saul Lieberman's

comment: "And if someone says to you, the biblical tales that appear in the Christian sources of the Christian Middle Ages were not even mentioned in the Jewish sources, you will tell him he is not right. If the scent of Christianity does not waft from them, they may well have come from a Jewish source, even if they were not mentioned in our literature." See Saul Lieberman, "Zniḥin," *Tarbiz* 42 (1992–1993), 51. Lieberman goes to great lengths to distinguish himself from folklore scholars, whether in the belittling title of his short article or in his opening words: "Folk narrative experts and lovers of Jewish folklore scramble after every crumb in the sources in order to rescue them and to bring them to the knowledge of the reading public. Since we received Rabbi L. Ginzberg's treasure chest, *The Legends of the Jews,* we have seen unraveled and revealed before us all the reams of legend that were woven around the biblical stories, and nothing is left for us but to add links and adornments to his great structure" (Lieberman, "Zniḥin," 42); and most of all in his conclusion: "Lovers of legend and folklore will find much material in the sources mentioned above, and we leave this Torah to its owners" (Lieberman, "Zniḥin," 52). However, between sarcastic opening and cynical closing, Lieberman himself added crumb to crumb—to use his words—in his characteristic meticulousness and as an expert and experienced traditional folklore scholar. See Goldberg on Lieberman as Ginzberg's successor at the Jewish Theological Seminary of America: Harvey E. Goldberg, "Becoming History: Perspectives on the Seminary Faculty at Mid-Century," in *Tradition Renewed: A History of the Jewish Theological Seminary,* I: *The Making of an Institution of Jewish Higher Learning,* ed. Jack Wertheimer (New York: Jewish Theological Seminary of America, 1997), 367; and, in the same essay, 375, on the assistance that Lieberman offered Eli Ginzberg in the writing of the book on his father, which has been extensively cited above.

73. Ginzberg, "East and West," 262 and nn. 67–68. There is, of course, particular importance in the fact that it was Heller who wrote the critical survey of Ginzberg's work for the leading American Jewish studies journal. See Heller, "Ginzberg's *Legends of the Jews.*"
74. David Weiss-Halivni, *The Book and the Sword: A Life of Learning in the Shadow of Destruction* (New York: Farrar, Straus and Giroux, 1996).

6

The Legend about *The Legends*

Methodological Reflections on Ginzberg's *The Legends of the Jews*

Ithamar Gruenwald

The Legend Factor in Jewish Literature

In this essay I examine some ramifications implied by the legend factor in the history of Jewish literature in antiquity in light of the monumental oeuvre of Ginzberg's *The Legends of the Jews.* I begin by addressing general aspects of the subject before engaging in specifics, with examples to clarify my points. Although Ginzberg does not explicitly refer to this point, he uses the term "legend" in the sense of the literary result of the fusion of a wide spectrum of what he calls "Haggadah" and specific biblical materials. In Ginzberg's view this fusion is justified by the fact that the "Haggadah" material "is thereby characterized first as being derived from the Holy Scriptures, and then as being of the nature of a story" (Preface, ix). Ginzberg views this constructive interplay between "Haggadah" and Scripture as dualism, and comments that "this dualism sums up the distinguishing features of Jewish Legend" (Preface, ix). While the first four volumes of *The Legends* show the results of that fusion, the fifth and sixth volumes contain annotated references that the huge body of aggadah used to accomplish the author's purposes.

The nineteenth and twentieth centuries saw the publication of a number of anthologies dealing in various ways with aggadic literature. Some of the most significant include Wilhelm Bacher's contribution to Tannaitic and Amoraic aggadah, Bialik and Ravnitzki's *The Book of Legends,* and Berdyczewski's *Mi-Mekor Yisrael.* Each of these followed its own literary modes of presentation, none resembling that adopted by Louis Ginzberg. In its unique manner, Ginzberg's work combines literary creativity with enormous erudition and intellectual acumen. Readers cannot fail to be impressed by the breadth and depth of this undertaking. Only through a masterful combination of these qualities could such a work come into being and its essentially literary and scholarly standards be adequately achieved.

In making use of Ginzberg's magnum opus, scholars could not fail being keenly aware of the impact that Ginzberg's research strategies have on our knowledge and understanding of Jewish literary traditions in antiquity and the dynamics of the modes of the expansion of these traditions in many areas of the spiritual spectra of Judaism. In this connection, the "Legend" factor has received scholarly promotion.

The breadth of knowledge and information embodied in the work invites the attention of readers and scholars from a variety of fields: literature, history, cultural studies, philology, theology, and folklore. This volume significantly adds to the list of scholars who have devoted themselves to the study of Ginzberg's oeuvre, adding comments, criticism, and valuable suggestions regarding the method Ginzberg adopted in gathering and presenting his material, including the annotated discussions in two volumes of notes.[1]

I first briefly discuss Ginzberg's Preface, in which he outlines the methodological considerations employed in the book, before venturing the possibility of assessing the work as a whole from a fresh perspective—one diverging from that advocated by the author and by several scholars who examined his work.[2] I do so in part in order to assess the significance of the work for our understanding of the various aspects of Jewish religious life and thought in a wider context than the one conceived by the author. In my view, the aggadic factor, as highlighted and outlined by Ginzberg, justifies an extension of the method and the scholarly practice of the author in his handling of the materials at hand. The context I have in mind is the study of ancient Judaism, its daily life and religion in the framework of cultural studies, religious studies, and anthropology.[3] I seek to highlight cross-referential vantage points, focusing attention on factors of divergence that take place within cultural points of convergence. This method attempts to cast new light on the kind of approach that Ginzberg adopted as the focal stance of his work and which is revealed in its structure—namely, an assemblage of biblical and para-biblical legend-materials associated with specific biblical figures and events.

My warrant for suggesting this kind of approach lies in the hope that it will introduce a new channel of discussion concerning the accumulative output of *The Legends* and its declared objectives and performance. While this is likely to lead to viewpoints whose existence Ginzberg did not take into consideration, it suggests vantage points for a new mode of handling the same materials, as well as their scholarly assessment in the presentation of Jewish culture as reflecting a religiously based and oriented civilization.

In its original English translation, *The Legends* comprises four volumes of biblical material interwoven with aggadic materials, two volumes of notes, and an index volume.[4] Ginzberg correctly perceived that the "legends" to which he devoted his learned attention constitute an important inventory of diversified and complex information concerning personages and events as shaped by and in modes of diverse forms of literary activity. Within this framework, biblical information concerning codes of behavior, belief, and social organization is regarded as stimulating the growth of materials that feed a wide range of derivative literary sources. As indicated, Ginzberg principally focused upon stories concerning personages and events related to these personages (Preface, xi), stressing the hermeneutico-creative and existential links forged by later generations in relation to the historical aspects of the biblical past. The materials at hand came to full cultural and historical fruition in literary units generically referred to as midrash or aggadah, which cover a wide range of hermeneutical and literary stances, but also much more.

Ginzberg conceived of the Rabbanan d'Aggadeta (the masters or teachers of Aggadah, a term used in medieval commentaries to talmudic literature) as being didactically intent on establishing "a close connection between the Scripture and the creations of the *popular fancy*, [and] to give the latter a firm basis and secure a long term of life for them" (Preface, xi; emphasis added). Here, however, a crucial question comes to mind. What did Ginzberg mean when referring to the notion of "popular fancy"? In his opinion, these teachers of aggadah "were *no folklorists,* from whom a faithful reproduction of legendary material may be expected" but "*homilists* who used legends for didactic purposes" (Preface, xi; emphasis added). I raise this question, since the volume in which this study is included places "folk literature" on its thematic platform. In my view, this may cause a cognitive dissonance. How close, or perhaps distant, are "homilists" from "folklorists," and what is included in "popular fancy"? Furthermore, how close are these notions to what is now termed "folklore"? The scope of folktale or folklore as a scholarly domain in its own right has branched out and specialized its terms of reference and research tools since Ginzberg wrote the Preface to *Legends.* Ginzberg was also aware of the fact that not much systematic, diachronic study of the materials at hand had been undertaken prior to the publication of his book, and thus he refrained from following certain desiderata in its full assessment (Preface, xi).

One of the consequences of this approach to the notion of aggadah was that extra-biblical literature found free passage into the literary setting of biblical materials as organized on principles set by the author himself.[5] As noted above, Ginzberg makes his point clear: "I have made the first attempt to gather from the original sources *all Jewish legends, as they refer to Biblical personages and events*, and reproduce them with the greatest attainable completeness and accuracy" (Preface, xi; emphasis added). Be that as it may, the manner in which Ginzberg organizes his work should not be viewed as merely constituting a formal principle of arranging the material but a substantive argument regarding the corpus of *The Legends.* Accordingly, people—biographical stances rather than topics (i.e., theological and ideological considerations)—and events dominate the world of *Legends.*

At this point, a question arises: Did Ginzberg convincingly succeed in creating the tight link—even bond—that he crafted between the para-biblical texts and their scriptural sources? If he did, one may argue that the doors are open for endeavors of a similar kind, but in the reverse direction. That is, we may ask to what extent can the homiletic materials be subjected to a similar process, infused with biblical materials. In this process, they may lose their principally homiletic stances and become "legends" in the sense that Ginzberg views the biblical materials infused with the homiletic ones.

In my discussion below, while following Ginzberg, I examine the extent to which the approach mentioned above is likely to show that tighter connections than those evolving in literary affiliations exist between the extra-biblical materials and the biblical ones to which they relate. While Ginzberg assumes the adequacy of the infusion of para-biblical materials *into* the biblical world,[6] my approach moves a step forward and suggests an examination of a paradigmatic case in which these connections are explored by relating biblical materials to the homiletic ones. If we accept the relevance of such an examination, we can reach conclusions that are significant to the assessment of the cases at hand, biblical and para-biblical, from the point of view of understanding essential aspects of the religious life in ancient Israel.

The para-biblical materials Ginzberg employs have undergone a process of crossing the boundaries. At the same time, the biblical texts have undergone considerable changes in light of the para-biblical materials inserted into them. Ginzberg may be understood as arguing that the materials accruing around the biblical texts had to wait for an outsider's—or scholarly—feat that facilitated their integration within the biblical texts. Whatever the case, in their new and unique setting, they do not show, though they should be given a chance to do so, their rich diachronic diversity or, as Ginzberg calls it, "dualism" (see above). In this respect, these texts easily open channels of dialectic discussion, in which cross-referential conclusions can be drawn in either direction.

In short, I examine the extent to which we can follow Ginzberg's work and explore—in both directions—the tracks he has opened. In doing so, we move a step forward and try to gain—in reference to a specific example—nuanced conclusions in regard to the vibrant dynamic of the cross-referential literary enrichment facilitated by what Ginzberg assumes is entailed by the term "Legend." One conclusion in this cross-referential process is clear: the extra-biblical sources constitute a fascinating replica of what sounds as the literary and theological polyphony of the biblical texts themselves.[7] While the trained ear can hardly miss the separate voices contributing to that polyphony, the overall tone of the biblical homiletics, as conceived in the first four volumes of *the Legends* seeks to ring a harmonic consistency and thematic coherence in the biblical text. However, in the ears of the expert and one who consults the two volumes of notes, the literary fusion of the extra-biblical with the biblical cannot be accepted without being fully aware of the dialectic dualism to which Ginzberg refers. From a methodological point of view, the arabesque-decorated weave of Ginzberg's intricately wrought artifact could not have been created had it not been conceived as it was in the mind of the author.

In my view, the question of whether the overall purpose of Ginzberg should be contained within the limits of the "Legends" factor, or if it has implications beyond that factor, has already received a positive answer. I believe that it has implications for a wide cultural and intellectual spectrum. Thus, further gleanings into its contents and nature are of great interest from a number of perspectives.

Speaking of the "dualism" between biblical text and its enriching para-biblical materials, one can give numerous examples that constitute precedents for that kind of "dualism" in Scripture itself. Comparatively and diachronically viewed, no textual and thematic agreement exists between many biblical passages which deal with the same specific subject.[8] Familiar examples are the two juxtaposed creation stories (Genesis 1–2), which diverge prominently from one another in character and content; the two versions of the Decalogue (Exodus 20 and Deuteronomy 5), which fail to correspond in essential details; the disparities in the description of the festivals, holy days, and sacrifices (Leviticus 23 and Numbers 27–29); and the essential differences regarding the divergent accounts of the spies (Numbers 13 and Deuteronomy 1 [here referred to as "men"]). Thus, in light of the recognition that similar processes are already at work in the scriptural sources themselves, the postulate that post-biblical literature is characterized by an innovative rewriting and reworking of the original text becomes a much less provocative, and in a sense *less legend-based*, statement. However, one should keep in mind one essential difference. Divergent versions of biblical accounts do not flow into one another, as they are called to do by Ginzberg in his *Legends*.

Thus, Ginzberg could argue that the rewriting of the Hebrew Bible in terms of "legends" serves as an essential element within every phase and aspect of Jewish religion, including Scripture itself.[9] The significance of this fact with respect to the programmatic foundations of the reworking of formative incidents in Jewish history should carry more weight than is usually granted. It only remains to speculate whether Ginzberg's oeuvre can be included in this kind of argument or whether it occupies a separate entity.

A few remarks are still in place with regard to the method applied by Ginzberg in his compendium. Notwithstanding the fact that Ginzberg confines himself, first and foremost, to *biblical* personalities and figures, the book contains noteworthy topical strata. One interesting aspect of this emerges when looking at the final volume of *Legends*—the index. The entries herein reveal that Ginzberg himself does not abide by his own declared principles. By way of example, the index contains eighteen entries relating to Rabbi Aqiba, including topical comments on biographical issues! Likewise, a great deal of attention is devoted to spirits and demons, among them Lilith, about whose existence and activity the Hebrew Bible seems to be uninformed. Likewise, the entry "Hell" contains dozens of references, many of which do not relate either to any biblical background or personages. In fact, the word (גיהינם) does not appear in the Hebrew Bible at all.

The sole warrant for introducing these topics derives from their presence in the para-biblical material that Ginzberg introduces as associated with the biblical personalities and events which he treats. However, a question comes to mind: What directed the authors of the para-biblical materials to offer them the way they did? Obviously, the answer changes from case to case. However, one question applies to all these cases: Was it by way of creatively expanding scriptural data or fulfilling the need to relate to it in homiletic terms? Furthermore, does the scriptural material warrant its discussion in a para-biblical context, or does the external material impose itself by literary and other means on the biblical text?

One possible answer to these questions may be inferred from the following example. According to Ginzberg (1:147–51), the story of Noah and the Flood includes the sins of the angels who rebelled against God and were punished. The details of this material are known from the apocryphal-pseudepigraphic literature and are liable to raise questions: Do they originate in an early version of Genesis 6 or derive from independent sources incorporating parallel ancient materials? Although most scholars opt for the second possibility, I have suggested elsewhere that the first need not be excluded.[10] In short, the conceptual umbrella of the *Legends* as forged under Ginzberg's hands creates a "chiastic" impression—namely, that the aggadah is "biblical" and the Hebrew Bible "aggadic." On numerous occasions, the first type of material slides almost imperceptibly into the domain of the second, the reverse circumstance prevailing on others. I would not take the time to indicate this matter in such detail were it not for the fact that I feel the need to fill what appears to me to be a scholarly lacuna in the scholarly assessment of Ginzberg's work.

One additional remark is due before concluding this introduction. It concerns the terminology at my disposal for the purposes of the present discussion. The academic language I employ constitutes a conceptual attempt to embed the terms of reference that serve the study of the scriptural and Rabbinic world in the context of religious and anthropological studies. I have discussed the reasons for doing so in another study.[11]

The Paradigmatic Case of Ḥoni the Circlemaker, Part 1

From the considerations adduced above, I now turn to a discussion concerning the person and activity of Ḥoni the Circlemaker.[12] Ḥoni's name and activity are mentioned in Rabbinic literature, and his works are closely related to the activity of central biblical characters such as Samuel (1 Samuel 12:13–25), Elijah (1 Kings 1:18), and Elisha (2 Kings 3:15ff.). He should thus have been given attention within *Legends*.[13] Certain acts performed by all these biblical figures resemble one another with respect to a key phenomenon—the bringing down of rain. Since this issue, whether wondrous or magical, has been fundamental to religious cultures throughout the ages, I consider it a proper and significant platform for inquiry and discussion.[14] While it should be noted that the calling down of rain represents a marginal event in the biographies of Samuel and Elisha, it stands at the center of Elijah's activity as recounted in 1 Kings.[15] More than being a "legend," it amounts to a cultural topos.

I refer to the issue at hand as a cultural topos due to the fact that the passages relating to Ḥoni in the Mishnah and Rabbinic literature are aggadic in the broad sense of the term. They include elements that have folkloristic aspects, sociological relevance, a halakhic context, and supernatural amplification. Ḥoni therefore constitutes a "legend" in the sense in which Ginzberg uses the term. The fact that the story about him occurs in the Mishnah enhances its narrative value in connection to Scripture. Although the link is not direct, this is the type of material Ginzberg uses in his *Legends*. In any event, legendary components—usually introduced by the term *ma'aseh* ("Once it happened that . . .")—run through the Mishnah and Tosefta, the two basic documents that configure halakhah. Tractate Ta'anit, which contains the source material concerning Ḥoni the Circlemaker, is no exception to this rule.[16] One may argue that a halakhic dimension exists in the stories inserted into the aggadic literature of the sages. From this perspective, the walls dividing aggadah from halakhah, or vice versa, are neither as lofty nor as solid as people who still hold to the obsolete distinction between halakhic and aggadic midrash are inclined to assert. The purpose of the present observations is to make clear that, however one assesses the story of Ḥoni—whether in the framework of aggadah or halakhah—its bearing on the type of discussion in which Ginzberg engages (the deeds of the biblical figures) poses no problem in my eyes. Its context is clearly that of the para-biblical.

I believe that, in failing to observe this association, Ginzberg missed an opportunity pregnant with tantalizing methodological ramifications. I return to this point below, simply noting at this junction that his methodology entails a selective process by which certain materials with a genuine claim to pertinence are excluded. At the same time, Ginzberg's work also contains an abundance of materials whose direct relevance to the biblical subject and/or personality is not as self-evident as he claims it to be.

Admittedly, the bulk of aggadic literature does not form a closed or monolithic literary-ideological artifact but warrants a multiplicity of scholarly approaches, each highlighting, in its own way, aspects of exegetical and scholarly technique. While one may play with it *ad libitum*, as Ginzberg does, we should also keep in mind the original and pioneering example propounded by Isaac Heinemann in his *Darkhei ha-aggadah* (The ways of the aggadah).[17] Heinemann argues that aggadah creates stances of creative hermeneutics, and may thus sanction, on methodological grounds, a wide range of midrashic possibilities that do not bypass what Ginzberg calls the aggadic dualism. My point is that by closing doors to certain materials, such as the story of Ḥoni, we shall lose an important aspect of the materials at hand. In this respect, the case of Ḥoni provides us with the opportunity to explore the pivotal axis linking aggadah and folk literature in light of the notions propounded by Ginzberg.[18]

Let us return to our topical center here. A discussion of the rain motif, as depicted in the sources—biblical and extra-biblical—instructively exemplifies the diversity and even dialectic tensions the Jewish religion has undergone over the generations with respect to one of the most fundamental phenomena of human existence. Some will say that themes of this kind should be addressed on the basis of *a priori* and even "wall to wall" agreement. Others maintain to the contrary that it is completely natural that such existential matters should be approached from different angles, employing variant attitudes and diverse methods of presentation—including, most importantly for our current discussion, the activities and deeds by charismatic figures of the kind discussed in the present essay.[19] We must not forget, however, that differences of opinion and practice exist in almost every subject relating to religious belief and practice—an endemic phenomenon in a living cultural tradition. In Judaism, *maḥloqet*—differences of opinion and views in matters relating to legal issues—have constituted a prevalent factor in Rabbinic literature, and in the life of those following in its wake throughout the ages.

In the daily experience of human beings, water supply is dependent upon several factors—rainwater, rivers, springs, and wells. To the modern mind, the falling of rain is a "natural," that is, climatic phenomenon, although human beings learn from experience that they lack the capacity to control it, its timing, or its quantity. If this is the state of affairs today, all the more so was it in ancient times, during which people believed that water resources depended on superhuman powers, such as the gods or angels. The latter were held—as they still are today in various societies and cultures—as the regulating factor behind the scenes. In daily life, God's question to Job—"Has the rain a father, or who has begotten the drops of dew?" (Job 38:28)—constantly resonates in the human mind.

During the Tannaitic period and in places receptive to such ideas, public prayers and fasts were instituted—or, alternatively, sages possessing special powers exercised them in order to bring about rainfall, controlling its timing and quantity. As noted above, at work here are factors associated with the creation of unique cultural topoi. The concept of "culture" serves in this respect in a broad and general sense, inclusive of religious rituals and miracles, as well as domains that, at times, have come to be regarded in a negative light—such as magic and other supernatural media. In any case, we possess a relatively wide and detailed range of documentation relating to the various means that served—as they still do today in various cultures—to guarantee the supply of water, in particular rainwater and its accumulation. In other words, a considerable amount of comparative material exists from an anthropological perspective.[20] This permits our discussion to branch out from the routine forms of the discourse on these matters as they arise in Rabbinic literature into a wide range of phenomenological data.

The following discussion focuses on the various aspects—literary and folkloristic—of water provision, principally in the form of rain. More precisely, I treat the subject in the framework of "the culture of water and rain." I prefer to employ the term "culture" since, in referring to the term "legends" (in our case, "of the Jews"), I may thereby be understood as delimiting the discussion to the literary realm of fable and fiction—even when the sources under discussion appear in a conceptual or halakhic framework. I am interested in anthropological factors with emphatically existential functions and implications. I have already provided a warrant for placing Ḥoni at the center of my analysis here in the specific thematic context that occasions his appearance in m. Ta'anit 3:8 and the parallels thereto. From a cultural point of view, it is apparent that in tractate Ta'anit—and its parallels in Rabbinic literature—the ritual protocols evinced reveal a formative shift in relation to the biblical passages dealing with corresponding phenomena.[21] Although the biblical texts are a general reference point for the detailed descriptions found in later sources, including the circumstances under which rain falls, one must be aware of the fact that later sources entail important shifts in the cultural and performative layout. Ginzberg perforce remains within a literary milieu in addressing the issues as "legends," an approach that virtually precludes the highlighting of a webbed texture woven from divergent cultural threads. Had he thus viewed the biblical materials in the context suggested here, more insights could have been gained into the complexities of Jewish life.

In principle, it may be said that not only the Mishnah but also the remainder of the extra-biblical sources that serve Ginzberg's enterprise consist of materials and data that signify—each in its own way—the inception of fresh and divergent cultural stages and configurations. Viewed together in their amalgamation and divergence, they paint a dynamic picture of a live religious tradition that, among other things, attaches increasing importance to a variety of ritual practices. These activities develop in ways and according to guidelines distinctive from those mentioned in Scripture. In other words, it is not coincidental that the relevant descriptions in the extra-biblical materials—including the Rabbinic sources—lack the features characteristic of the Hebrew Bible. They clearly demand the ingenuity of a scholarly magician to bring them together, thus creating a coherent streamlining capable of bridging cultural distances and differences.

I shall immediately proceed to explore in what manner m. Ta'anit makes its point via topics and ritual protocols, the likes of which are unprecedented in Scripture. The basic statements of Mishnah regarding general and individual principles alike are presented in such a way as to highlight the existence of controversial views—or one trend of opinion against its antithesis. This is not the nature of the Hebrew Bible, which, as we have seen above, promotes the existence of diverse versions of the same event or ritual act—sometimes in two consecutive verses or passages. Significantly, these versions are not attributed—as in halakhah—to specific persons or easily identifiable legal schools. It is thus possible to claim, in principle, that halakhic materials such as those found in m. Ta'anit and elsewhere are appropriate for use in *The Legends of the Jews.* One kind of diversity meets the other. Despite the inner variation these texts tolerate, they do not lose their paradigmatic status.[22]

Whatever the case may be in this regard, Ḥoni's case in the Mishnah is presented as a *ma'aseh* or ritual exemplum. In other words, the force of the argument that his story possesses derives from the realization that a practical, alternative act exists and is likely to become normative. We should not forget that Ḥoni's *ma'aseh* is performed in the face of a previously specified halakhic procedure that has proved inefficacious.[23] It should be noted, however, that numerous discussions in Rabbinic literature adduce cases which raise issues that verge on topics bearing the status of ritual exempla as opposed to halakhic rules. At times, they succeed in making a meta-halakhic point.[24]

As just remarked, the context of the exemplum related to Ḥoni in m. Ta'anit concerns the detailing of the ritual protocols to be performed when rain fails to fall by specified dates during the winter. I would like to suggest that Shimon b. Shetaḥ's words to the effect that Ḥoni deserved to be excommunicated signal an attempt to declare Ḥoni's act to be a relativizing protestation vis-à-vis the stipulated efficacy of the various ritual protocols previously specified in the Rabbinic code of rituals. The Rabbinic authorities responsible for formulating these protocols evidently sought to determine normative facts within the framework of the establishment they endeavored to maintain, perhaps—if I may be allowed to turn around my statements above—precisely in the face of deeds such as that performed by Ḥoni.[25] In general, however, the mishnaic text and the rituals it refers to constitute an attempt to establish standards of normative status. This is particularly true in places where Scripture does not detail any specific or binding ritual or fails to provide one at all.[26]

The Paradigmatic Case of Ḥoni the Circlemaker, Part 2

As suggested above, the story of Ḥoni does not, *prima facie,* belong to a discussion of Ginzberg's anthology. Not constituting an explicit case of para-biblical expansion, it does not fall within the immediate paradigm of *Legends*. However, since the story is linked in a special way to the narratives concerning Samuel, Elijah, and Elisha (each in its own specific setting), it creates a bridgehead between the cultural milieu and the textual evidence in Rabbinic literature, on the one hand, and the biblical sources that tend to attribute the cessation of rain to the sins of the people, on the other. Whatever the case in all these accounts, they respectively convey the idea that special individuals mediate the bringing down of rain or the provision of water. On this basis, Ḥoni and his conceptual framework deserve to function as a unique example in the para-biblical framework that Ginzberg adopted as a meta-literary principle.

We now understand that the alleged connection with the story of Ḥoni the Circlemaker forces upon us suggestive notions concerning the rainwater stories recounted in relation to Samuel, Elijah, and Elisha. These incidents may contain historical truth, or, paradigmatically speaking, they project trajectories of the realm of aggadic-mythic narratives designed to promote specific goals beyond the particular events they report.[27] As indicated above, the framework of the study of folk literature adds special resonance to this question. Folk narratives, especially legends, constitute a cultural framework in which the issue of verisimilitude takes on a unique dimension. In this context, the customary critical and methodological objections in regard to the absolute distinction between the self-appraisement of historiographical reports concerning a specific historical reality and the status of literature dealing with the same event are often suspended.[28] A recurrent claim, supported by cognitive studies and psychological and psychoanalytic approaches, is that concrete historical-biographical reality—verisimilitude—is a multi-faceted factor that enables the shaping of reality in various modes. While it may boast that it presents the true version of proceedings, it is likely to include elements that verge on being "mythic." By the same token, myth can include correct details concerning historical reality.[29] In any event, it opens multi-directional paths that permit free transition from one realm to the other, and thus enable the inclusion or exclusion of heterogeneous materials.

These statements are made primarily in light of the fact, noted above, that the first four volumes of *Legends* integrate aggadic material that variously elaborates and expands the narrative aspect of the scriptural text. In certain groups or sects these materials were regarded as historical truth, necessary and responsible—beyond any exegetical function—for the shaping of a certain historical reality. The issue of overwriting the original scriptural setting did not arise as a possible option in these cases.[30] In fact, in taking material(s) from an extensive and loosely marked range of multi-vocal and extra-biblical inventory of materials, *The Legends of the Jews* creates a "rewritten Bible" in a modern and, practically speaking, self-solicited scholarly style. In this respect, stories such as those regarding Ḥoni must be recontextualized, from a cognitive point of view, in order find their way into the broadly conceived notion of the legends-construct of the kind Ginzberg creates.

To put the issue in focus, we must ask ourselves to what extent the ideas developed in m. Ta'anit can be seamlessly connected to the biblical material.[31] My answer has in effect already been given: as long as we keep in mind and are aware of the fact that an essential and recognizable difference exists between Scripture and the interpretative "legends," any creative move that follows Ginzberg's methodology is worthy of serious consideration. If, however, such a division is not maintained or a trend prevails toward disregarding the exegetical expansions of the scriptural story as an integral part of it, critical caution and restraint must be engaged to direct the scholarly enterprise.

A telling example of such moderation is found in regard to the Feast of Tabernacles (Sukkot), mentioned both in the Hebrew Bible and the Mishnah as a festival on which various rituals are performed in order to ensure the falling of rain in the forthcoming winter.[32] While the connection between the Feast of Tabernacles and rain is not documented in Scripture until the days of Zechariah (Zechariah 14:16–18), this link dominates the accounts given in the Mishnah, Talmud, and Midrash. Although the stories of Samuel, Elijah, and Elisha are not connected to any particular festival, they contain features that associate them with the world of the supernatural, and thus prepare the way for what becomes magically oriented material. In the study of religion, the supernatural is treated as not far removed from that which claims the right to constitute an integral part of religious reality. In the case of Ḥoni and similar figures, the sages evince a need to enlist a conceptual mechanism intended to legitimize the acts of persons performing such acts. While calling them *ḥasidim* (pious men), *ba'alei shem* (*tov*) (miracle workers), or *tsaddiqim* (righteous men) may be effective in creating a separation between them and the biblical figures, the affinity remains on the level of the noteworthy from a phenomenological point of view.

Draught and Rain in the Perspective of Cultural Changes

Here I address additional features whose general outlines I discussed in the preceding section. The Book of Genesis recounts that, during the patriarchal period, the Land of Canaan suffered occasional periods of famine and drought. In line with his general layout, Ginzberg offers wider horizons and counts ten cases of famine. While the majority of these are scriptural, some—such as the famine that will plague "the generation in which the Son of David will appear"—occur in post-biblical times.[33] In principle, such a list prepares the way for the inclusion of hermeneutical comments. Ginzberg consequently argues that conditions of famine usually constitute a means for the "chastisement of men."

The narratives in Genesis do not fall under this category, however, rather being facts of nature unassociated with any punitive stance. The food shortages from which the patriarchs suffer force them to leave their place of residence and even the Land of Canaan itself. Thus, even when the length of the famine is predicted ahead of time—as in the days of Joseph—neither dearth nor drought is associated with a theological framework or system. At best, the shortage is placed within a non-specific framework that aligns the divine plan with historical events. In other words, the famines of those days do not require a specific ritual act to bring rain or avert the suffering caused by aridity. On the contrary, it is precisely the customary behavioral norms, surprising as these may be, within the life of the family—in particular between man and wife (Abraham, Sarah, Pharaoh [Genesis 12]; Isaac, Rebecca, Abimelech [Genesis 26])—which are determined in the wake of the decisions and acts taken by the patriarchs during times of famine. The explicated norms do not fall under the exegetical category of whatever has happened to the patriarchs is a sign to the children. I do not need to detail these phenomena here, since they resolve themselves within what I have defined elsewhere as the "ethos-stage" wherein norms of personal behavior crystallize as pre-religion, not being considered as binding as the everlasting laws and commandments specified in other parts of the Torah or Prophets.[34]

Once the cessation of rain is perceived as a divinely enforced punitive intervention, the arrival of rain in its proper season enters the domain of dependence on human conduct. In this context, it acquires a conditional status: it comes when people do the will of God and ceases when they disobey Him.[35] Since this issue concerns modes of ritual behavior, further elaboration on this matter is necessary. M. Ta'anit and similar texts clearly constitute, each in its own way, models in a complex line of development in the ritual realm vis-à-vis scriptural antecedents.

In essence, m. Ta'anit contains detailed references to penitential rituals performed in order to correct a situation whose smooth running has been disturbed. Apart from their general penitential character, no directly obvious connection exists between the various rituals and their purpose. It is only via the performance of the reparative ritual(s) that we hear, retrospectively, that something has interfered with/in the ordinary processes of nature. We do not hear what obstructed the normal procedures and caused the drought, however. Clearly, in the mishnaic context it is not linked to what we consider meteorological factors. Normally, lack of rain does not constitute a meteorological reality that can be ritually—or, as the case might be, miraculously—corrected. Furthermore, as we shall see, the assertions concerning the efficacy of ritual protocols made in m. Ta'anit evince a departure not only from the natural sciences but also—and even more significantly in the present context—from the biblical theology according to which the supply of rain is dependent on human obedience to the divine will. While the connection may be implied, it is not specifically stated.

As remarked above, however, a specified ritual protocol does not always have the desired effect. The customary protocols of blowing the horn, fasting, and praying as stipulated in the Mishnah are frequently exposed as ineffective. In such cases, an alternative factor is adduced, as m. Ta'anit demonstrates via the story of Ḥoni.[36] While I discuss the account in detail below, I have already noted that, in principle, it opens the door to alternative ritual channels, such as the application of adjuration-like prayers, which brings us into close proximity with the miracles performed by the Prophets if not the realm of magic. In any event, as noted above, the figure of Ḥoni is not without parallels.[37] From this perspective, the intriguing vista he provides of the religious world of the sages is significant beyond the single case he represents. In this respect, I would argue that he is more relevant for inclusion in the para-scriptural materials adduced by Ginzberg in *The Legends of the Jews* than may appear at first glance.

In addition to the above comments, room also exists to conjecture that the polemical background reflected in the attempt to excommunicate Ḥoni is already present in the story of Elijah. In contrast to the account of Elijah given in the Book of Kings, the Book of Chronicles makes no allusion to the prophet, ignoring his conflict with the prophets of Baal and the calling down of rain upon his multi-structured sacrificial rite. We can thus assume the existence of polemical tones in Elijah's "evaporation" from Chronicles.[38]

Before Magic Sets In: From Providence to Provision—Water and Rain in the Biblical Context

Let me now expand on the biblical material, and its nature, as presented in the first four volumes of Ginzberg's *Legends.* The reader of the compendium is likely to receive an impression of sequential stories coherently refashioned and edited. I have already remarked that Ginzberg's work lacks any indication regarding the inner diversity and dialectic characteristic of the biblical texts themselves, even when dealing with a single person or event — a fact Ginzberg himself recognized as constituting a significant principle. More accurately, one of the things that makes it difficult to retain any impression of continuity or unity within the biblical materials is the fact that the same themes appear in various, polyphonic forms in different biblical documents—on occasion even within the same book. The three basic literary "unities" applied in classical art—plot, time, and place—are absent not only from the extra-biblical sources that occupy such a substantial place in Ginzberg's compendium but even more conspicuously from Scripture itself. No linear unity of literary exposition, giving rise to a façade of literary coherence, can therefore be sustained on the basis of the manner in which Ginzberg presents his material to his readers. A notable example, in this respect, are the two chapters in *Legends*—representing Genesis 1 and 2—in which Ginzberg handles as a sequential continuum, albeit giving them separate names (and subsections): "The Creation of the World" and "Adam." As the reader can see for himself, these chapters are loaded—I would dare say, overloaded—with legendary para-biblical materials that obscure the unique manner in which Ginzberg handles his materials. Clearly, they do not serve any exegetical purpose.

Another example to the same effect, but more relevant to our topical discussion of the rain/water culture, sheds light on the present discussion. This relates to the plight of Moses and Aaron in face of the demand of the Israelites for the supply of life-saving water in the desert. In Numbers 20:8, God says to Moses, "You and your brother Aaron take the rod and assemble the community, and before their very eyes speak to the rock to yield its water. Thus you shall produce water for them from the rock." I do not address the dual striking of the rock here, which eventually drew forth great amounts of water and gave the Israelites and their livestock to drink. Instead I draw attention to a statement made in the following chapter, which describes the Israelites' wanderings in the wilderness: "and from there to Be'er, which is the well where the Lord said to Moses, 'Assemble the people that I may give them water.' Then Israel sang this song: Spring up, O well—sing to it—the well which the chieftains dug" (Numbers 21:16–18).[39] Here, the term "well" replaces the word "rock," both being distinguished from the *tsur* used in Exodus 17 (cf. also Psalm 78:20, 105:41, etc.), which depicts a similar miracle.[40]

It is also interesting to note that, whereas in Exodus, the Israelites are called "people," in Numbers 20 they are referred to as a "community" (*'edah*) and then once again as "people."[41] Although these terminological nuances, which find expression—and of course gain significance—in the various biblical texts, should have served Ginzberg in configuring the "aggadah of Moses," they are in fact absent from *Legends.*[42] I relate to the subject merely because an examination of the approach to the sources that Ginzberg adduces and their integration into a synthetic system—which he designates "Legends of the Jews"—fails to elucidate these subtleties.

Indeed, the subject of the supply of rain and water constitutes a complex issue as early as the creation stories in Genesis 1–2. It could—or rather should—have received more emphatic attention to enhance the impact of the "Legends" already in its biblical context. Let me explain this point. On the second day of creation the waters are "separated"—those above the firmament from those below (Genesis 1:6–8), the latter being said to "be gathered into one place, that the dry land may appear" (1:9). In the following verses, which refer to the fifth and sixth days of creation (20ff.), the accounts focus upon the bringing forth of living beings in the sea, in the air, and on the earth. While the blessings given to everything created relate to their reproduction ("Let them be fruitful and multiply"), no mention is made of the provision of the forms of subsistence necessary for their existence and growth. Only in Genesis 2, which alludes to an alternative story of creation, do we find the expected reference to the supply of water necessary for their sustenance: "No shrub of the field was yet on the earth and no grasses of the field had yet sprouted, *because the Lord God had not sent rain upon the earth*" (Genesis 2:5). The following verse immediately corrects this defect: "but a stream would well up from the ground and water the whole surface of the earth" (2:6). In short, this section of the account informs us that the "watering" came up from below and then formed into clouds that watered the earth. This itself, however, is quickly supplemented by an additional system—one of irrigation, which also finds various echoes in Scripture: "A river issued from Eden to water the garden, and it then divided and became four major supplying sources" (2:10). The four rivers are subsequently named as the Pishon, Giḥon, Tigris, and Euphrates (2:11–14).[43] These two methods of irrigation and water supply—rainwater and rivers—are thus condensed into a single chapter and constitute complementary cultural "topoi" featuring interesting ramifications in Jewish culture from the biblical times onward. While, as noted above, they play a central role in determining the deeds of the God of Israel and His providence in the world, Ginzberg pays them virtually no attention. In itself this case constitutes the prototype of a "legend," which deserves attention, before it is inflated with heterogeneous materials.

A second, complementary example comes from Deuteronomy, which relates to both systems noted above. While the rivers appear to be constantly full of water supply, the rain is dependent upon the mercy of the heavens. Moses says to the people, "For the Lord your God is bringing you into a good land, a land with streams and springs and fountains issuing from plain and hill" (Deuteronomy 8:7)—adding that in this respect the land of Israel is different from Egypt: "For the land that you are about to enter and possess is not like the land of Egypt from which you have come. There the grain you sowed had to be watered by your own labors, like a vegetable garden" (Deuteronomy 11:10). Moses then immediately explains that in "the land you are about to cross into and possess, a land of hills and valleys," the people would drink "from the rains of heaven" (1:11).

All these statements bypass the obvious connection that makes the rivers dependent on rainwater. Rain is the major issue in the people's lives—and consequently in the theology implied by their religious obedience. Moses makes this point clear: "If, then, you obey the commandments that I enjoin upon you this day . . . I will grant the rain for your land in season, the early rain and the late. You shall gather in your new grain and wine and oil" (Deuteronomy 11:13–14). He further admonishes the people: "Take care not to be lured away to serve other gods and bow to them. For the Lord's anger will flare up against you, and He will shut up the skies so that there will be no rain and the ground will not yield its produce; and you will soon perish from the good land that the Lord is assigning to you" (1:16–17). In short, the "key of rain" mentioned in several Rabbinic texts lies in God's hands and is not handed over to any emissary.[44] According to Moses, God can employ it for blessing or for cursing.

These latter acts appear in similar fashion in the following passages. Deuteronomy 28 states: "The Lord will open for you His bounteous store, the heavens, to provide rain for your land in season and to bless all your undertakings" (v. 12)—contrasted with the warning: "The Lord will make the rain of your land dust, and sand shall drop on you from the sky, until you are wiped out" (v. 24). The transition from one state to the other is dependent upon two antithetical factors: "Now, if you obey the Lord your God" (v. 1) versus "But if you do not obey the Lord your God" (v. 15). It is important to note here that the biblical text nowhere mentions any direct means—ritually performed—for restoring the situation to its original status, namely, the falling of rain in its season.[45] While Ginzberg devotes more than a complete volume to Moses, including aggadic sources detailing his death, he fails to refer to any of the issues discussed here, despite the fact that they are of great significance for Moses' teaching and the theological position represented by the book of Deuteronomy, and fit into a macro-cultural system related to rain that serves as the forerunner of m. Ta'anit and related sources.

The biblical story does not end at this point, however. The first allusion to any ritual intervention in which the people are involved when the heavens are shut up occurs in Solomon's prayer at the dedication of the First Temple: "Should the heavens be shut up and there be no rain, because they have sinned against You, and they pray toward this place and acknowledge Your name and repent of their sins, when You hear them . . . [you will] send down rain upon the land which You gave to Your people as their heritage" (1 Kings 8:35–36). It is significant to note here that Solomon prays and does so next to the altar on which the sacrifices were to be offered. No sacrificial offerings are mentioned: "Then Solomon stood before the altar of the Lord in the presence of the whole community of Israel; he spread the palms of his hands toward heaven" (8:22).[46] Ginzberg ignores this unique fact, however, adducing instead Moses' encounter with Samael (3:466) and Solomon's with Beelzebub and Ashmedai (4:149f.)—neither of which incidents, of course, appear in the biblical texts.

While I cannot survey all the biblical references to the conditional status of water and rain, they are not, in fact, particularly copious. The majority deal with rain or dew, noting that God is somehow involved in their provision. Furthermore, as I have remarked above, no detailed ritual protocols intended to bring about rainfall are mentioned. The exceptions are Solomon and a passage in Zechariah, which states: "Ask the Lord for rain in the season of the late rain. It is the Lord who causes storms; and He will provide rainstorms for them, grass in the fields for everyone" (Zechariah 10:1). Subsequently, however (14:12–17), Zechariah cautions concerning another noteworthy event: a great plague will fall upon "all those peoples that warred against Jerusalem," adding an unprecedented assertion with regard to "all those who survive of those nations that came up against Jerusalem": "[They] shall make a pilgrimage year by year to bow low to the King Lord of Hosts and to observe the Feast of Booths. [But] any of the earth's communities that does not make the pilgrimage to Jerusalem to bow low to the King Lord of Hosts shall receive no rain" (14:16–17). In other words, a contrapuntal legend emerges.

In addition to the previously adduced references to rain, three new conditional requirements make their appearance here: (1) The nations—not "all of Israel"—must go up to Jerusalem; (2) the idea of worshiping God—rather than pilgrimage in the sense of seeing God and appearing before Him with sacrifices; and (3) the linking of this matter to the Feast of Tabernacles. Zechariah bestows a special status on Sukkot here, not one associated, as we have seen, with the cycle of the annual three pilgrimage festivals as described in the Torah. He completely ignores the sacrifices commanded by Moses (Numbers 29:12–38), the making of the booths (*sukkot;* Leviticus 23:42), and the taking up of the four species (Leviticus 23:40).

Is Zechariah autonomously adding a new element to the feast, thus creating a para-scriptural prototype? While we cannot give a definitive answer to this question, Nehemiah's reference to Sukkot offers a possible explanation: "The whole community that returned from the captivity made booths and dwelt in the booths—the Israelites had not done so from the days of Joshua son of Nun to that day" (Nehemiah 8:17).[47] While Nehemiah's words serve as background and foundation for the subsequent developments in Israelite religion, Ginzberg fails to include them.[48] If we accept his literary approach of adducing stories concerning the lives and/or biographies of biblical figures, we must also recognize that he proffers no explanation for leaving certain aspects of their lives in obscurity. While the issue of selectivity in choice of material governs in many cases, the above-mentioned topics relating to Solomon and Nehemiah are left out of *Legends*—a fact barely noted by most readers.

With this comment in mind, let me conclude this section with a discussion of Elijah, the story of whom, prominently linked to drought and rainfall, is "rejected" in Chronicles. We may perceive in this act yet another biblical precedent for Ginzberg's application of fact-censorship. Elijah forms the sole biblical account in which a ritual—miraculous or magical—is performed in association with the bringing down of rain. This rite serves a clear purpose: to demonstrate to the northern Israelites, with King Ahab at their head, who is the true God—Baal or the God of Israel. The victory of the latter comes in the wake of the failure of the 450 "prophets" of Baal to arouse their god by means of special rites to cause rain to fall.

Whatever the case may be in this respect, it should be noted here that Elijah "prays" and even offers a sacrifice. I emphasize these elements because they are preliminary to m. Ta'anit in general and the story of Ḥoni in particular. B. Ta'anit 23a informs us that Ḥoni was overwhelmed by the huge burst of rainfall that erupted in the wake of his prayer. In light of the fact that it might have destroyed the world, he tells his worried "disciples": "I have it as a tradition that we may not pray on account of an excess of good. Despite this, bring unto me a bullock for a thanksgiving offering. They brought unto him a bullock for a thanksgiving offering [Rashi: to confess over it] and he laid his two hands on it and said. . . ."[49]

These words are consistent with the opening statement of the Mishnah prefacing Ḥoni's "ritual/act," which stipulates that the rituals connected with the alarm-blowing of the shofar are enacted whenever any calamity is likely to occur in the public domain—with the exception of "an overabundance of rain" (m. Ta'anit 3:8). Since m. Ta'anit makes clear what the ritual procedure entails, it is *a priori* clear that Ḥoni should not have prayed for "an overabundance of rain" but only on account of its shortfall or failure to arrive. According to the Talmud, when the people pleaded with Ḥoni to interfere following the excessive measure of rain, he realized that he must sacrifice a bullock for a sin-offering.[50] In line with the present discussion, Ginzberg should have included these details—and similar ones—in his work in any way he thought fit, due primarily to its association with the story of Elijah. No need exists to speculate how he should have done so. What concerns us here is the fact that he ignored the material entirely.

Ḥoni in Light of Categorized Folktales

One of the prominent scholars to examine the materials discussed here, especially those related to Ḥoni and similar figures, was the late Dov Noy.[51] Even if we disagree with him on certain points, Noy's line of argumentation is a helpful example of methodology applicable to the study of aggadic materials in general. To the best of my understanding, he demonstrates what Ginzberg should have done in order to elevate the value of his compendium beyond its status as an erudite anthology. Noy classifies the "folktale" known as "miraculous rainfall during times of drought by means of prayer" as type 827* in "the index of types in Jewish folktales," placing it under the heading "Prayers of the Morally Perfect (*tamim*)."[52] In my opinion, this category is appropriate to the type of pious people dealt with by Haim Lapin—although Lapin abstained from dealing with the complexity of the stories of Ḥoni and Elijah.[53] Since I have discussed the case of Ḥoni here within my present frame of reference, I bring this discussion to an end with an analysis of the category-framework that Noy adds to it.[54]

Noy classifies six topics as constituting "a prototype of rain-story formulations" (34–36). The fifth topic forms the starting point mentioned in the mishnaic account of Ḥoni and discussed above in the context of the ritual of the "horn-blowing alarm" performed on the occasion of any disastrous visitation upon the community. As noted above, the only exception recognized by the Mishnah is the case of the "overabundance of rain." Noy remarks that although the people initially ask Ḥoni to pray for rain to fall, when they realize "that the miracle is too great and too beneficial" (m. Ta'anit 3.8), Ḥoni "*prays again* to stop it" (35, column B end; emphasis added). Although, in my opinion, this account should be expanded—a task to which I hope to devote myself at some future point—the manner in which Noy presents the case is correct in principle. The Mishnah tells us that Ḥoni first "prayed"—but that "no rain fell." In other words, even Ḥoni's first attempt to do the will of the people, in line with the protocol specified in the Mishnah, fails. In this respect, his decision to apply his alternative capabilities—marking a circle, with all the implications thereof—should have reduced its polemical stance. Shimon ben Shetaḥ had different thoughts on the matter, however, regarding the circle and Ḥoni's unique prayer, as marking his distinction from the community controlled by the sages. In any event, the appeal of the people to Ḥoni to employ his special skills tells an interesting story, one highlighting existential plight versus Rabbinic norms.

In the third section of his article Noy aptly includes a category relating to the "confidence of the *ḥasid* (pious man)." Ḥoni is so sure of his success that he says to those who turn to him for help: "Go and bring in the ovens [on which you are going to roast] the Paschal offerings." Noy rightly draws attention to the fact that the guilelessness of the one performing the wonders (praying) "borders on absolute confidence. He is utterly convinced that his prayer will be heard, accepted, and answered." In Noy's view, this is a natural and legitimate belief (35). The question which must be answered is whether Ḥoni belongs to the category of the "pure and innocent" (in line with Lapin's emphasis on the prerequisites of piety) or to a more complex class, one employing magical protocols. One of the standard categories employed in the field of comparative religion permits us to perceive him as a charismatic figure capable of performing acts beyond the normal capacity of human beings and thereby impacting the community of believers.

In the fourth section Noy addresses the "The Miracle Itself." In Ḥoni's case, however, the miracle that occurs does not do so in the customary sense of the word but in an enhanced form. Miracles occur when God instructs things to move or directly intervenes. Human initiative, on the other hand, is restricted to the realm of magic. The magician performs—by means of uniquely constructed prayers (i.e., adjurations), sacrifices, and other extraordinary means—an act of coercion whose aim is to produce a specific state or circumstance. Next, Noy denotes the "Preparatory Act," in which the guileless person prefaces his prayer with an act whose purpose is to bring about a situation wherein a coercive decree is imposed on heavenly beings.[55] Where Ḥoni is concerned, however, he marks a "circle" in whose middle he stands and says, "Master of the Universe, Thy children have turned to me because they consider me to be a 'son of Thy household'; I swear by Thy great name that I will not move from here until Thou hast mercy upon Thy children."

While, *prima facie,* these words do not invoke any sense of the extraordinary in the mind of the reader, on a closer look they contain elements that deserve attention. In Rabbinic parlance, the term "son of the household (*ben bayit*)" customarily signifies a servant with special, confidential status. The sages rarely designate themselves by this term, particularly in the sense denoted by Ḥoni. Likewise, the swearing of an oath transposes the event to another plane, essentially initiating a magic shift. As a rule, prayers do not contain this element, which introduces a coercive aspect. In other words, Ḥoni utters a prayer that contains an element of adjuration, albeit not in the fully-fledged magic formulation characteristic of the texts known from the Greek magical papyri and similar texts in other languages.[56] This constitutes what Noy classifies as a "Preparatory Act." Pace Goldin, the "Rabbinic" rebuke uttered by Shimon b. Shetaḥ strengthens this interpretation.[57] Comparatively speaking, however, this particular element is absent from the story of Elijah, as well as that of Elisha, as discussed by Noy—although the latter does remark upon the affinities the story demonstrates with magic, stressing that the "preparatory act" "utterly contradicts the element of the prayer that issues from the heart of the contrite person."

Here, it is worth examining Noy's argument that the details in the story of Ḥoni are well forged from the point of view of monotheistic faith. Despite exceptions to the rule, the world of aggadah does not aspire to promote or preserve theological-philosophical tenets such as monotheism and its corollaries. Although in many instances halakhic laws and norms develop into folkloristic customs, in certain cases aggadah contains elements located in territories in which conventional theological and halakhic rulings become blurred. *Mutatis mutandis,* neither theology nor halakhah *a priori* serve the basic traits of folk narratives and/or aggadah. Accordingly, discussions of any associations with the issue of monotheism do not, in my opinion, promote the debate of subjects such as those referred to here. In general, work done in the area of religious studies has demonstrated that what has traditionally been defined as "rational monotheism" can in fact be included amongst ideational and ritual elements, the likes of which are also found in religions that are not monotheistic in the pure theological-philosophical sense.

The "circle" which Ḥoni marks—the enclosed magical territory and, particularly, everything said or done in it—sets him apart from the regular and routine aspects of religious experience, whether that known from the world of aggadah or halakhah.[58] The circle enables the enactment of a "different"—alternative—means that demands skills not common in the religious praxis customarily found amongst the sages of the Mishnah as representatives of the establishment. The magic ring creates a special space that marks a reality closed and guarded against external threats. In this sense, it creates the locale that contributes to the intensification of the power of the "performer," whether evil, or—significantly—the divine. Deeds such as Ḥoni's are to be found in abundance in the literature dealing with Jewish magic and in rituals from other religious cultures.[59]

In order to round off the discussion and establish the link with Ḥoni, I must address here the story of Elisha (2 Kings 3:15–19), which also contains a unique preparatory act, albeit one not intended to bring down rain: "For thus says the Lord: You shall see no wind, you shall see no rain, and yet the riverbed [dry valley] shall be filled with water; and you and your cattle and your pack animals shall drink" (3:17). This incident takes us back to the form of irrigation by way of rivers and streams (Genesis 2) discussed above. It should be noted that Noy's comment regarding the "Preparatory Act" is valid here. Elisha says: "'Now then, get me a musician.' As the musician played, the hand of the Lord came upon him" (3:15).[60] We must also note here that, like Elijah—and the version of the story of Ḥoni given in the Babylonian Talmud—Elisha also offers a sacrifice: "And in the morning, when it was time to present the meal offering, water suddenly came from the direction of Edom and the land was covered by the water" (3:20).

In summary, let me remark that the present discussion concerning Samuel, Elijah, Elisha, and Ḥoni the Circlemaker has suggested interesting lines of correspondence. It is difficult to determine to which type of genre these accounts belong: story, historical report, aggadah, or folk narrative. Whatever the perspective may be, whether synchronic or diachronic, they deserved to be included in such a thematic anthology as *The Legends of the Jews,* which deals with biblical figures. While the stories of Elisha and Ḥoni do not gain the kind of resonance they deserve in Ginzberg's work, the story of Elijah on Mount Carmel is subject to an elaborate aggadic expansion. I have endeavored to demonstrate the sense in which the case of Ḥoni the Circlemaker could have added an illuminating dimension to this expansion. At this concluding point we are reminded of Ginzberg's admonition regarding the inclusion of "the supplemental work of scholars in the products of the popular fancy" (Preface, xi). I hope that my present work—and that of the scholars included in the present volume—fit this elaborative scheme by establishing "a close connection between Scripture and the creations of the popular fancy, to give the latter a firm basis and secure a long term of life for them" (Preface, xi). I should note, however, that Ginzberg does not call the scholarly domain of folklore by its generic name. In my view, the systematic collection of folk narratives, or folktales, possesses its own and unique system of boundary creation. In any event, its widely ranging concepts are the method that justifies the creation of *The Legends of the Jews.*

Notes

This is a considerably revised and enlarged version of a Hebrew article, with the same title, published in *Jewish Studies* 47 (2011). The new version owes a lot to Ms. Liat Keren, who put at my disposal an inspiring initial English translation. I wish also to thank Prof. Galit Hasan-Rokem for her insightful comments that were instrumental in upgrading my argument in this version of the essay. I owe thanks to Professors Eli Yassif and Ishay Rosen-Zvi for their careful reading of the Hebrew version. Their suggestions and comments have significantly contributed to its scholarly qualities. I have done my best to ensure that their efforts have not been in vain. I have also endeavored not to overlap with other contributions in this volume.

1. Yonah Fraenkel has approached this subject from a broad disciplinary angle in *Darkhei ha-aggadah veha-midrash* [The methods

of the aggadah and midrash] (Tel Aviv: Modan, 1991), 553–61. While referring to the work of Louis Ginzberg and arguing—correctly in my opinion—that *The Legends of the Jews* is a *mixtum compositum* of "a most unusual nature" (555), in a chapter entitled "Darkhei ha-aggadah ba-meḥkar" (The methods of the aggadah in research) Fraenkel fails to provide the type of analysis of the work as I am currently undertaking. Let me further remark that in the notes to this essay I have endeavored to refer primarily to recent studies, which contain references to earlier publications. In this context, the reader should be made aware that various issues arising in this essay have been dealt with more comprehensively by Eli Yassif,*The Hebrew Folktale: History, Genre Meaning* (Folklore Studies in Translation), trans. Jacqueline S. Teitelbaum, with foreword by Dan Ben-Amos (Bloomington, Ind.: Indiana University Press 1999). While some points of contact and affinity exist between Yassif's extensive treatment of the subject and the discussion as presented here, Yassif is not concerned with Ginzberg's methodology. Although I frequently concur with his insights, I have found no necessity to turn the reader's attention to every point at which this happens. See also Galit Hasan-Rokem, *Web of Life: Folklore and Midrash in Rabbinic Literature,* trans. Batya Stein (Stanford, Calif.: Stanford University Press, 2000), and the discussion of these two works by Dinah Stein, "'Let the People Go': The 'Folk' and Their 'Lore' as Tropes in the Reconstruction of Rabbinic Culture," *Prooftexts* 29/2 (2009), 206–41. See also Galit Hasan-Rokem, "Did the Rabbis Recognize the Category of Folk Narrative?" *European Journal of Jewish Studies* 3/1 (2009), 19–55.

2. It should be noted that the term "religion" occurs on only a single occasion in Ginzberg's preface (in adjectival form). The terms "popular character," "Rabbinic Judaism," and "legends of the Jews" are generally preferred! See also the following note.
3. In this respect, I shall not enter the discussion as to whether the biblical stories of ancient Israel are reliable from a historical point of view or mere late and tendentious "fiction." The modern trend to read them as the latter treats them as open texts. On this reading, they may be used for a variety of purposes, including the introduction of additional layers of information, which are as para-historical as the biblical stories themselves. During Ginzberg's own lifetime, these hotly debated issues—to which I return—had not yet ignited.
4. I am relating in this article to the first edition of 1910, translated from the German by Henrietta Szold and published in Philadel-

phia by the Jewish Publication Society of America. Any reference to other editions—principally translations or abridgements—would have necessitated an examination of a subject into which I do not wish to be drawn at present.

5. See, further, Louis Ginzberg, "Some Observations on the Attitude of the Synagogue towards the Apocalyptic-Eschatological Writings," *Journal of Biblical Literature* 41/1–2 (1922), 115–36.
6. In this context, we should mention Joshua Levinson, *The Untold Story: Art of the Expanded Biblical Narrative in Rabbinic Midrash* [in Hebrew] (Jerusalem: Magnes Press, 2005), which seeks to demonstrate how the biblical story becomes a rich, multi-faceted narrative in Rabbinic midrashic literature by bridging the conceptual gaps between the biblical source and the various modes of narrative hermeneutics adopted by the sages. In contrast, the present discussion is based on the claim that, in Ginzberg's unique approach, the biblical texts are expanded by aggadic materials that permeate the biblical narrative without exposing the literary seams weaving them together. This point is further elaborated upon below.
7. In this respect, no innovation is visible—in principle—in the literary fashioning of *The Legends of the Jews.* Its commingling of midrashic additions and other material with the biblical text is foreshadowed, for example, in such ancient compositions as *Jubilees* and the *Biblical Antiquities,* both of which form part of the Pseudepigrapha. As I emphasize below, the ordinance in Deuteronomy 4:2—"You shall not add anything to what I command you or take anything away from it"—was abrogated in the Hebrew Bible itself, not to speak of the midrashic literature, including the halakhic midrashim. As a matter of method and principle, it may be noted that Jewish exegesis across the ages—including aggadah, for our purposes—has taken three principal forms: (a) alteration of the biblical text, as exemplified by the apocryphal and pseudepigraphic literature and the Qumran Temple Scroll; (b) exegesis of the text in such a way as to distinguish between the biblical text and the interpretative stance, whether by way of clearly articulated terms of literal or midrashic hermeneutics—as, for example, in the Qumran *pesharim,* the Midrash, and medieval commentaries; and (c) a re-presentation of the content of the biblical text either by way of implementation (as in the halakhah) or by way of its core meaning—as, for example, in the philosophical approach of *The Guide for the Perplexed* or the kabbalistic (or mystical) stance taken by the Zohar and its derived literature. For *Jubilees,* which serves as a model for various modes of biblical exegesis from the

Second Temple period onward, and particularly the editorial problems it presents, deriving or influenced by its tendentious motives, see Michael Segal, *The Book of Jubilees: Rewritten Bible, Redaction, Ideology and Theology* (Leiden: Brill, 2007). See also Vered Noam, *From Qumran to the Rabbinic Revolution: Conceptions of Impurity* [in Hebrew] (Jerusalem: Yad Ben-Zvi, 2010).

8. For an impressive, sharply articulated, and structured study that develops this direction, see James L. Kugel, *Traditions of the Bible: A Guide to the Bible as It Was at the Start of the Common Era* (Cambridge, Mass.: Harvard University Press, 1998), which stresses the various ways of exegeting the Torah during the period closely paralleling the rise of Christianity. Not all the sources cited by Kugel necessarily have a Jewish provenance.
9. To the best of my knowledge, the subject of alternative phrases and textual versions in the Hebrew texts of Scripture and its early translations was first systematically discussed by Shemaryahu Talmon, "Double Readings: A Basic Phenomenon in the Transmission of the Old Testament Text" [in Hebrew] (Ph.D. diss., Hebrew University of Jerusalem, 1956). I am grateful to Mr. Shlomo Goldberg of the National and University Library, Jerusalem, for his efforts in recovering this dissertation from the library archives.
10. For precisely such an endeavor, see Michael Fishbane, *Biblical Interpretation in Ancient Israel* (Oxford: Oxford University Press, 1985).
11. See Ithamar Gruenwald, "The Commentary on 1 Enoch," in *George W.E. Nickelsburg in Perspective: An Ongoing Dialogue of Learning*, ed. Jacob Neusner and Alan J. Avery-Peck (Leiden: Brill, 2003), 395–408.
12. See in particular Ithamar Gruenwald, *Rituals and Ritual Theory in Ancient Israel* (Leiden: Brill, 2003).
13. Space constrains the present discussion and compels me to forgo an in-depth analysis of all the information given in the talmudic sources concerning Ḥoni and to content myself with a discussion of one or two points of interest alone.
14. The index to the English edition of *Legends* contains only three (!) entries for Ḥoni, none of them relating to the subject of rain, which is the center of the ensuing discussion.
15. In addition to biblical and other sources, which I treat below, the heightened concern over the falling of rain in Seder Mo'ed in the Mishnah should be mentioned: "At four seasons of the year the world is judged . . . on the Festival [of Tabernacles] they are judged in regard to water" (m. Rosh Hashanah 1:2); and "the water libation" (m. Sukkah 4:1), the procedure of which is de-

tailed in m. Sukkah 4:9. In fact, m. Ta'anit as a whole deals with crises in regard to the supply of rain, drought, and the ceremonies performed in order to procure the belated falling of rain, special rituals coming into effect in such cases. It is noteworthy that the subject is discussed in Seder Mo'ed ("Times") rather than Seder Zera'im ("Seeds"), the tractate dealing with agricultural and related issues.

16. Here it is proper to note that, while volume 4 of *Legends* contains several chapters devoted to Samuel, Elijah, and Elisha, none of these refer to the calling down of rain. I believe that an awareness of the importance and relevance of the story of Ḥoni would have enriched Ginzberg's discussion of these biblical figures. In this respect, we are required to sharpen our review of Ginzberg's method and performance. Although he mentions Elijah's conflict with the prophets of Baal and Elijah's bringing down of rain (199), he devotes a mere paragraph to these incidents. Furthermore, like the remainder of the texts concerning Elijah in *Legends*, this contains materials that are problematic. At the same time, however, it must be remarked that the Book of Chronicles ignores this episode altogether. We discuss this point later on.
17. For this issue, see—indirectly—Assnat Bartor, *Reading Law as Narrative: A Study in the Casuistic Laws of the Pentateuch* (Atlanta: Society of Biblical Literature, 2010).
18. Itzhak Heinemann, *Darkhei ha-aggadah* (The ways of the aggadah) (Jerusalem: Magnes Press, 1954). Heinemann refers to "creative historiography" and "creative philology." The modern reader cannot ignore this concept, despite the fact that it was hardly in use during the period in which Heinemann wrote his book. His approach falls within the field currently referred to as "cognitive studies" or hermeneutics. I am not embarrassed to admit that such a statement as "the article attributed to Luther . . . notwithstanding the fact that it never issued from his mouth, is 'true' in the highest sense because it describes Luther's mind-set more accurately than lengthy descriptions [= historical facts]" (9), preempted my own initial forays into the field by many years, primarily with respect to the notion of "myth" in the sense I attribute to it elsewhere and in my recent studies. At this juncture, it is also proper to mention Ofra Meir's *The Darshanic Story in Genesis Rabbah* [in Hebrew] (Tel Aviv: Ha-kibbutz ha-Meuchad, 1987), which, in its own way, raises various issues I am addressing in the present framework.
19. When speaking of folklore, Raphael Patai immediately comes to mind. In the context of the materials discussed below, Patai has

dealt with the subject of water, rain, and the rainbow. For my present purposes, however, and the English reader, I find most relevant his study "The Control of Rain in Ancient Palestine: A Study in Comparative Religion," *Hebrew Union College Annual* 14 (1939), 251–86, which analyzes an extensive array of sources, some of which I address here, albeit from a divergent perspective.

20. Since this subject has been extensively studied, I suffice myself here with reference to a recently published volume: Yuval Harari, *Early Jewish Magic: Research, Method, Sources* [in Hebrew] (Jerusalem: Yad Ben-Zvi, 2010), 76, 275, 287. For purposes of comparison with the present study, see Gideon Bohak, *Ancient Jewish Magic: A History* (Cambridge: Cambridge University Press, 2008), whose focus lies primarily on human coercion of the deity, perceiving this to constitute the principal reason behind Shimon b. Shetaḥ's opposition to Ḥoni (53, 345). In contrast, in *Studies in Midrash and Related Literature* (Philadelphia: Jewish Publication Society, 1988), 331–35, "On Ḥoni the Circlemaker: A Demanding Prayer," Judah Goldin argued—contrary to the position he himself had supported, to the effect that Ḥoni was criticized on account of the drawing of the circle, allegedly signaling a magical act—that the story represents an example of a "demanding prayer." In Goldin's opinion, the circle marks a confined area that the petitioner does not leave before his request is granted, the story thus containing no magical implications. While Goldin adduces supporting documents, which, in my view, add an interesting aspect to the customary understanding of the story, I find it difficult to accept his line of argumentation. I return to this point toward the end of this study.
21. For the background of the present discussion, including a detailed analysis of Ḥoni's prayer in light of his standing in the eyes of his Rabbinic colleagues, see Adolf Büchler, *Types of Palestinian Piety from 70 B.C.E. to 70 C.E.: The Ancient Pious Men* (New York: Ktav, 1968), 196–264. It should be noted, however, that detailed and informative as it is, Büchler's discussion does not address the problem I discuss in this paper.
22. A parenthetical question not possessed of any binding nature concerns the status held by stories in which the halakhic statements they contain do not validate themselves in real life. In other words, the ritual component in the material fails to confirm the inevitability of the halakhic norm, because the rites prove to be inefficacious. The legal case discussed thus merely serves as a pretext for the raising of a particular halakhic issue, valid in theory but not in practice. Several cases are referred to in the Babylonian

Talmud to the effect that "This is halakhah but it is not to be followed" (*halakhah ve-ein morin ken*). Put differently, we frequently sense that halakhah indicates a theoretical reality resembling case stories, the latter serving as non-binding exempla. See Ishay Rosen-Zvi, *The Rite That Was Not: Temple, Midrash and Gender in Tractate Sotah* [in Hebrew] (Jerusalem: Magnes Press, 2008).

23. This subject is worthy of a more detailed examination than the present framework permits. See the reference below, note 26.
24. See Haim Lapin, "Rabbis and Public Prayers for Rain in Later Roman Palestine," in *Religion and Politics in the Ancient Near East,* ed. Adele Berlin (Bethesda: University Press of Maryland, 1996), 105–29. Lapin adduces a list of rabbis who, due to their pious deeds and status, successfully prayed for rain (107n.3). He refers briefly to Ḥoni, alluding to two articles devoted to him in note 2. Relevant to the present discussion, though from a different perspective than the one offered here, is Gad Ben-Ami Sarfatti, "Pious Men, Men of Deeds, and the Early Prophets" [in Hebrew], *Tarbiz* 26 (1956–57), 126–53.
25. See also b. Ta'anit 25b, where it is recounted that R. Aqiba prayed—apparently a personal prayer—for rain to fall. The Gemara comments that הוו מרנני רבנן ("the Rabbis were suspiciously critical"), however, indicating their disapproval of his ritual stance.
26. Various studies of this subject are now available, not all of which have been published to date: see Moshe Simon-Shoshan, *Stories of the Law: Narrative Discourse and the Construction of Authority in the Mishnah* (Oxford: Oxford University Press, 2013). My thanks go to Ishay Rosen-Zvi for bringing this work to my attention and to Moshe Simon-Shoshan for his help with additional references.
27. Christian study of the New Testament contains a branch that even today continues to treat this subject, particularly with regard to the Synoptic problem (the relation between the first three Gospels, Matthew, Mark, and Luke).
28. To the best of my knowledge, this trend in relation to aggadic literature was initiated by A. G. Wright, *The Literary Genre Midrash* (New York: Alba House, 1967). In my opinion, it began with the "quest for the historical Jesus." While space prevents me from reviewing the extensive body of literature dealing with this subject, it has recently been the object of a comprehensive examination by Robert Bonfil, *The Family Chronicle of Ahima'az ben Paltiel in a Medieval Jewish Chronicle* (Leiden: Brill, 2009).
29. In this context, see especially my article "Myth and Historical Truth: Can Myths Be Shattered," in *Myth in Judaism* [in Hebrew],

ed. Ithamar Gruenwald and Moshe Idel (Jerusalem: Zalman Shazar Center, 2004), 15–52, which discusses these psychological questions, and the research literature, in the framework of the epistemological study of myth.

30. Here, perhaps, is the place to reemphasize the fact that, with respect to the essential subject, this article takes a different direction to that followed by Galit Hasan-Rokem in *Web of Life* and Eli Yassif in *The Hebrew Folktale.* See above, note 1.
31. We have already referred to the fact that in his preface to Genesis (1:11), Ginzberg raises an interesting point with respect to the issue under discussion here, suggesting that an important part of the modern study of aggadah is to make a "clean separation between the original elements [the Hebrew Bible] and the later learned additions." The question must be asked, however: Does aggadah fall within the framework of "learned additions"? As long as this division is not maintained, Ginzberg argues, it is impossible "to write out the Biblical legends of the Jews without including the supplemental work of scholars in the products of the popular fancy." See further below.
32. Cf. Zechariah 14:16 and Nehemiah 8:16—which speak of the booths built, among other places, "in the square of the Water Gate"—with Nehemiah 3:26 and m. Rosh Hashanah. 1:2; et al.
33. See Ginzberg, *Legends* 1:221. Cf. b. Sanhedrin 97a.
34. See Gruenwald, *Rituals and Ritual Theory in Ancient Israel,* 40–93.
35. Moshe Weinfeld, *Deuteronomy and the Deuteronomic School* (Oxford: Clarendon Press, 1972), 59–157, aptly links the blessing-cursing alternatives with the treaty/covenant pattern modeled on the Mesopotamian monarch's relationship with the vassals to whom he granted agricultural land.
36. See Moshe Simon-Shoshan, ""The Story of Honi Ha-Me'agel in Mishnah Taanit 3:8: A Case Study in the Art of Mishnaic Narrative," *Jerusalem Studies in Hebrew Literature* 26, (2013), 1–20, which also relates to the extensive scholarly literature on the subject. My thanks to Moshe Simon-Shoshan for permitting me to read this article prior to its publication. In contrast to Simon-Shoshan's paper, which adopts a broadly based literary approach, my focus herein lies on the ritual dimension of the "act" or "deed" in Tannaitic literature.
37. In a footnote in his article cited above in note 24, Haim Lapin refers to Tannaim (the Rabbinic sages of the mishnaic period) who prayed for rain to fall, although he focuses his attention on Palestinian pious figures who were not necessarily Rabbis. Despite its fascinating character, his discussion fails to perceive the key factors in the shaping of prominent personalities belonging to the liminal territory constituting the difference between "scholars"

and "popular" figures. Likewise, he does not elucidate the possible link with the story of Elijah and the other biblical figures referred to above, thus missing the crucial point of the cross-references between the biblical materials and the relevant parallels in later texts. I consider this recognition vital for a comprehensive assessment of Ginzberg's work, such as I am attempting herein.

38. Parenthetically, it should be noted that Ḥoni's epithet—"Circlemaker"—has caused several people who have studied the subject some wonder. Despite the fact that other figures brought down rain—such as R. Ḥaninah b. Dosa (see Hasan-Rokem, "Did the Rabbis Recognize the Category of Folk Narrative?")—he appears to constitute a special case. It is interesting that the formulation in t. Ta'anit (Saul Lieberman, *Tosefa Mo'ed*, 334) contains slight variations, which in my view modify the magical elements of the story by referring to "a [certain, unnamed] pious man" (*hasid*) rather than to "Ḥoni the Circlemaker." Lieberman argues—in my opinion rather arbitrarily—that "we have here *another similar act*" (*Tosefta Kifshuta, Ta'anyot,* 1096; emphasis added). Whatever the case might be in this regard, b. Ta'anit 23a, which brings the story with significant changes and refers to Ḥoni by way of his unique epithet, emphasizes his outstanding erudition in halakhic Torah study: "Whenever [Ḥoni] came to the Beth Ha-Midrash he would resolve for the scholars any difficult issue they faced." Shimon b. Shetaḥ's weighty reservations regarding Ḥoni (m. Ta'anit 3:8–9) therefore represent an alternative attitude that the Babylonian Talmud seeks to replace. We may conjecture that the incident as related in the Tosefta account takes an intermediate line, endeavoring to transpose the scene into the world of the *hasidim,* known for their ability to perform miracles: see Ithamar Gruenwald, "Ma efshar lilmod me-ha-typologia shel ha-tnuot ha-ḥasidyot be-Yisrael al tnu'ot eleh 'atzman ve-'al dat Yisrael bi-khlal?" (What can we learn from the typology of the groups of ḥasidim in Israel about these movements and about Judaism in general?), in *Studies in Talmudic and Midrashic Literature in Memory of Tirzah Lifshitz,* ed. Moshe Bar-Asher, Joshua Levinson, and Berachyahu Lifshitz (Jerusalem: Bialik Institute, 2005), 113–26. The issue discussed there (119) should be supplemented by the present article. At any rate, y. Ta'anit 3, 9 (66d) mentions Ḥoni without any reservations. See also Berachyahu Lifshitz's extensive treatment in "'Aggadah' and Its Role in the History of the Oral Law (*Torah she-be'al peh*)" [in Hebrew], *Annual of the Institute for Research in Jewish Law* 22 (2001–2004), 233–328.

39. Attention should be drawn to Jacob Milgrom, *Numbers* (Philadelphia: Jewish Publication Society, 1990), 460–62 ("The Song of the Well").

40. Compare also the desalination of the bitter water (Exodus 15:23f). Other similar cases occur in Scripture. In this context, Deuteronomy 32:13 should also be noted: "He fed him with honey from the crag (*sela*), and oil from the flinty rock (*tsur*)." See, in contrast, Psalm 105:41: "He opened a rock (*tsur*) so that water gushed forth." Cf. Psalm 78:20, which employs similar language. The descriptive discrepancy between the rock and the well is already noted in t. Sukkah 3:11, which endeavors to solve the problem by forging a reality in which the well resembles an "itinerant" rock that follows the people of Israel during their years of wandering in the desert. Lieberman in his *Tosefta Kifshuta* (876) somewhat whimsically concludes: "It is a simple matter that all the *derashot* [homiletic utterances] are the same, as is usual in the aggadah."
41. It is thus possible to conjecture that the verses in Numbers allude to the water Moses drew from the rock as described in Exodus.
42. Ginzberg deals with the material from Exodus by expanding the narrative to include matters given in direct speech (!) not mentioned in the Torah—all under the heading "Miriam's Well" (3:50–54). According to the Gemara (b. Ta'anit 9a), the well accompanied the Israelites for forty years in the wilderness, until Miriam's death, when it ceased to gush. The immediately following passage (Numbers 20:2) recounts the story of the renewing of the emission of water from the rock. Ginzberg brings all this material in one volume (3:307–11) under the heading "The Waters of Meribah"—together with an excursus, whose sources, as is the case in so many other places, are difficult to ascertain.
43. While the last three are known to us from other biblical texts, Rashi and Ibn Ezra identify the Pishon with the river of Egypt—the Nile.
44. Cf. b. Ta'anit 2a. Elijah is considered a rare exception: cf. Tanḥuma, Buber Va-yetse no. 16.
45. See similarly the blessings and curses given in Leviticus 26, especially vv. 3, 14, and 27.
46. In this respect, the status of this circumstance is surprising, especially since the content of the desired prayer is only referred to in general terms. We might have expected the description of the Temple's dedication to have included a reference to the efficacy of the sacrifices rather than that of prayer. For this reason some scholars have assumed that this case conceals a polemical stance (also attested in the words of the classical prophets) against the sacrificial cult of the Temple. Only at the very end of the lengthy prayer does Solomon conclude the ceremonial events with the offering of sacrifices, over the prescribed period of seven days (see Leviticus 8:33). While the Book of Kings devotes a mere three ex-

plicit verses to this event (1 Kings 8:42–44), the parallel in Chronicles is more liberal, providing us with seven verses (2 Chronicles 1:1–7). It should also be noted in this connection that the Chronicler's version of Solomon's prayer assumes a correspondence between the shutting up of heaven and sin and the renewal of rain and penitential prayer, respectively (2 Chronicles 6:26–27).

47. This verse recalls that dealing with Passover in 2 Kings 23:22: "Now the Passover sacrifice had not been offered in that manner in the days of the chieftains who ruled Israel, or during the days of the kings of Israel and the kings of Judah." This is not the place to discuss in detail the significance of these statements.
48. Since prophets are not included in Ginzberg's programmatic layout, he does not bring the crucial material found in Zechariah.
49. One should note that Ḥoni does not ask for a penitential bullock but one "for a thanksgiving offering (פר הודאה)." A similar offering is mentioned in b. Yoma 50a (end), although it should be noted that the printed editions read בפר הודאה. The textual witnesses (two manuscripts) read פר הודאה. The discussion therein vacillates with regard to whether this bullock should be considered a public or individual sacrifice. The comparison given with the bullock of the Day of Atonement ultimately clarifies the point: it is regarded as constituting a public sacrifice.
50. The sacrificial act is not specifically mentioned, however!
51. See Dov Noy, "Tefilat ha-tamim moridah geshamim" [The prayer of the righteous brings down rain]," *Maḥanayim* 51 (1961), 34–45. My thanks go to Galit Hasan-Rokem for bringing this article to my attention.
52. In support of Noy's thesis we can bring examples of figures who did not succeed in making rain fall, the sages noting the reason for such failure. Thus, for example, R. Yose bey R. Bun (R. Yose of the house of R. Abin) asserts that Ḥoni did not bring rain down on 20 Nisan because "he did not come with humility" (y. Ta'anit 3, 9, 16b).
53. See Lapin, "Rabbis and Public Prayers for Rain in Later Roman Palestine."
54. Ibid. I have already remarked that a slightly different discussion can be found in Bohak, *Ancient Jewish Magic,* 53.
55. In Rabbinic literature, the Hebrew term derives from *g-z-r,* a root that denotes divine decrees or a humanly solicited—and hence magical—enforcement of will.
56. The essence of the oath lies in the term "great name" (שם גדול). The qualifier הגדול, or in Aramaic רבא (Greek μεγάλη), served in various connections in magic and those forms of ancient mysticism deriving from it.

57. See above, note 21.
58. On the contrary, if we rely on the witness of Josephus (*Antiquities* 14.22–24), Ḥoni refrains from cursing Aristobulus II at Hyrcanos II's instigation and is thus stoned by the crowd! See Bohak, *Ancient Jewish Magic,* 128.
59. See above, note 20. See further the broad discussion in Nikki Bado-Fralick, *Coming to the Edge of the Circle: A Wiccan Initiation Ritual* (Oxford: Oxford University Press, 2005). Bado-Fralick deals with magical texts relating to initiation into groups practicing unique magical forms of activity in modern-day America, the magical circle comprising a constitutive feature in these rituals. As increasingly common in anthropological research dealing with magic rituals, Bado-Fralick is herself a "scholar-practitioner" versed in both fields, thereby allowing practice to be put in the service of research and providing a theoretical and insider's view of the subject matter alike.
60. Music is often connected with the prophetic spirit, although its effects can be counterproductive—as in the case of David playing for King Saul (1 Samuel 18:10).

7

Aggadah in "Higher Unity"

The German Manuscript of *The Legends of the Jews*

Johannes Sabel

The Legends of the Jews is unanimously held to be an epoch-making work. It is marked not only by monumentality on various levels, but also by totality. Consisting of seven volumes, the work is meant, as Ginzberg states in the German manuscript, to "represent all of the Jewish legends, insofar as they touch upon biblical figures and events, as faithfully and completely as possible, according to the original sources."[1] The 1998 paperback reprint edition—coming almost ninety years after the publication of the first volume—announces that this aim has been achieved: Ginzberg has reproduced the aggadic material "completely, accurately, and vividly."[2] The reviews sound a similar note: "From the vast and scattered mass of haggadic material, Ginzberg has selected all the stories that concern biblical events and characters."[3] To this day the two volumes containing the annotations are the standard reference work for locating rabbinic, pseudepigraphical, apocryphal, Hellenistic, patristic, and other sources dealing with biblical matters. The high esteem in which *Legends* has been held from the start also becomes apparent when one considers that immediately after the publication of the first volume, there were attempts to publish *Legends* in German.[4] Ginzberg's former teacher in Strasbourg, the orientalist Theodor Nöldeke, proposed a German edition as early as 1910.[5] In September 1933, Martin Buber directed Moritz Spitzer, secretary of the Schocken publishing house, to ask Ginzberg whether he would be willing to hand in his original manuscript so that a German edition might also be prepared.[6]

This instant classic of traditional Jewish storytelling is among the very first modern attempts to collect and narrate the aggadic tradition as related to biblical matters. At the same time, it is also the completion of said task. A similar project has never since been undertaken, and even adding to, or merely checking, the sources seems to be an impossible project; 38,000 references, leading in part to the most obscure and inaccessible texts, cannot be revised. The work as well as the author have, according to James Kugel, taken on a "legendary" status.[7] Both have thus metaphorically been elevated to the realm of the supernatural events with which *The Legends of the Jews* is concerned.

Apart from the sheer number and comprehensiveness of the cited sources, the totality suggested by *Legends* also has a more important, literary reason: Ginzberg's retelling harmonizes the stories, and the diverse, polyphonic accounts are combined to form one grand narrative. The foreword to the German manuscript explicitly states this intention: "differing versions of one and the same legend" have been "dissolved into higher unity" (German manuscript [henceforth *mL*], 1:7).[8]

However, the characteristics of unification are only part of the story—there is an opposing account, straight from the "workshop" and the "source" of *Legends of the Jews.* For the most part, the features described above refer to a later and, if you will, derivative text: the American edition, an English translation by Henrietta Szold and Paul Radin, that deviates from the German manuscript in many respects (only the volumes containing the annotations were translated by Ginzberg himself). If we consider research on Ginzberg, it is a more than surprising fact that the original text of *Legends,* the German manuscript written by Ginzberg himself, has never been scrutinized. Until well into 2009, one hundred years after the publication of the first volume, the manuscript had not even been archived properly, and accordingly is in less than satisfactory shape. It seems as if the English edition, with all the superlatives it attracts, has outshone its very source.

In spite of these circumstances, it is a valid and accepted stance to consider the edited and published text when it comes to evaluating and contextualizing any given work. With this background in mind, it can be said that, in the future, one will have to differentiate between two texts of *Legends*—the English one, reflecting the language of Szold and Radin (this claim shall be proved later on), and the German one, penned by Ginzberg himself.

When analyzing the "work in progress" of *Legends,* two lines of inquiry must be distinguished. One interrogates the external conditions of its composition, including Ginzberg's personal situation during his first years in the United States and his association with the Jewish Publication Society (JPS) and Henrietta Szold, both the secretary of said society and Ginzberg's most intimate confidante. The second line of inquiry is concerned with the writing process of the first four volumes, the composition of the two annotation volumes, and lastly the final index volume, created without Ginzberg's involvement. In this essay I discuss the German manuscript and the writing process as far as it can be reconstructed. Not only has the manuscript never been studied before, but also, and more importantly, it allows us to gain an understanding of the dynamic and heterogeneous composition of *Legends.*

Notwithstanding the emphasis this article places on the writing process, the following account sheds at least some light on the institutional framework of *Legends.* The scholarly core of *Legends,* the two annotation volumes, drove two translators to despair, so that Ginzberg eventually had to translate them himself. The proceedings of a meeting of the JPS publishing committee on May 7, 1916, state that the annotations for the first and second volumes were approaching completion, and that Dr. Julius H. Greenstone was to be commissioned to translate the manuscript of the annotation volumes.[9] On May 23, Greenstone accepted the job.[10] As it turns out, the annotations had not progressed as far as had been assumed earlier. On November 5, 1916, Ginzberg reported at a JPS meeting that "nearly all the notes to his four volumes of the *Legends of the Jews* were now ready and that he hoped to deliver the manuscript by December 16."[11] Yet only on April 1, 1917, did the secretary of the JPS report that he had received the annotations and had passed them on to Greenstone.[12] On May 6, roughly one year after engaging Greenstone, the proceedings state: "The Secretary reported that Dr. Julius Greenstone, to whom was assigned the translation of the notes and the preparation of the index to the *Legends of the Jews,* had, after examining the manuscript, declined to do the work because he found it difficult to decipher the cursive hand of the author."[13] This is a surprising turn of events, especially because Greenstone's explanation is not convincing at all. All of the *Legends* manuscript is written in an easily legible hand, and the annotation volumes are no exception.

After a sample translation by Dr. Joseph Medoff, based on part of the annotations, had been judged sufficient, the JPS committee decided that he should translate the annotations instead of Greenstone.[14] In October 1918, in order to check on Medoff's progress, the committee demanded one hundred pages of what he had translated thus far.[15] But there was a sudden reversal once again. The committee proceedings of January 5, 1919, state the following:

> Under date of January 3, 1919, Dr. Louis Ginzberg wrote that after examining a part of Dr. Medoff's translation of his notes he became fairly convinced that the translator's knowledge of German as well as his acquaintance with the subject matter was entirely inadequate for purpose of publication. The Committee directed the Secretary to write to Dr. Medoff to the effect that the translation prepared by him was not deemed satisfactory by the author and that he should discontinue further work on the manuscript.[16]

A month later, the "list of agenda" for another JPS meeting laconically states: "Translator wanted."[17] After yet another month, it was decided that Ginzberg should translate the annotations himself.[18] The proceedings then fall silent, and there is no further news until November 1924: "The notes to the *Legends of the Jews,* volumes I and II, are now in plates."[19] In 1925, nine years after the first attempt to translate the annotations, the first of the two volumes was published. The index volume has a similarly long, drawn-out story—after two failures, Boaz Cohen took over, and he completed the task in 1938.

It is hard to find the actual reasons for these conspicuous delays. At least in the case of the two annotation volumes, it may be assumed that Ginzberg held to an especially high standard because these volumes were meant to showcase the scholarly quality and completeness of *Legends* for a professional audience. The process of composition and translation shows—in its external, institutional, and organizational contexts—that the project of a "complete" collection bordered on failure at the exact point where this completeness was to be demonstrated.

The same tension also accompanied the actual writing of the text. The German manuscript shows that, as in the case of the annotations, here, too, the very act of translation was a crucial and precarious one for Ginzberg. Studying it makes the complex work on the material, as well as the significant deviations in comparison to the English text, become apparent.

Selection and Synthesis: Working on Traditions

The German manuscript is marked by changes, some of which are extensive. Deletions, corrections, and insertions are typical of writing processes in general. Critical editions try to give an account of these changes because they offer an insight into the genesis of the text; that is, alternative readings to the edited text which is the final product of the whole process. These allow the reader to have insight into the mental and textual processes of composition that have led to the result. In the case of *Legends,* these changes are particularly important: they make it possible to trace Ginzberg's attempts at selecting and synthesizing multifarious traditions.

In order to show this, I discuss an exemplary passage taken from the chapter on "Creation" in the first volume. Leviathan is described as one of the beings that, according to Rabbinic tradition, was created on the fifth day of creation:[20]

> Der Leviathan ist ein solch' Ungeheuer, dass (es) all das Wasser das ~~im~~ (vom) Jordan ~~während eines Jahres~~ (ins Meer) fliesst (zur Stillung seines Durstes braucht) ~~nicht mal dazu ausreicht die Kehle desselben zu benetzen, wesswegen Gott aus dem Paradiese einen Fluss hervorkommen lässt, der das Ungeheuer mit Wasser versieht.~~[119]

When compared to the annotations, this deletion shows how Ginzberg dealt with the Leviathan and Behemoth traditions and attempted to produce a single narrative. Rather than a spontaneous change, it seems to be a correction made in retrospect. This impression is further consolidated by the revisions of note 119. The first version says:

> *Pesikta,* Buber VI, 58a, *Pesikta R.* XVI, 81a, *Lev. R.* XXII gegen Ende; ~~nach~~ *Bava Batra* 74b ~~trinkt der Leviathan das Jordan-water nachdem dieser Fluss sich ins Meer ergossen hat.~~ vgl. weiter ~~unten~~ unten Note . . .[21]

Another version that has not been crossed out supposedly succeeded the first: "*B. Bat.* 74b; etwas verschieden in den palästinensischen Midrashim, *PK.* VI, 58a und (Parallelstellen)."[22] Finally, this is the version on which the English rendering of the note is based:

> *Bava Batra* 74b. ~~*Pinhas 12.*~~ Die Midrashim (*PK.* VI, 58; *PR.* XVI, 81a; *WR* XXVII XII, 9; *BaR* XXI, 18; *Tan. Pinhas* 12) schildern noch mit grelleren Farben den gewaltigen Bedarf des ~~Leviathan~~ (*Behemot*) an Wasser und citieren eine Ansicht, wonach aus dem Paradies täglich ein Fluss ausströmt für den Durst dieses Ungeheuers. Vgl. N. 142.[23]

In the process of composition, three unresolved issues become apparent. First, there is the central question of attributing the various elements to the Leviathan or the Behemoth myths. Second, it has to be decided which aspects of the tradition should be taken up in the main text and which should be given in the notes. Lastly, there is the question of how thoroughly the sources should be documented.

The first, deleted version of the main text provides a narrative that is, strictly speaking, part of the Behemoth myth: the wetting of the mouth and the creation of the river so that—it is mistakenly said—Leviathan might quench his thirst. The corresponding, and likewise deleted, first draft of the footnote furnishes this main text with a description of Leviathan drinking the water of the Jordan that has flowed into the sea. In terms of the Rabbinic tradition on this topic, this is equally wrong. The second version of the note, which has not been crossed out, does not feature this addition and is also much shorter: it only mentions the two main sources, Baba Batra and Pesikta de-Rab Kahana. In the third version, which provides the basis for the English translation, Ginzberg finally corrects the attribution of the various elements, also correcting the main text. His rendering of both now conforms to the tradition as it is provided in the main midrashic source, Pesikta de-Rab Kahana: Behemoth, not Leviathan, drinks the water of the river that flows out of paradise. It is striking that Ginzberg, after having corrected his error, crosses out the interesting, vivid description of Behemoth's thirst. As the Pesikta de-Rab Kahana, Ginzberg's source, has it:

> And the Rabbis said: He makes a single draught of all [the water] that the Jordan brings down in twelve months. And the proof? The verse, "He is confident, because the Jordan rushes forth to his mouth" (Job 40:23). *And yet this draught is only enough to moisten the Behemoth's mouth.* R. Huna said in the name of R. Jose: There is not even enough to moisten his mouth. Then where does he drink from? [R. Jose thereupon quoted the answer of] R. Simeon ben Yoḥai: "Out of Eden there goes forth a river" (Genesis 2:10) whose name is Yubal . . . and from its limitless waters he drinks.[24]

In this particular section, Ginzberg violated his own claim to a comprehensive treatment, as stated in the foreword, and went against his declared method of providing variants and "marginal" details in other contexts or in the notes. Since the main text deals with Leviathan, he could have given in the corresponding note the description of how the Jordan barely carries enough water to wet the mouth of Behemoth. Yet another and possibly the best option would have been to provide this detail as part of the narrative dealing with the sixth day of creation on which, as tradition has it, Behemoth is created. However, Ginzberg eliminated this particular element altogether and only mentions the last bit of the source, the immeasurable supply of water carried by the river flowing out of Eden that is able to quench Behemoth's thirst. This detail is actually repeated in the succeeding chapter on the sixth day of creation.[25]

One can only speculate on Ginzberg's reasons for wholly discarding the narrative detail concerning Behemoth and the Jordan. It may be that the desire to deliver a "smooth presentation without any irregularities" (*mL*, "Foreword," 1:7) overruled the objective of a comprehensive representation. This serves to confirm the thesis that between Ginzberg's goal—a well-rounded, complete, and homogeneous narrative—and the actual process of composition, there is a significant tension that has left its traces in the manuscript. In addition, the highly complex process of composition has come to the fore: here we see how, starting with an erroneous rendition, Ginzberg eventually arrived at the corrected, selective, and completely revised text for which the annotation had to be changed no fewer than three times.

The Language of "Dispersed" Traditions: Code-Switching in the German Manuscript

Another peculiarity hinted at in the passage discussed above, which is taken from the chapter on the fifth day of creation, is the phenomenon of code-switching. One of the crossed-out phrases reads: "trinkt der Leviathan das *Jordanwater*" (emphasis mine; see n. 21). In the process of writing, the English "water" seems to have sneaked into the German text. There is another example, however, which has not been crossed out: "Die fünfte *Earth*gattung, 'Arka' genannt ist genau in derselben Weise von der sechsten getrennt wie die sechste von der siebenten" (emphasis mine).[26] In both cases, these instances of sudden code-switching are involuntary and unintentional. Nevertheless, they fit in well with the overall profile of the first and second volumes. Apparently, when he first began his project (that is, while writing the first two volumes), Ginzberg was ambivalent concerning the proper language in which to compose his manuscript.[27] In addition to extended passages written in English ranging between two and four manuscript pages, there are a number of spontaneous but slightly longer English bits of text interspersed among the German:

> Die Hölle ist in sieben Abteilungen eingeteilt, einer unter der anderen. Die oberste ist "Sheol," the height thereof is 300 years' journey and the width 300 years' journey and its length 300 years journey.[28]

As with the first two examples, the flow of the text is not interrupted. But due to the length of these passages, it seems likely that they are intentional.

Ginzberg's use of the German language itself completes the impression. Ginzberg's German is marked by many irregularities that cannot be put down to "historical" spellings and are thus outright mistakes. Throughout the text, there is an uncertainty regarding the use of double consonants. Examples include *kamm* instead of *kam* ("came") (*mL,* "Moses," 3:124); or the other way around, *Flage* instead of *Flagge* ("flag") (*mL,* "Moses," 3:172). The conjunction *dass* ("that") is often spelled with only one "s." The inappropriate use of double "s" is problematic as well; hence the consistent use of *wesswegen* instead of *weswegen* ("because of which") (*mL,* "Creation," 1:41). Also, "ie" and "i" pose problems to Ginzberg: *erwiedert* appears instead of *erwidert* ("replied") (*mL,* "Moses," 3:186), and *giebt* instead of *gibt* ("gives") (*mL,* "Creation," 1:35). There are even uncertainties regarding grammar and syntax:

> Ferner pflegte die Lade das Zeichen zum Aufbruch geben in dem sie sich in die Höhe schwang[703] und dann vor das Lager rasch herzog. . . . Kaum dass sie [die Israeliten] vom Sinai sich entfernt hatten als dass sie auch ihr früheren sündhaften Leben(swandel) dass sie für einige Zeit abgelegt hatten von neuem zu führen bega(nnen).[29]

It is no coincidence that this passage is taken from a later volume, the third. As time and the manuscript progressed, there were more and more syntactical mistakes. Obviously, during the long years of his stay in the United States, Ginzberg was slowly losing his German.

When we consider this aspect of Ginzberg's use of language in the German manuscript of *Legends,* in comparison to the smooth English version, a specific and important condition of his writing becomes apparent. In the beginning, there was notable indecision, resulting in code-switching between German and English. In the later volumes, Ginzberg settled on German as the language of composition, but his skills steadily declined and mistakes abound. The context in which the *Legends* were being written is thus caused, characterized, and conditioned by diaspora. The linguistic homogeneity of the English *Legends,* the source material of which was composed in a vast array of different languages, is not achieved in Ginzberg's own manuscript. To put it another way, the linguistically "dispersed" position of the material is reflected in the linguistically "dispersed" situation of the author. Between his native Yiddish, German, the language of his studies, and English, his professional language, he was unable to find a linguistic home. This was Ginzberg's situation of writing in diaspora.

English Reworkings: Differences between the German Manuscript and the English Edition

Even the English passages of Ginzberg's manuscript have been "translated"; in the American edition, they differ from the manuscript in many cases. Indeed, it seems to have been a significantly altered version of Ginzberg's original, revised by Szold and then Radin, that was eventually published. There is no way to tell how strongly Ginzberg was involved in the production of the English version. In the following example from the "Creation" section, the differences are highlighted:

manuscript (mL)	***English Edition***
And they undergo	And they undergo
Three	**Four**
Transformations	Transformations
	every day,
passing through	passing through
Three	**Four**
states. In the first the righteous is changed into a child. He enters the division for children, and tastes the joy of childhood. Then he is changed into a youth, and enters the division for the youths, with whom he enjoys the delights of youth.	states. In the first the righteous is changed into a child. He enters the division of children, and tastes the joy of childhood. Then he is changed into a youth, and enters the division for the youths, with whom he enjoys the delights of youth.
	Next he becomes an adult, in the prime of life, and he enters the division of men, and enjoys the pleasures of manhood.
Then for the last time	**Finally,**
he is changed into an old man, he enters the (division for) the old, and enjoys the pleasures of ~~the old~~ (~~old~~) (age).[1]	he is changed into an old man, he enters the division for the old, and enjoys the pleasures of age.[2]

1 *mL*, "Creation," 1:18<N>19. 2 English ed. (1947), 1:20.

A comparison of the German foreword and the English preface to the first volume sheds light on these differences. Often, the German text is more succinct, and there is a subtle but significant difference of emphasis in the statement of objectives that accounts for this circumstance. When Ginzberg explains his narrative agenda of distributing individual motifs across various parts of his *magnum opus,* he states: "[M]ein Bestreben war eine glatte von Unebenheiten freie Darstellung zu geben."[30] The corresponding passage in the English preface says: "My aim [is] to give a smooth presentation of the matter, with as few interruptions to the course of the narrative as possible" (English ed., 1:xiv). Here, both the generality and the determination of Ginzberg's original statement are weakened. The aim of the German manuscript is to give "a smooth presentation *without any* irregularities," whereas the English text is satisfied with "*as few* interruptions to the course of the narrative *as possible*" (emphasis mine).

When Ginzberg mentions the volumes of *Legends* planned for the future, there is another difference that consolidates this impression. On the one hand, the German manuscript says the following: "Da beinah das ganze Werk in den Händen des Druckers ist, so wird wohl das Ganze noch innerhalb dieses Jahres erscheinen."[31] On the other hand, the English version refrains from giving any precise information. In contrast to the German original, there is some ostentatious formulating that pushes the date of publication into a vague, and possibly distant, future: "As the first three volumes are in the hands of the printer almost in their entirety, I venture to express the hope that the whole work will appear within measurable time, the parts following each other in short intervals" (English ed., 1:xv).

The preface of the English edition ends with this disheartened gesture. From the composition of the German text through to the finalized English translation, the anticipation of the work's completion seems to have waned: the last lines of the German foreword sound much more enthusiastic. They suggest other issues that I do not discuss here, but they show, once more, the transformations the text had undergone on various levels, including a very personal one:

> Es ist mir eine angenehme Pflicht an dieser Stelle Fräulein Henriette Szold meinen innigsten Dank auszusprechen, nicht

> allein für die meisterhafte Übersetzung, sondern auch für die vielen ~~Verbesserungen des~~ Vorschläge mit Bezug auf Form und Inhalt des Buches, die demselben von grossem Werth waren.[32]

"Folktales," "Legends," or "Sacred Legends" of the Jews: The Question of Genre

In considering the foreword, where Ginzberg explains his method and agenda, the question of genre is of import. James Kugel declares this to be the crucial issue for scholarly engagement with *Legends.* In the German, there is a clear distinction between *Sage* (legend) and *Legende* ("sacred legend"; strictly speaking, the account of a saint's life), but both terms are usually translated into English as "legend." Based on the English edition, it is impossible to decide whether Ginzberg has written *The Legends of the Jews* or *The Sacred Legends of the Jews.* Notwithstanding Kugel's assertion, discussing the question of genre only with regard to the English text will not lead very far. Nevertheless, from the point of view of literary history, the answer to said question has far-reaching consequences for the role assigned to *Legends.*

The issue comes to seem even more important when we realize that Ginzberg has an understanding of these terms that is, at first glance, surprising. The relevant sentence, however, has not become part of the English translation. Ginzberg talks about "the Jewish legend or, to use *a more comprehensive term,* the Jewish sacred legend."[33] Ranking the terms in this order is more than astonishing, since it contradicts the classical understanding.[34] In the classic scholarly discussions, as well as in the contemporary academic context of the writing of *Legends,* the legend (*Sage*) is clearly conceived as being the more comprehensive generic category than the sacred legend (*Legende*).[35]

The definitions provided by the Brothers Grimm in their studies, especially their *Deutsche Sagen* (1816/18), Jacob Grimm's *Deutsche Mythologie* (1835), and their letters, are summarized in their *Deutsches Wörterbuch* (1854–1960). The *Sage,* according to them, is able to "touch upon everything to which a people has a mental claim, heavenly or earthly," whereas the *Legende* is more narrowly "a tale of the life of saints." They adhered almost literally to the definition put forward by Johann Gottfried Herder in his essay "Über die Legende" (1797).[36] In his lecture series, "Sagengeschichte der germanischen und romanischen Völker" (1830/31), Ludwig Uhland provided a more generous definition of the *Sage:*[37] "Der Sagengeschichte in unserem Sinne fallen alle Überlieferungen anheim, welche das Leben der Völker, in göttlichen und menschlichen Beziehungen zurückspiegeln."[38] The Hebrew Bible scholar Hermann Gunkel also defined the legend as an umbrella term:

> Sage ist—das Wort wird hier in keinem anderen Sinne als dem allgemein anerkannten gebraucht—volkstümliche, altüberlieferte, poetische Erzählung, die Personen oder Ereignisse der Vergangenheit behandelt.[39]

Finally, in a letter mentioned above, Martin Buber contrasted the proposed German edition of *The Legends of the Jews* to the American one and suggested the title *Sagen der Bibel* (*Legends of the Bible*).[40]

In his stance on the relationship between legend and sacred legend, Ginzberg seems to oppose both the traditional and the contemporary views. This peculiar twist that sets the German foreword apart from the English text, from which it has been omitted, deserves to be investigated. I therefore attempt here to trace Ginzberg's usage of both terms in the foreword.

In various passages in the foreword to volume 1, *Sage* and *Legende* are used interchangeably. The reason for this lies in the labeling traditionally applied to the Rabbinic corpus: "Sage, Märchen, Legende und Verwandtes führen in der Sprache des nachbiblischen Schriftthums den gemeinsamen Namen Haggadah."[41] Aggadah is understood as the superordinate category that also encompasses legend, sacred legend, and folktale. At the same time, the listing of these terms makes it clear that there are differences between them—when trying to show the inclusive nature of the aggadah, a listing of synonymous terms for identical genres would be rather pointless.

Regarding Ginzberg's usage of the term *Sage,* in most cases it is used to refer to material for narratives, "raw material," if you will. Ginzberg often talks about *Sagenstoff* (the "matter" of legends); the terms *Sage* (legend) and *Sagenkreis* (cycle of legends) are used less often. According to this understanding, *Volkssage* (folk legend) designates the original form of a collectively authored narrative. The folk legend is that which has existed prior to another kind of record, or stage of adaptation, into which the legend is then integrated.

A few examples can illustrate this understanding of *Sage* as involving a pattern of original, collectively authored narrative and its later adaptation. The first two passages come from the foreword (*mL*, 1:2) and were later crossed out: (1) the "personal imprint the aggadists gave the legend"; (2) "in aggadic literature, the original folkloristic creations are for the most part very much overgrown by scholarly ingredients."[42] Third, Ginzberg says that originally the Rabbis were "preachers first and foremost, who were using the legend for didactical purposes, and in most cases they were trying to conform to Scripture the flow of *folk*-fantasies."[43] The fourth and final example is this statement:

> Die Lehrer der Haggadah, die vom Talmud genannten Rabbanan d'Aggadta, waren keine Folkloristen, so dass wir von ihnen eine treue Wiedergabe des Sagenstoffes erwarten können.[44]

According to this conception, the legend (*Sage*) is an original creation of the people, an unrefined, archetypal narrative. By repeatedly stressing the notion of collective authorship, Ginzberg incorporates the classic understanding of the legend as it can be found in Jacob Grimm's essay, "Gedanken wie sich die Sagen zur Poesie und Geschichte verhalte" (1808).[45]

In contrast, Ginzberg associates the sacred legend—*Legende*—with the later stage of adaptation that has been mentioned several times. Ginzberg uses the term when referring to the written sources to which he has access:

> Bei verschiedenen unter sich abweichenden Versionen einer und derselben Legende habe ich ~~häufig~~ ~~manchmal~~ (entweder) nur die eine im Text gegeben während die übrigen in den Noten folgen. . . . Manchmal wiederum sind die verschiedenen untereinander sich widersprechenden Legenden an verschiedenen Orten ~~behandelt~~ gegeben.[46]

Thus, it is the sacred legend that can be presented through a text; it is the readable form of the folk narrative, legend material that has been handed down by tradition. Considering this, it makes sense that Ginzberg speaks of Jewish "Legendenkunde" (the study of sacred legends) instead of "Sagenkunde" (the study of legends). The philologist has access only to the written and adapted form. By the term "*Legende,*" Ginzberg refers to that adapted form of folkloristic modes of expression which has been turned into literature, written down by individuals.

For Ginzberg, what matters most is thus the difference in media that is also apparent in the etymology of both terms. Just as the English noun "tale" is related to the verb "to tell," German *Sage* is derived from *sagen* ("to say") and hints at an oral tradition. It contrasts with the *Legende* as that which has to be read or even read out loud.[47] The *Legende* also alludes to the orally held sermon, which Zunz holds to be the source of the aggadah in general. In sketching a contrast between the legend as a primitive, collective, oral narrative and the sacred legend as a later form of adaption written down by individuals, Ginzberg is not wholly original. Near the end of the nineteenth century, a controversy took place around Wilhelm Bacher's monumental work on the aggadah of the Tannaim and Amoraim.[48] In Ginzberg's manuscript, a succinct statement refers to this: "Von der Haggada der Tannaim und Amoraim ~~zu~~ zu sprechen ist im Grunde genommen (ebenso falsch) als wenn man von den Sagen Shakespears [sic] und ~~Uhlands~~ (Walter Scotts) ~~zu~~ sprechen wollte."[49] By definition, "Legends" cannot be attributed to a single compiler.

Ginzberg defines aggadah by yet another term altogether, namely *Märchen,* in English usually rendered as "folktale," in a way that leads to a further refinement of his understanding of "legend" and "sacred legend": "Märchen, diese unmittelbaren Schöpfungen des Volkes, die in der jüdischen Literatur die Form von heiligen Legenden (häufig) annehmen."[50] Analogous to the legend, the folktale is another folkloristic genre that later on, as it is made into literature, may become a legend. More precisely, these are "sacred" legends, a conception that corresponds to the classical understanding of legend as a narrative concerned with the life of a saint. Since this definition is obviously rooted in Christian and ecclesiastical traditions, its transformation in the foreword must be noted. According to Ginzberg, legends are always connected to the Bible. This is why he also refers to the "*biblical* legend,"[51] whereas there can be no such thing as a biblical folktale. In a way Ginzberg substitutes the life of the holy people, as it is recorded in Scripture, for the lives of the saints. Finally, the adjective "holy" also designates the stage of adaptation and distribution of the folk narrative material: folk legends have become sacred legends because they are now part of the canonical, sacred texts, part of the formative literature of a formerly oral tradition.

The understanding of legend in the foreword is completed by a third definition: The legend is "the appraisal of history on the part of the people."[52] Here, too, the connections to the understanding of legend as the account of a saint's life are apparent. Just as a legendary narrative turns the saint into a saint by means of evaluation and interpretation (beyond any processes of sanctification through the Church), the biblical legend appraises the journey of Israel. In this section, there is another striking difference between the German manuscript and the American edition. In the former, the evaluative function of the legend is attributed to the aggadah as well:

> Die Begebenheiten der alten Geschichte Israels, die man nicht allein studierte sondern jeden Tag (zum) Neuen durchlebte erzeugte das Bedürfnis die biblische Geschichte zu beurteilen. Daher die eigenthümliche Form der Haggadah.[53]

Here Ginzberg equates the aggadah and the sacred legend. This move is suppressed by the English text. The sentence "This explains the peculiar form of the Aggadah" is placed at a later point.[54] In a different context the statement fails to establish the significant connection between the aggadah and the sacred legend that can be found in the German manuscript.

A marginal correction in the German text provides a clue to the literary and the philological point of reference for Ginzberg's distinction between the sacred legend and the legend. In his reference to Shakespeare and Walter Scott, Ginzberg names canonical writers who adapted folkloristic material. From the standpoint of the subject matter of his poems and plays, Uhland actually fits right in, and yet Ginzberg crosses out his name. One explanation might suggest that Ginzberg here bears in mind Uhland's scholarly engagement with folktales (his *Sagengeschichte*) rather than his literary works. In Uhland's eight-volume *Schriften zur Geschichte von Dichtung und Sage* (1865–1873) and *Der Mythus von Thôr nach nordischen Quellen* (1826), he is primarily concerned with the field of folkloristic *literature* (as opposed to the collection of folklore in its preliterary, unedited forms, represented by the efforts of the Brothers Grimm, as well as Achim von Arnim and Clemens Brentano). The deletion lets us assume beyond reasonable doubt that Ginzberg was familiar with Uhland's work, but could also signify that he was unsure about the familiarity of his U.S. audience with it.

This hint leads us to an important precursor of the genre definitions in the foreword of *Legends.* Uhland's "Sagengeschichte der germanischen und romanischen Völker" (1830/31) lays the foundations for Ginzberg's understanding of the two genres, sacred legend and legend. Uhland expands upon the difference in media, the distinction between "telling"—*Sage*—and "reading"—*Legende*—which is taken up by Ginzberg. The strong connection of speech and writing to two different forms of authorship—collective and individual, respectively—are also emphasized by Uhland. During the "life" of "folk literature" (a term that, in Uhland's understanding, corresponds to the legend),[55] the individual is still embedded into the collective production of narratives.[56]

> Allerdings wird die Schrift das Mittel, wodurch der Anteil der Einzelnen an den geistigen Gesammtleben und den gesonderten Richtungen desselben zur Erscheinung kommt und in immer schärferen Individualitäten sich ausprägt. Und so besteht auch umgekehrt die Sage nicht bloß in Ermangelung des noch unerfundenden Buchstabens, sondern weil für diesen noch gar kein Bedürfnis vorhanden ist, weil die Bilderschrift poetischer Gestaltung ihn gar nicht vermissen läßt.[57]

Uhland's exclusion of *Sage* from the realm of writing paved the way for Ginzberg's reconfiguration of *Sage* and *Legende,* which seems conspicuously different from the traditional understanding of the

Legende as the account of a saint's life. Uhland, foreshadowing Ginzberg, does not refer to the saint as the point of reference for a sacred legend. Instead, he privileges Scripture. According to him, a sacred legend is the result of the following "sequence of steps . . . : first, the poetic treatment of Holy Scripture, and afterwards also the apocryphal writings of the New Testament, and beyond these a more and more widespread and multiplied creation of legends."[58]

Finally, one more work shaped the contemporary context of Ginzberg's conception of the legend. Gunkel's commentary on Genesis led to the conception of Genesis as a folkloristic part of the Bible. Although the context is that of justifying the classification of Genesis as legend,[59] Gunkel's description of the point at which a legend becomes a sacred legend is nonetheless apt:

> So hat denn diese Zeit [der Entstehung der Genesiserzählungen] Geschichten gebildet, die im eigentlichen Sinne "geistlich" sind, d. h. die nur von Gott und von Frömmigkeit handeln, und in denen die profanen Motive zurücktreten; solche Sagen sind die von Abrahams Auszug, von der Bundesschliessung, von Isaaks Opferung u. a. Hier ist die vormals volkstümliche Sage im Begriff, "Legende" d. h. "geistliche" Erzählung zu werden.[60]

Gunkel's study provides the immediately contemporary context for Ginzberg's transformation of the ecclesiastical understanding of the legend within a Jewish context: sacred legends are to be distinguished from profane folk legends.

Against the background of the definitions of legend and sacred legend as presented in Ginzberg's foreword and the relevant philological works, it becomes clear why Ginzberg subordinates the folk legend to the sacred legend, and takes the latter to be a more comprehensive term. Any investigation of the question of genre is only possible on the basis of the German manuscript and the process of composition that can be traced therein, the "workshop" of *The Legends of the Jews.*

Conclusion

Ginzberg's *Legends* forms the climax of a long tradition of Jewish anthologies, compiled throughout the nineteenth and early twentieth centuries. In his ground-breaking essay "Etwas über die rabbinische Litteratur" (1818), Leopold Zunz defined the ambitious goal of the *Wissenschaft des Judentums* (the academic study of Judaism) as the complete collection of all Jewish literature by philological means. Later, in his monumental *Gottesdienstliche Vorträge der Juden, historisch entwickelt* (1832), he narrows the focus of this endeavor to the aggadah. Due to Zunz's influence, an intense engagement with the literary rather than the non-canonical and not strictly speaking ritual or religious part of Jewish tradition acquired the primary emphasis of nineteenth-century Jewish studies. For nineteenth-century Jewish and Christian scholars such as Moritz Steinschneider, Franz Delitzsch (a Protestant, unlike most scholars of this school), Gustav Karpeles, Adolf Jellinek, and Delitzsch's student August Wünsche, as well as Jakob Winter, Wilhelm Bacher, and Sigmund Maybaum, their main interest was in the aggadah. This circumstance led to many anthologies in which aggadic material was collected, among them Jakob Weil's *Fragmente aus dem Talmud und den Rabbinen* (1809–1811); Raphael J. Fürstenthal's *Rabbinische Anthologie* (1835); Ludwig August Frankl's *Libanon* (1855); Michael Sachs' *Stimmen von Jordan und Euphrat* (1891); and many more. Marking the end of this tradition, the early twentieth century saw the rise of the large-scale projects associated with names such as Micha Josef Berdyczewski, Ḥaim N. Bialik, and Louis Ginzberg. Prior to these monumental works, there are merely anthologies, deserving of this label due to their nature: they are highly selective compilations of, among other things, Jewish tales, biographies, proverbs, and exemplary tales. Although this is a generalization, their common tendency may be called emancipatory. Especially for the early anthologizers, working during the first decades of the nineteenth century, the aim was to deny the prejudice regarding the inferiority of Jewish culture and to establish its equal status in a Christian world. The very best that Rabbinic and later traditions have to offer was presented to the public.

Ginzberg's *Legends of the Jews,* however, aims also at something else—it is not anthological, but comprehensive, and thus the so-called *nugae rabbinorum*[61] of the talmudic and midrashic traditions are not filtered out. A new self-confidence and a new take on tradition coincide: the formerly unpopular tendencies of Jewish tradition are now appreciated and presented to the public. Ginzberg's goal is to display all of thc biblical aggadah in a new manner that is distinctly Judeo-American and that contrasts with the German anthologies. But at the very same time, *Legends* thwarts its own potential of presenting its heterogeneity as the unifying characteristic of Jewish tradition, paradoxical though this may sound. *Legends* offers no synopsis of the manifold variants that are connected to biblical narratives or matters. Instead, the accounts are synthesized to represent the "typical legend,"[62] as Ginzberg put it in the English translation. The entertainment value, the manageability of tradition due to the claim of an all-encompassing treatment, and, finally, the epic form used to provide American Jews with a grand narrative of the biblical history of Israel—all these cannot be united within the presentation of a heterogeneous tradition. In the context of the intended Judeo-American renaissance, the stated objective of the Jewish Publication Society—to obtain an easily readable presentation of Jewish tradition that is both educating and entertaining for the general American public—cannot be reconciled with the nature of the sources on which Ginzberg drew.

Given this background, only once the forgotten German text is published may the qualities claimed for the American edition be actualized. Solely through the coexistence of both texts, the German and the English one, does the specific, transitional position occupied by *Legends* become apparent. The collection is situated between the Judeo-German scholarly and literary tradition, on the one hand, and an attempt to establish and promote a genuinely Judeo-American culture, on the other. Both of these contexts, the dominant German scholarly tradition and an American Jewish culture that virtually did not exist until the beginning of the twentieth century, are brought to the fore through an examination of history and interrelationship of both texts and their differences. The fact that, until now, there have only been American editions reflects the specific social location of *Legends.* Through this work, the New World articulated a claim both to originality and to its very own Jewish literature. Behind and prior to the American edition lies the German original, which exhibits the traces of the *Legends*' ambivalent position between a German Jewish heritage and a new beginning in America.

Notes

I thank Michael A. Zuber for translating this article from the German. All translations of quoted material are his, unless otherwise indicated. I thank Ruth A. Clements for editing the English translation.

1. Foreword to the six-volume German manuscript, 1:5: "Den gesammten jüdischen Sagenkreis, soweit er biblische Personen oder Begebenheiten berührt mit möglichster Treue und Vollständigkeit nach den Originalquellen zu Darstellung . . . bringen." Ginzberg's original spelling is retained throughout this essay. The manuscript is to be found in the archive of the Library of the Jewish Theological Seminary in New York, catalogued as ARC 42:30, Boxes 1–14. The JTS Library is in the process of putting the complete manuscript online, as part of its Digital Collections.
2. Louis Ginzberg, *The Legends of the Jews,* 7 vols., with a foreword by James L. Kugel (Baltimore: Johns Hopkins University Press, 1998), vol. 1, cover.
3. Robert H. Pfeiffer, "Review: *The Legends of the Jews* by Louis Ginzberg," *Journal of Bible and Religion* 7/3 (1939), 139–42, 142. See also Bernhard Heller's detailed discussion at the beginning of his detailed, five-part review in *JQR:* "Nothing less is attempted than the complete collection of the Aggada material which refers to the stories and personages of the Bible" ("Review: Ginzberg's *Legends of the Jews* [1909–1928]," *JQR* 24/1 [1933], 51–66; 24/2 (1933), 165–90; 24/3 [1934], 281–307; 24/4 [1934], 393–418; 25/1 [1934], 29–52); the quotation is from 24/1 (1933), 52. See also Herbert Danby, "Review: *The Legends of the Jews* by Louis Ginzberg," *JBL* 58/4 (1939), 389–91.
4. *Legends* was commissioned in 1901 by the Jewish Publication Society for an English-speaking audience. Ginzberg, as a relative newcomer to the United States, wrote the manuscript in German, the language of his earlier scholarship; but translation into English was always in view. Hence the notion of a German edition was not integral to the original conception of the work. See Jonathan Sarna, *JPS: The Americanization of Jewish Culture, 1888–1988* (Philadelphia: Jewish Publication Society, 1989), 130–31.
5. Theodor Nöldeke in a letter to Ginzberg dated June 21, 1910: "Would it not be desirable to publish your German original as well?" JTS Archive, *Louis Ginzberg Collection,* ARC 42.
6. Moritz Spitzer in a letter to Ginzberg dated September 28, 1933. An edition of the German manuscript is currently being prepared.
7. Kugel, "Foreword," in Ginzberg, *Legends of the Jews* (1998), 1:xii.
8. ". . . Verschiedenen unter sich abweichenden Versionen einen und derselben Legende . . . in höhere Einheit aufgelöst." Regarding

Ginzberg's harmonizing narration, see also the analysis by Rebecca Schorsch, "The Making of a Legend: Louis Ginzberg's *Legends of the Jews*" (Ph.D. diss., University of Chicago, 2002), 24. Note that "Higher unity" ("höhere Einheit") has a quantitative denotation (i.e., pointing to a larger textual unit) as well as a qualitative one (designating a higher order).

9. The proceedings of the publication committee of the Jewish Publication Society are found in the JTS Archive, *Alexander Marx Collection,* ARC 80. See Proceedings of May 7, 1916.
10. Proceedings, June 4, 1916.
11. Proceedings, November 5, 1916.
12. Proceedings, April 1, 1917.
13. Proceedings, May 6, 1917.
14. Ibid.
15. Proceedings, October 6, 1918.
16. Proceedings, January 5, 1919.
17. List of agenda, February 2, 1919; JTS Archive, *Alexander Marx Collection,* ARC 80.
18. Proceedings, March 2, 1919.
19. Proceedings, November 2, 1924.
20. "Leviathan is such a monstrous creature that (it) (needs) all the water that flows ~~in~~ (from) the Jordan ~~in the space of one year~~ (to the sea) ~~is not even sufficient to wet its throat, wherefore God has a river come out of paradise that provides the monstrous creature with water~~.[119]" (*mL,* "Creation," 1:26 [see also the seven-volume English edition (Philadelphia: Jewish Publication Society, 1946–1947, a reprint of the 1909–1938 edition), 1:27]). In the translations of the German manuscript, Ginzberg's additions are marked by round brackets, while English terms and phrases in the German text remain untranslated and are italicized. Citations of the English publication are given according to the 1947 reprint edition.
21. "*Pesikta,* Buber VI, 58a, *Pesikta R.* XVI, 81a, *Lev. R.* XXII towards the end; ~~according to~~ *Bava Batra* 74b ~~Leviathan drinks the *Jordanwater* after this river has flowed into the sea.~~ comp. further ~~down~~ down note . . ." (*mL,* annotations to "Creation,"[b] 1:47). Where more than one version of a note exists, "a" denotes the version that was eventually published; "b" denotes the version that was not used.
22. "*B. Bat.* 47b; slightly different in the Palestinian Midrashim, *PK.* VI, 58a and (parallel passages)" (*mL,* annotations to "Creation,"[a] 1:47).
23. "*Bava Batra* 74b. *Pinhas* 12. The Midrashim . . . describe ~~Leviathan's~~ (Behemoth's) enormous demand for water in even more striking colours and quote an account according to which a river daily

flows out of paradise for the thirst of this monstrous creature. Comp. n. 142" (*mL,* annotations to "Creation,"[b] 1:47).

24. *Pesiqta de-Rab Kahana: R. Kahana's Compilation of Discourses for Sabbaths and Festal Days,* trans. William G. [Gershon Zev] Braude and Israel J. Kapstein (Philadelphia: Jewish Publication Society, 2002), 170, *Piska* 6:1; emphasis mine.
25. See *mL,* 1:31, and also the English edition, 1:30.
26. "The fifth kind of *earth,* called 'Arka,' is separated from the sixth in exactly the same way as the sixth is from the seventh" (*mL,* "Creation," 1:8).
27. James Kugel, however, assumes that Ginzberg had been planning to write in German from the start and have a translation made afterward; Kugel, "Foreword," in Ginzberg, *The Legends of the Jews* (1998), 1:xi.
28. "Hell is divided into seven divisions, one beneath the other. The uppermost is 'Sheol' . . ." (*mL,* "Creation," 1:15).
29. "Further the Ark used give the sign for departure by raising itself up and then in front of the camp quickly advanced. . . . As soon as they [the Israelites] had moved away from Sinai they also bega(n) leading they're sinful life(style) anew whom they had laid down for some time" (*mL,* "Moses," 3:177). [Translator's note: The English translation tries to bring across the kinds of mistakes that are to be found in Ginzberg's original (omission of words, uncertainty with regard to homophones, awkward syntax, and so on) rather than the very mistakes themselves, which is impossible in most cases. It remains to be pointed out that there are more mistakes in the German original than it has been possible to translate.]
30. "My intention was to give a smooth presentation without any irregularities" (*mL,* "Creation," 1:18–19).
31. "Since almost all of the work is in the hands of the printer by now, the whole should be published within this year" (*mL,* "Foreword," 1:7–8).
32. "At this point, it is an honourable obligation of mine to express my heartfelt gratitude to Miss Henrietta Szold, not only for her masterful translation, but also for the many ~~improvements of~~ suggestions with regard to the form and content of the book, which were of great value for it" (*mL,* "Foreword," 1:8).
33. "Und in der That ist dieser Dualismus das Charakteristische der jüdischen Sage oder um *einen umfassenden Ausdruck* zu gebrauchen der jüdischen Legende" (*mL,* "Foreword," 1:3, emphasis added).
34. The possibility that this is a mistake due to insufficient German skills on Ginzberg's part can be ruled out: there is yet another passage where he talks about the difficult project of collecting

"The Legends of the Jews" without also including literary tales in addition to folk narratives. See *mL,* "Foreword," 1:5.

35. For the classical treatment, see the writings of the Brothers Grimm and the lectures of Ludwig Uhland mentioned in the main text. For the contemporary discussion, see Hermann Gunkel's *Schöpfung und Chaos in Urzeit und Endzeit: Eine religionsgeschichtliche Untersuchung zu Gen 1 und Ap Joh 12* (Göttingen: Vandenhoek & Ruprecht, 1895), as well as his *Genesis* (Handkommentar zum Alten Testament, Part 1.1) (Göttingen: Vandenhoek & Ruprecht, 1901).
36. Johann Gottfried Herder, "Über die Legende," *Zerstreute Blätter* 6 (1797), 249–74, 250.
37. Hereafter, "legend" is used as the translation of *Sage;* "folktale," *Märchen;* and "sacred legend," *Legende.*
38. "According to our usage, the history of the folktale [*Sagengeschichte*] covers all the traditions that reflect the life of peoples in their godly and human interactions"; Ludwig Uhland, "Sagengeschichte der germanischen und romanischen Völker," *Uhlands Schriften zur Geschichte der Dichtung und Sage* (Stuttgart: Cotta, 1865–1873), 7:8.
39. "A legend is—here the term is used in no other than the commonly accepted way—a folkloristic, poetic narrative handed down from days of old, dealing with people or events of the past": Hermann Gunkel, *Genesis,* "Die Sagen der Genesis," 1:viii. [Editor's note: Oddly, this sentence was omitted from the published English translation of Gunkel's foreword; see n. 62 below. The translation used here is that of Michael Zuber.]
40. Cited by M[oses]. Spitzer in a letter to Ginzberg dated September 28, 1933, JTS Archive, *Louis Ginzberg Collection,* ARC 42.
41. "In the language of postbiblical literature, folktale, fairy tale, legend, and related forms all share the name Aggadah" (*mL,* "Foreword," 1:3).
42. (1) The "persönliche Gepräge, welches die Haggadisten der . . . Volkssage gaben"; (2) "In der haggadischen Literatur sind sogar meistentheils die ursprünglichen Volksschöpfungen so sehr von den gelehrten Zuthaten so sehr überwuchert."
43. "[Rabbis sind in erster Reihe] Prediger gewesen, die für didaktische Zwecke der Sage sich bedienten und sie waren meistens bestrebt die Ausströmungen der Folksphantasie an die Schrift anzulehnen" (*mL,* "Foreword," 1:2).
44. "The teachers of the Aggadah, called 'Rabbanan d'Aggadta' in the Talmud, were folklorists, from whom we could expect a faithful presentation of the folktale material" (*mL,* "Foreword," 1:2).
45. Jacob Grimm, "Gedanken wie sich die Sage zur Poesie und Ge-

schichte verhalte," in *Kleinere Schriften* (Berlin: Dümmler 1864), 1:399–403, 400 (originally published in the *Zeitung für Einsiedler* 19/20 [1808]).

46. "With regard to different, variant versions of one and the same legend, I ~~often sometimes~~ (either) gave one in the main text only, while the others follow in the notes. . . . Sometimes the different, contradicting legends are ~~treated~~ given in various places" (*mL,* "Foreword," 1:7).
47. See also Herder, "Über die Legende," 266.
48. After the publication of Bacher's studies on the Babylonian Amoraim (1878) and the Tannaim (1884–1890), and continuing after Bacher's death, scholars discussed the value and the accuracy of his work. The discussion mainly took place in the *Monatsschrift für Geschichte und Wissenschaft des Judentums* and the *Jahrbuch für jüdische Geschichte und Literatur;* see, for instance, Felix Perles's article on Wilhelm Bacher in the *Jahrbuch für jüdische Geschichte und Literatur* (1915), 177–91, esp. 187–91. A strong critique was formulated by M. Aschkenaze: *Tempus Loquendi: Über die Agada der palästinensischen Amoräer nach der neuesten Darstellung* (Strassburg Fr. Engelhardt , 1897), 6.
49. "Basically, ~~to~~ to speak of the Aggadah of the Tannaim and Amoraim is (just as mistaken) as to speak of Shakespeare's and ~~Uhland's~~ (Walter Scott's) folktales" (*mL,* "Foreword," 1:2).
50. "Folktales, these immediate creations of the people, which in Jewish literature often take on the form of sacred legends" (*mL,* "Foreword," 1:1).
51. "Biblischen Legende" (*mL,* "Foreword," 1:5; emphasis added).
52. "Die Beurteilung der Geschichte seitens des Volkes" (*mL,* "Foreword," 1:4).
53. "The events of the ancient history of Israel—which are not only studied, but relived (a)new each day—have led to the need for evaluating biblical history. Hence the peculiar form of the Aggadah" (*mL,* "Foreword," 1:7).
54. English ed., 1:x.
55. "Die Sage der Völker ist hiernach wesentlich Volkspoesie; alle Volkspoesie aber ist ihrem Hauptbestande nach sagenhaft, sofern wir unter Sage die Überlieferung durch Erzählen, das epische Element der Poesie, zu verstehen pflegen." Uhland, "Sagengeschichte der germanischen und romanischen Völker," *Schriften,* 7:4.
56. Uhland, "Geschichte der altdeutschen Poesie: Vorlesungen an der Universität Tübingen gehalten in den Jahren 1830 und 1831, Erster Theil," *Schriften,* 1:26.
57. "However, writing becomes the means through which the con-

tribution of the individual to socio-mental life, and the specific tendencies thereof, becomes apparent and expresses itself in ever greater individuality. And thus, conversely, the folk legend does not hinge on the lack of an invented letter that has not been invented yet. There is yet no need for it at all, since the imagery of poetic composition does not leave room for wanting it." Uhland, "Sagengeschichte der germanischen und romanischen Völker," *Schriften,* 7:3–4.

58. "Stufengang . . . : zuerst poetische Bearbeitung der heiligen Schrift, dann auch Apokryphen des Neuen Testaments und über diese hinaus eine stets mehr verbreitete und vervielfachte Legendendichtung." Uhland, "Geschichte der altdeutschen Poesie: Zweiter Theil," *Schriften* 2:2.
59. Gunkel's *Schöpfung und Chaos in Urzeit und Endzeit* is also quoted by Ginzberg.
60. "Accordingly this later time constructed stories which are specifically 'sacred,' that is, which deal only with God and piety, and in which profane interests are relegated to the background. Such legends are those of Abraham's exodus, of the covenant, of the sacrifice of Isaac, and so on. Here the formerly popular saga is on the point of becoming 'legend,' that is, a characteristically 'sacred' or 'priestly' [*sic*] narrative." Gunkel, *Genesis*, "Die Sagen der Genesis," l [50]. This seventy-one-page foreword to Gunkel's commentary was published separately in both German (also 1901, as an offprint from the commentary) and English, as *The Legends of Genesis: The Biblical Saga and History,* trans W. H. Carruth (Chicago: Open Court, 1901); the translation used here is from 110–11 of the English edition.
61. "Rabbinic trivia," English ed., 1:vii.
62. Ibid., 1:xiv.

Contributors

Daniel Boyarin is the Taubman Professor of Talmudic Culture in the Departments of Near Eastern Studies and Rhetoric at the University of California, Berkeley. His latest book is *The Jewish Gospels: The Story of the Jewish Christ* (2011). He is currently completing a book entitled *A Traveling Homeland: The Talmud as Diaspora.*

Jacob Elbaum is Professor Emeritus in the Department of Hebrew Literature at the Hebrew University of Jerusalem. He has published books and papers about midrashic literature (mainly on the late midrashim) and about medieval and early modern Hebrew and Yiddish Literature.

Rabbi Prof. David Golinkin is the president of the Schechter Institute of Jewish Studies in Jerusalem, where he is also the Jerome and Miriam Katzin Professor of Jewish Studies. He is the author or editor of forty-five books, including *The Responsa of Prof. Louis Ginzberg* and the second Hebrew edition of Ginzberg's *Legends of the Jews.*

Ithamar Gruenwald is Professor Emeritus at Tel Aviv University, where he chaired the Department of Jewish Philosophy (now the Department of the History of Jewish Culture) and the Program of Religious Studies. He has published extensively, mostly on methodological issues in the areas of ancient Jewish apocalyptic, mysticism, and ritual studies. His books include *Apocalyptic and Merkavah Mysticism*, *From Apocalypticism to Gnosticism*, and *Rituals and Ritual Theory in Ancient Israel.*

Galit Hasan-Rokem is Max and Margarethe Grunwald Professor of Folklore and Professor (emerita) of Hebrew Literature at the Hebrew University of Jerusalem. She studies folk literary and ethnographic aspects of classical late antique Rabbinic literature and its intercultural and interreligious aspects; folklore and literary theory; the proverb genre; and Jewish motifs in European folklore, especially the traditions on the Wandering Jew, and contemporary Israeli culture. Her books include *Web of Life: Folklore and Midrash in Rabbinic Literature* (2000), *Tales of the Neighborhood: Jewish Narrative Dialogues in Late Antiquity* (2003), and *A Companion to Folklore* (2012), coedited with Regina F. Bendix.

Hillel I. Newman is a senior lecturer in the Department of Jewish History at the University of Haifa.

Johannes Sabel received his doctorate in German literature from the University of Tübingen. From 2009 to 2011 he collaborated on the German edition of Louis Ginzberg's *Legends of the Jews.* Among his publications is *Die Geburt der Literatur aus der Aggada. Formationen eines deutsch-jüdischen Literaturparadigmas* (Tübingen, 2010). Currently he is the head of Katholisches Bildungswerk Bonn.

Rebecca Schorsch is the director of Jewish studies at the Chicagoland Jewish High School, where she is a member of the administrative team and also teaches Rabbinics, Bible, and Jewish thought. In addition, Dr. Schorsch teaches adult Jewish education and lectures and serves as scholar-in-residence in a range of formal and informal educational and religious settings. Dr. Schorsch holds degrees from the University of Chicago (Ph.D., history of Judaism), the Jewish Theological Seminary (M.A., Jewish history), and Columbia University (B.A., European history).

Index